Creativity is Forever

Third Edition

Gary A. Davis

University of Wisconsin

KENDALL/HUNT PUBLISHING COMPANY

2460 Kerper Boulevard P.O. Box 539 Dubuque, Iowa 52004-0539

**To Paul Torrance and
Pansy Torrance**

Contents

10 Let's Be a Cuckoo Clock: Creative Dramatics 267

11 Teaching for Creative Growth 281

Preface

Creative leader E. Paul Torrance (1988) recently described creativity as:

Wanting to Know	Digging Deeper
Looking twice	Crossing out mistakes
Listening for smells	Listening to a cat
Getting in	Getting out
Cutting corners	Cutting holes to see through
Building sand castles	
Singing in our own key	Plugging into the sun
Shaking hands with tomorrow	Having a ball

Together, these analogies translate roughly as seeing what is not there, looking beyond the habitual and ordinary, imagining, experimenting, clarifying and solving problems, making mistakes, and especially, growing personally and professionally and becoming all that one is capable of becoming. Creativity is these and more. Creativity is essential to one's personal growth and success; it is vital to society.

This book was prepared for any adult reader interested in better understanding the topic of creativity, becoming a more creative person, or teaching others to think more creatively. It is absolutely true that much about human creativity remains—and will remain—an intriguing mystery. However, it also is absolutely true that we do understand much about creativity and creative people—their energetic and curious personalities, their idea-finding processes and strategies, and the circumstances that support or squelch their innovative thinking.

Further, it is absolutely true that despite genetic differences in cognitive and affective creative gifts, everyone can become a more flexible and creative thinker. The central and indispensable ingredient is simply an elevated level of *creativity consciousness,* a goal that is aided by a better understanding of and appreciation for the topic of creativity.

This book will help the dedicated teacher understand creative students, barriers and blocks to creative thinking, mental processes of creativity, techniques for creative thinking and problem solving, creativity testing, the role of creativity in gifted education, exercises for creative dramatics, strategies for strengthening creative abilities, and generally "what to teach when you teach creativity." Teachers have a great direct impact on the day-to-day lives of children. This text hopefully will enrich the professional development of teachers and other educators so they may nurture the creative gifts of students.

The book also aims at several needs of the business person interested in developing his or her own creative thinking potential or in helping others to be more creatively productive. Particularly valuable will be the illustrations of creativity and problem solving techniques that, in fact, originated in the corporate and business setting.

An understanding of creativity can change your life just as it has changed the lives of many others. The reader will discover that creativity is more than art, theatre, new consumer products, and zany TV commercials. These are important. But more important to you personally is the full development of your own capabilities and talents, and an increase in your flexibility, curiosity, open-mindedness, and sense of adventure which also are part of becoming a more creative person. Creative people invest more in life and they reap bigger, more satisfying returns. They live all aspects of life in a more creative, innovative, and enjoyable fashion.

GAD

1

creativity, self-actualization, and you

[*Scene: Enchanted forest home of two lovable gnomes, Rodney Dangergnome and Gnome Rickles. The dear friends are trying to help each other with difficult personal problems.*]

Gnome Rickles: Look, dummy, you can't sit around all yer life sweatin' an' straightenin' yer tie an' mumblin' "I don't get no respect! I don't get no respect!" Of course you don't get no respect. Yer a failure! Ya' gotta' get self-actualized an' realize yer potential—like me!

Rodney Dangergnome (straightening his tie): You dunno' how tough it's been, Rickles. When I wuz a kid even my mother said she just liked me as a friend! An' I couldn't play hide an' seek 'cause nobody wanted to find me!

Rickles: Maybe it's yer creativity, fish face! Have you ever thought of using yer imagination? Trying to solve a problem once in a while? And yer personality! Yer neurotic! Self-actualized people ain't neurotic!

Dangergnome: Okay, okay, I'm self-actualized! But it ain't easy being well-adjusted when you're me. My dad took me to the chimp cage at the zoo, the zookeeper said "Thanks for bringin' 'im back!" Last week my psychiatrist said I was crazy. I tol' him I wanted a second opinion, so he said I was ugly, too!

Rickles: Just one more time, nincompoop! I'll talk slow. Try to read my lips. Ya' gotta' be more creative, more confident, better adjusted, an' ya' gotta' develop yer skills as much as ya' can. I don't expect much, yer too stupid. But ya' gotta' give it a try!

Dangergnome: Watch it, Rickles! You ain't exactly Prince Charmin', ya' know what I mean? Next to you, a sore rattesnake is a very beautiful person!

Rickles: Tell you what. Let's both sit down, you keep yer yap shut, an' let's read Chapter 1 together! Real careful like!

Self-
Actualization
Is Profoundly
Important:
Abraham
Maslow, Carl
Rogers

One of the most profoundly important concepts in the field of creativity is the relationship between creativity and self-actualization. Humanistic psychologists Abraham Maslow and Carl Rogers define *self-actualization* as using all of one's talents to become what one is capable of becoming—actualizing one's potential. Further, the self-actualizing person is mentally healthy, self-accepting, forward growing, fully functioning, democratic minded, and more. In Maslow's (1954) words, self-actualization ". . . refers to our desire for self-fulfillment, namely, to the tendency for a person to become actual-

Realizing One's
Potential

ized in what he or she is potentially . . . the desire to become more and more what one is, to become everything that one is capable of becoming . . . what one can be, one must be." [1] Maslow (1968, p. 138) added, "We are dealing with a fundamental characteristic, inherent in human nature, a potentiality given to all or most human beings at birth, which most often is lost or buried or inhibited as the person gets enculturated." Maslow (1968) further observed that self-actualization includes an ever-increasing move toward unity, integration, or synergy within the person.

Look carefully at Maslow's description of self-actualized people in Insert 1.1. The thoughtful reader may agree that few things in life are more important than one's self-actualization.

Inset 1.1
Maslow's 15 Characteristics of Self-Actualized People

In view of the proposition that a creative person also is a self-actualized person, perhaps we should look more closely at Maslow's notion of self-actualization. According to Maslow (1954), self-actualized people:

1. Perceive reality more accurately and objectively; tolerate and even like ambiguity; are not threatened by the unknown.

2. Accept themselves, others, and human nature.

3. Are spontaneous, natural, genuine.

[1]"Him" and "he" in the original quote were replaced with the gender neutral "one" and "he or she." Maslow would understand.

4. Are problem-centered (not self-centered), non-egotistical; have a philosophy of life and probably a mission in life.

5. Need some privacy and solitude more than others do; are able to concentrate intensely.

6. Are independent, self-sufficient and autonomous; have less need for praise or popularity.

7. Have capacity to appreciate again and again simple and common-place experiences; have zest in living, ability to handle stress, high humor.

8. Have (and are aware of) their rich, alive, fulfilling "peak experiences"—moments of intense enjoyment.

9. Have deep feelings of brotherhood with all mankind; are benevolent, altruistic.

10. Form strong friendship ties with relatively few people; are capable of greater love.

11. Are democratic, unprejudiced in the deepest possible sense.

12. Are strongly ethical and moral in individual (not necessarily conventional) ways; enjoy work in achieving a goal as much as the goal itself; are patient, for the most part.

13. Have a more thoughtful, philosophical sense of humor that is constructive, not destructive.

14. Are creative, original, inventive with a fresh, naive, simple and direct way of looking at life; tend to do most things creatively—but do not necessarily possess great talent.

15. Are capable of detachment from their culture; can objectively compare cultures; can take or leave conventions.

It is important to develop your self-actualized creativity.

Creativity Equals Self-Actualization

Rogers (1962) tied self-actualization to creativity with these words: "The mainspring of creativity appears to be the same tendency which we discover so deeply as the curative force in psychotherapy—one's tendency to actualize oneself, to become one's potentialities . . . the urge to expand, extend, develop, mature—the tendency to express and activate all the capabilities of the organism . . ." (pp. 65–66).[2] Similarly, Maslow (1971), in a scientifically cautious statement, noted ". . . the concept of creativeness and the concept of the healthy, self-actualizing, fully human person seem to be coming closer and closer together, and may turn out to be the same thing."

Moustakis Agrees

To add further credibility to this significant relationship, Clark Moustakis (1967), another prominent humanistic psychologist, maintained that "It is this experience of expressing and actualizing one's individual identity in an integrated form in communication with one's self, with nature, and with other persons that I call creative."

Research Evidence

There also is research evidence that self-actualization and creativity go hand-in-hand. Based on the 15 characteristis of self-actualization in Inset 1.1, Buckmaster created an adult-level inventory designed to measure self-actualization entitled *Reflections on Self and Environment* (ROSE; Buckmaster & Davis, 1985). College students' scores on the ROSE were compared with their scores on a shortened version of the *How Do You Think* inventory (Davis, 1975; 1991, see Chapter 8), which measures personality and biographical characteristics of creative people. The statistical correlation between scores on the two inventories was a solid .73 (on a scale from 0 to 1.0). Almost every individual who scored high in self-actualization also scored high in creativity, and vice versa. Further, scores on both tests were significantly correlated with ratings of the creativeness of students' art and writing projects.

Creativity Plus Intelligence: Highest Self-Actualization

Yonge (1975) earlier reviewed research that showed positive correlations between scores on another measure of self-actualization, the *Personal Orientation Inventory* (Shostrum, 1963), and various measures of creativity, for example, scores on a creativity scale of the *Adjective Check List* (Chapter 8). Finally, Damm (1970) concluded that it helps to be smart, too. While creativity and intelligence were each related to self-actualization, the highest levels of self-actualization were reached by his high school students who were both creative and intelligent.

---

[2]"Man's," "himself," and "his" were replaced with "one's" and "oneself."

"Yes dear, you finally became what you were capable of becoming." (The Museum of Modern Art / Film Stills Archive.)

SELF-ACTUALIZED CREATIVITY AND SPECIAL TALENT CREATIVITY

Neurotic
Creative Genius

Now the on-his-or-her-toes reader may be thinking about world-class creative people who are, or were, highly neurotic and not at all self-actualized in the mentally healthy sense. History is full of neurotic but creative people. The names of Vincent van Gogh and Edgar Allen Poe come to mind, and perhaps Beethoven, Mozart, Howard Hughes, Judy Garland, John Belushi, Janis Joplin, and introvert Yves St. Laurent. (Can you think of others?)

Special Talent
Creativity

May or May Not
Be Self-
Actualized
in Mentally
Healthy Sense

The solution to this apparent dilemma lies in Maslow's (1954) perceptive distinction between *self-actualized* versus *special talent* creative people. Special talent creative people, by definition, possess an extraordinary creative talent or gift in art, literature, music, theatre, science, business, or other area. These persons might be well-adjusted and live reasonably happy, self-actualized existences. Or they might be neurotically disturbed and habitually uncomfortable, if not miserable, in their personal, professional, and social lives (see Figure 1.1).

Three
Implications

There are at least three important implications of distinguishing between self-actualized and special talent creativity that relate to (1) being creative without a specific great creative talent, (2) the core role of personality and affective traits in creativity, and (3) whether creativity must be taught within a subject area. We will look briefly at each.

One Can Be Creative without a Great Creative Talent

Self-Actualized
Creative People
May Not Have a
Great Creative
Talent

The first implication of the distinction between self-actualized and special talent creativity is tucked in Maslow's item 14 in Inset 1. Under no circumstances should the reader stop right now and look at item 14 in Inset 1. Self-actualized creative people are mentally healthy, live full and productive lives, and tend to approach all aspects of their lives in a flexible, creative fashion. They do

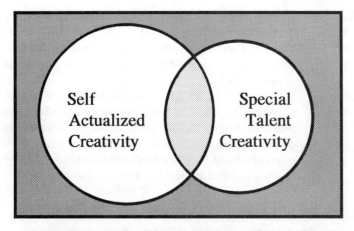

Figure 1.1. Self actualized creativity and special talent creativity.

not necessarily have an outstanding creative talent in a specific area (e.g., art or science). *That is, you need not possess exceptional artistic, literary, scientific, or entrepreneurial talent to consider yourself a creative person and live a creative life.* It is unfortunate that the word "creativity" is too-strongly associated with the possession of extraordinary and distinguished talent.

Emphasis on Personality and Affective Traits

Highlights Importance of Affective Traits

Creative Thinking Is a Way of Living

The second implication of distinguishing between self-actualized versus special talent creativity is the built-in emphasis on the importance of affective traits of creative people—personality characteristics, attitudes, motivations, and conscious predispositions to think creatively. Creativity is a lifestyle, a way of living, a way of growing, and a way of perceiving the world. Living creatively is developing your talents, learning to use your abilities, and striving to become what you are capable of becoming. Being creative is exploring new ideas, new places, and new activities. Being creative is developing a sensitivity to problems of others and problems of humankind. The reader may wish to look again at Inset 1.1. Is this what life is (or should be) about?

Humanistic
Approach
Deemphasizes
Abilities,
Processes

The humanistic, self-actualization approach to creativity deemphasizes creative abilities and creative processes. From this perspective, creative abilities and processes are by-products of the more important personological traits.

Creative
Personality
Traits Essential

In Chapter 4 we will examine the creative personality more closely. Most of the creative personality characteristics described in that chapter—for example, independence, adventurousness, curiosity, a sense of humor, perceptiveness, open-mindedness—mesh nicely with Maslow's description of self-actualization.

Creativity Need Not Be Taught Within a Subject Matter

A third important implication of the self-actualized versus special talent distinction relates to whether creativity must be taught within a subject area. Schiever and Maker (1990) and Keating (1980), for example, have claimed that creativity cannot be taught "in the abstract"; students must have something to think about, to create with. Absolutely wrong, nonsense. Creativity may be taught in a completely content-free context; or the training may be embedded within a specific content or subject area.

Self-Actualized
Creativity Is
Content Free

And May Be
Taught and
Learned

Self-actualized creativity is a *general* creativeness which is content free. Many successful creativity courses, programs, workshops, and educational workbooks try to (a) raise creativity consciousness, (b) strengthen creative attitudes, such as valuing novel ideas, (c) teach idea-finding techniques and creative problem solving techniques, and (d) strengthen underlying creative abilities through exercise. Such courses and programs seek to help the learner understand creativity and approach personal, academic, and professional problems in a more creative fashion. The approach is sensible, common, and effective (e.g., Davis & Bull, 1978; Edwards, 1968; Parnes, 1978; Smith, 1985; Stanish, 1977, 1981, 1988; Torrance, 1979, 1987b; Torrance & Myers, 1970; Von Oech, 1981). Consistent with self-actualized creativity, this approach does not tie creativity training to a particular subject or content.

Special Talent
Creativity Is
Taught within a
Subject Area

On the other hand, a goal might well be to strengthen creative thinking and problem solving skills as they relate directly to a specific subject such as creative writing, photography, theatre, botany, architecture, astronomy, or dinosaurs. With the typical independent projects approach, students are given (or find) a project or problem and proceed to clarify it, consider various approaches, settle on a main solution or resolution, and then create or prepare the project or problem for presentation. Throughout, students identify and resolve numerous subproblems, evaluate their methods and results, acquire knowledge and develop technical skills in the content area, and their creative abilities and skills are strengthened. This strategy clearly fits Maslow's special talent type of creativeness. It is an appropriate and effective teaching method.

Independent
Projects

Teaches
Knowledge,
Technical
Skills,
Creativity

Creativity
Training May
Be in a Content
Area or Content
Free

We will see in Chapter 9 that independent projects are a common strategy for teaching academic content, technical skills, and creativity to gifted children. Content-free creativity training also is widely employed, for example, in brainstorming sessions that teach creativity consciousness, receptiveness to wild ideas, deferring criticism and evaluation, and principles of looking for many ideas and building upon others' ideas.

Self-Actualized and Special Talent Creativity Overlap

Components
of Each Are
in the Other

Logically, components of *special talent* creativity will be strengthened while teaching a general, *self-actualized* creativeness. For example, within a "content-free" creativity session students might brainstorm ideas for a science-, history-, or math-related problem or they might do creative writing or art exercises. Conversely, creative projects in a subject area (special talent creativity) will help develop general creative attitudes and abilities that extend beyond the subject area at hand.

The history of civilization is a history of creative innovations. Traffic accidents were reduced to zero when this dangerous intersection became the site of the world's first stop-and-go signal. Unfortunately, the policeman operating the signal was immobilized by a tuna sandwich from the corner restaurant. (Wisconsin Center for Film and Theater Research.)

CIVILIZATION: A HISTORY OF CREATIVE IDEAS

Civilization:
History of
Creative Ideas

Cottontail
Drumstick
Anyone?

Because the main purpose of this chapter is to increase awareness of the importance of creativity, we might remind the reader that the history of civilization is more than a sequence of famous wars. Civilization is a history of creative ideas that have been modified, combined, transformed, and transferred—building upon each other—into ever new creations. It has happened, and continues to happen, in any area we might look at—art, science, mathematics, technology, law, medicine, politics, music, philosophy, agriculture, economics, consumer products, and even more imaginative ways to conduct those wars.[3] Without creative ideas and creative thinkers, we still would be living in caves and trees, picking berries and clubbing bunny rabbits for breakfast.

Civilization will continue to have problems and aesthetic needs, and creative people will continue to provide solutions and aesthetic experiences.

COMPLEXITY OF CREATIVITY

Mystery of
Creativity

Lots of
Poppycock

It may be trivial and obvious to point out that creativity is intricate and complicated. Artistic and scientific creativity are enticingly mysterious processes, capabilities, and experiences that have confused scholars, philosophers, and creative people themselves for centuries. Creative people may not understand where their ideas come from, which is why ancient poets and composers credited their ideas to inspiration from their *muses.* A few people, with more imagination than objectivity, have attributed creativity to somehow tapping into a *universal mind* or *universal consciousness*—a mysterious information source that supposedly is floating throughout the universe. Early Greeks chalked up creativity to inspiration from their Gods, an unscientific idea with remarkable endurance. Some have argued that psychical abilities and experiences are important for creativity.

[3]Creativity may be used constructively or, unfortunately, destructively.

Can Be Forced or Intuitive

Creativity can be forced in brainstorming sessions or it can happen spontaneously, as when poetry, music, or a problem solution suddenly "comes alive" in the creative person's mind.

Children, Senior Citizens Can Be Creative

Children can be creative, and so were Grandma Moses and Picasso at 90. Some experts assume that the creative process is the same in art as in science; other experts assert that there are as many creative processes as there are creative people.

Strange Theories

Some theories of creativity (Chapter 4) are frankly bizarre, products of intelligent but baffled imaginations. An easy example is Sigmund Freud's assumption that creativity is motivated by an unconscious conflict between the sex drive (libido) of the *id* and the social conscience (*superego*). The neurotic conflict supposedly is resolved by rechanneling the sex urge into creative outlets—so the id is happy, the superego is happy, the ego is well-adjusted, and everybody goes to Mexico for a vacation.[4]

Torrance: Suprarational Processes

Worldwide creativity authority Paul Torrance (1979) emphasized that creative processes are *suprarational,* a concept he borrowed from psychologist Rollo May. By suprarational he means that creativity involves the intellect, volitional factors (deliberate intent), nonrational factors (being illogical, playful, far-fetched), and emotional functions—all brought into play together. He is right.

Is Insight Important?

Or Just Planning

Some experts claim that creativity is building on an initial insight; others say creativity is just the result of a lot of work—and sudden insights have almost nothing to do with it. Some emphasize the role of chance and randomness in creative discovery and problem solving; others stress intentional, mindful planning (Tardif & Sternberg, 1988).

Creativity: Partly Genetic, Partly Environment

But Can Be Increased

Some have argued that creativity cannot be taught, you either have it or you don't—which is partially true. Like all other human capabilities, creative talent stems in part from genetics and in part from the environment (learning). It therefore follows that no amount of training will create a Da Vinci or Edison. But it also is true that everyone's capacity for creative living and creative productivity can be increased.

---

[4]Freud also said that only men can be creative, because women's creative urges are fulfilled in reproduction. So much for Freud's credibility.

Creative Abilities, Personality, Motivation Important

In creative thinking and behavior generally there is a big role of natural creative abilities, and as we have seen in this chapter a big role of personality characteristics. There is a very big role of motivation—commitment, persistence, enthusiasm, adventurousness, and a strong drive for accomplishment and recognition.

Social Circumstance, Too

There is a big role of social circumstances; the social atmosphere can support or repress creativity. Further, society can reward or ignore particular creative achievements—that is, society will determine what products and ideas are "creative."

Training and Experience

There is a big role of training and experience in a content area. If we are talking world-class, special-talent creative contributions, such as making major medical discoveries, writing broadway plays, or creating a successful business or corporation, it may take years or even decades of training, experience, and skill development before high-level creative achievements are possible.

Chance

There also is a role of *chance*, unfortunately. Many inventions and discoveries are accidental, as when Eli Whitney saw a cat reach through a fence to grab a chicken, but came back with only a pawful of feathers, thus inspiring the cotton gin. Pasteur's pasteurization also was rooted in chance, as was Roentgen's discovery of x-rays, Nobel's research with dynamite, Foucault's discovery that a pendulum would illustrate the rotation of the earth, Galvani's discovery that electricity could be chemically produced, and several discoveries by Edison. Columbus accidentally found a Carribean island while looking for China (was he ever lost!). If you wish to be a successful ballerina or Sumo wrestler you had better have the right genes for the right physique.

Great accomplishments in most areas require the existence of appropriate cultural knowledge and technology and high-level instruction. Therefore, you cannot, by chance, be born too soon.

Comment

We Do Understand Much about Creativity and Creative People

Despite its intrinsically puzzling nature, there is much we do understand about creativity. This book will help clarify creativity by examining definitions and theories, characteristics and traits, internal creative processes, idea-finding techniques used by creative people, creativity tests and their assumptions, and realistic strategies for teaching for creative growth.

Your Creative Development Is Important

A core message of this book is that everyone can increase their creative potential and live more creative lives. It is important for you: it is important for society.

SUMMARY

Self-actualization is developing your talents to become what you are capable of becoming; it includes being mentally healthy, forward growing, democratic-minded, and more. Creativity and self-actualization are intimately related, perhaps identical, says Carl Rogers, Abraham Maslow, and Clark Moustakis. Research supports this relationship.

The self-actualized creative person is mentally-healthy and approaches all aspects of his or her life in a creative fashion. The special talent creative person has a great creative talent, but may or may not be self-actualized in the mentally healthy sense.

The first implication of this distinction is that one need not possess a great creative talent to consider oneself creative and live a creative life. The distinction also stresses the importance of affective, personality characteristics in creativity. A third implication is that a general, self-actualized creativeness may be taught in a content-free fashion. Special talent creativity must be taught within a content area, most often by engaging students in independent projects.

The history of civilization is a history of creative ideas in every area.

For centuries creativity has confused scholars, philosophers, and even creative people themselves, leading, for example, to the invention of muses, a "universal mind," and to psychical ability as explanations.

Creativity can be forced or it can happen spontaneously, and it happens at all ages. Scholars disagree on whether the creative process is the same in art as in science.

Freud attributed creativity to an unconscious conflict between the libido and the superego.

Torrance recognized suprarational components: intellect, volition, nonrationality, and emotions.

Various experts have emphasized sudden insight or systematic work; chance or planning.

Creativity is due partly to genetics and partly to environment, which means that creativity can be taught and learned to some degree.

There is a role in creativity for natural abilities, personality characteristics, motivation, social circumstances, training and experience, and chance.

Despite its complexity, there is much we do understand about creativity.

Your creative development is important.

barriers, blocks, and squelchers: why we are not more creative

[*Scene: Small girl scout camp deep in forest of Southern California. Scout Leader Rita Rambo is discussing plans to rescue pet duck, held hostage without sardines by disgruntled political group. Small girl scouts Darcy, Jennifer, and others listen intently. Darcy opens the creative problem solving.*]

Darcy: We need a plan. Something creative to surprise those people—maybe distract them while we sneak in and grab Daffy!

Rita Rambo: No thanks, kiddo! Somebody would have suggested it before if it were any good! You've got to be kidding. What bubblehead thought that up! I say let's hit 'em with everything we got. Jennifer, did you bring your little bazooka?

Jennifer: No, Ms. Rambo, but I have my brother's baseball bat.

Darcy: But Ms. Rambo, we shouldn't be violent. Besides, we might hurt Daffy!

Rambo: You don't understand the situation, small fry! And don't forget the chain of command. I learned how to deal with duck-nappers on Wake Island! Soften 'em up with artillery, then we go in! That's the way it's always been done!

Darcy: What about disguising ourselves as Groucho Marx, Ben Turpin, Charlie Chaplin, and W. C. Fields. We could walk in, argue about who is the funniest, and when Jennifer says "That's the most ridiculous thing I ever hoid!" I'll sneak off with Daffy!

Rambo: Not this girl scout, cookie! It just won't work, we've never done that before, too blue sky, we need more lead time. I don't see the connection, the comedians' union will scream, it'll mean more work, don't step on any toes, don't rock the boat, and you can't teach this old dog new tricks!

Jennifer: Do you imagine that . . .

Rambo: No, I never imagine.

Jennifer: Well, do you suppose sometimes?

Rambo: Sometimes I suppose, if it's not difficult.

Jennifer: Suppose we hire a mariachi band. While everyone is drinking
margueritas and dancing the New Mexican Hat Dance, Darcy could pop
Daffy into her big siesta.

Darcy: You mean my sombrero.

Rambo: We did all right without a mariachi band, it'll mean more work, our people
won't accept it, let's be practical, and what will the other Girl Scouts
think? Besides, we tried that before!

Darcy: Maybe we could negotiate a trade—a dozen Big Macs, some french fries,
and a winning season for the Los Angeles Rams!

Jennifer: Let's just buy a new duck! Daffy's in the soup by now anyway!

We Do Not Use
the Creative
Abilities We
Have

A good case could be made for the proposition that all
of us would be more creative if it were not for internal and
external barriers to creative thinking. That is, because of
their insecurities, well-learned habits, or an unsupportive
or even repressive environment, most people do not use
the creative abilities with which they were born.

Lots of Blocks
and Barriers

In this chapter we will look at some common barriers
to creative thinking: habit and learning, perceptual
blocks, cultural blocks, emotional blocks, and resource
barriers. We also will review Von Oech's (1983) 10 types
of mental blocks—which may take a whack on the side
of the head to jar loose. Finally, we will itemize a list of
probably-too-familiar "idea squelchers."

*The challenge to anyone wishing to increase their per-
sonal creativeness is to understand, expect, and be ready
to cope with barriers to creativity.*

HABIT AND LEARNING

Language
Habits

Response
Routines

The first and most obvious barrier to creative thinking
and innovation is just *habit;* that is, our well-learned and
habitual ways of thinking and responding. It begins when
we are munchkins. We learn language habits and the
conceptual categories that things and ideas belong in; we
learn responses, routines and patterns of behavior; we
learn "the way things have always been done," and "the
way things are supposed to be done." Over the years it
becomes more and more difficult to break away from these
habits; to see and create new possibilities.

Have You Been
Creative Lately?

When did you last try a new restaurant? Was it exotic and creative? When did you last try a new sport or take a college course in some intriguing topic? When *did* you last do something truly novel? Are your old habits and expectations interfering with new ideas and activities?

Habits Are
Necessary

Of course, the ability to form habits and expectations is an adaptive and necessary capability for humankind and lower animals. It would be troublesome indeed to open your eyes each morning, look at the ceiling, and wonder where you are and what you are supposed to do next. Being a "creature of habit" is a boon and a curse.

RULES AND TRADITIONS

Rules and
Traditions:
Necessary but
Restrictive

It also is obvious that social groups, from the family to corporate, national, and international groups, could not function without the rules, regulations, policies, and traditions that guide personal, social, and institutional behavior. However, "guide" often means "restrict" or "inhibit."

Van Gundy (1987) described several organizational barriers to creative innovation that clearly are rooted in rules and traditions. While aimed at corporate organizations, these barriers apply to educational and other organizations as well.

Status
Hierarchy

One traditional barrier lies in the *status hierarchy.* Lower-status persons are reluctant to suggest ideas to those in higher positions due to insecurity and fear of evaluation. If there is little lower-level participation in decision-making, it is even less likely that new ideas will "trickle up."

Further, if a new idea threatens to reduce status differences ("Hey, we can increase sales if we make everybody a vice president!"), the idea is sure to be resisted by higher status persons.

Enforcement of
Rule Following

Understatement?

The *formalization* barrier refers to the degree to which following rules and procedures is enforced. Observed Van Gundy in a mild-mannered understatement: "It is thought that formalization is detrimental to initiation of innovations. . . . If organizational members are expected to behave in prescribed ways, and innovation is not prescribed, fewer idea proposals will be generated" (p. 361).

Habit, tradition, rules, regulations—all will interfere with versatile creative problem solving. "He's forcing you to take money and threatening you with a banana? Sheesh!" (Wisconsin Center for Film and Theater Research.)

However, he also rightfully observed that after an innovation is accepted, an efficient formal structure expedites its implementation.

Procedural Barriers

Van Gundy's *procedural* barriers include policies, procedures, and regulations (including unwritten ones) that inhibit creative innovation. Some examples are:

Promoting administrators based on analytic skills, not on their ability to create a creative atmosphere.

Emphasizing short-term (translation: short-sighted) planning.

Avoiding expenditures that do not produce an immediate payback.

Overemphasizing external rewards rather than internal, personal commitment.

Insisting on an orderly advancement with an innovation, with too much detailed control early in its development.

Rules and traditions keep the system working. However, like habits, such predetermined guides work against creative thinking.

PERCEPTUAL BLOCKS

Perceptual Set, Mental Set, Functional Fixity

Perceptual blocks are based in learning and habit. We become accustomed to perceiving things in familiar ways, and it is difficult to see new meanings, new relationships, or new applications and uses. Psychologists refer to our predisposition to perceive things in certain ways as *perceptual set, mental set,* or *functional fixity.* Perceptual sets are different for different people, rooted in our unique interests, needs, biases, values, and past learning.

Jumping to Conclusions

Perceptual sets also are tied to our tendency to make quick decisions and jump to conclusions, rather than flexibly see alternatives. One old problem solving experiment demonstrated that when a piece of string was needed to solve a problem, the string would be perceived and used if it were dangling from a nail on the wall—but not if it were engaged hanging a *No Smoking* sign, mirror, or calendar (Sheerer, 1963).

Perceptual barriers lead us to "kick ourselves" for not seeing a solution sooner. Try the following puzzles. The solutions appear at the end of the chapter.

1. Punctuate the following set of words to make a meaningful statement:

   TIME FLIES YOU CANNOT THEY FLY TOO FAST

A Puzzle a Day Keeps the Doctor Away

2. Consider this puzzle:

   The police entered the gym containing five wrestlers just as the dying man looked at the ceiling and mumbled the words, "He did it." They immediately arrested one of the wrestlers. How did they know which one?

3. Remove six letters from ASIPXPLETLTERES. What word is left?

Can Miss the "Real" Problem

Perceptual blocks can prevent one from identifying "the real problem." For example, based on symptoms that seem familiar, a physician or auto mechanic may persist in misclassifying a problem and will treat it incorrectly.

Failure to
See Other
Possibilities

Perceptual blocks also prevent us from getting a complete and accurate picture of the world around us. For example, school teachers who fixate on IQ scores will fail to perceive students who are highly creative, highly artistic, or who are gifted in just one area. A teacher who has successfully used a particular teaching technique for many years will not recognize another technique as being even more effective. If a salesperson is invited by a client to demonstrate a computer desk, and is "mentally set" to do just that, he or she may fail to perceive that the client needs other products and supplies. A new product developer, who tries to make his or her product exactly right for one purpose, may fail to see other uses or markets for modified versions of the product.

Making the
Familiar
Strange:
Seeing New
Possibilities

Creativity leader William J. J. Gordon (1961) described how *making the familiar strange*—perceiving common objects and ideas in new ways—is a central creative process. Indeed it is. Much creativity involves a mental transformation, the perception of new meanings, combinations, and relationships that depend upon overcoming perceptual blocks.

CULTURAL BLOCKS

Expectations,
Conformity

Fear of Being
Different

Cultural blocks amount to social influence, expectations, and conformity pressures, all based on social or institutional norms. Cultural blocks thus include more than a dab of learning and habit and rules and traditions. There are several dabs of "fear of being different" and a few dashes of "the way we think others expect us to behave." The result is a loss of individuality and creativity.

Kindergarten
Slump

Torrance (1977, 1983) concluded that creativity (fantasy, imagination) drops when children enter kindergarten, an early time when conformity and regimentation suddenly become the rule. Said Torrance (1977, p. 21), ". . . this drop . . . is a societal or cultural phenomenon rather than a biological or natural one."

Fourth-Grade
Slump

There has been an even larger drop in creativity at the fourth grade—Torrance's famous *fourth-grade slump.* Repeated Torrance (1977, p. 22), ". . . the drop which

**Fifth-Grade
Slump in Korea**

occurs in the fourth grade is a societal rather than a biological phenomenon." The cultural source of the fourth-grade slump was confirmed in a recent study of 1,100 Korean elementary children by Kang (1989). Kang also found a substantial drop in creativity test scores, but in the fifth grade rather than fourth. The fourth-grade slump cannot be biological in origin if it occurs at age 9–10 in one country and age 10–11 in another.

**Fourth-Grade
Slump
Disappearing**

There is a silver lining around the dark fourth-grade cloud, particularly in western cultures. A growing emphasis on teaching for creative development in recent years has helped offset the conformity-based fourth-grade slump; it seems to be disappearing.

**Seventh-Grade
Slump, Too**

Perhaps the most visible monkey-see monkey-do conformity pressures exert themselves at adolescence, when new-found abstract thinking abilities (Piaget's formal operational thinking) increase students' self-awareness and self-consciousness. Is it surprising that Torrance (1977) described another drop in creative thinking at the seventh-grade level? This drop is not as large as the infamous fourth-grade slump.

**Dynamics:
Uncomfortable
to Be Different**

On the surface, the dynamics of conformity pressures are not extraordinarily mysterious: It simply is uncomfortable to be different, to challenge accepted ways of thinking and behaving.[1] We learn that it is good to be correct and bad to make mistakes. Rewards normally follow correctness, but being wrong can elicit disapproval, criticism, or even sarcasm and ridicule. "Being different" or "being wrong" raises fears of being judged foolish, incompetent, or just plain stupid.[2]

**More Subtle
Dynamics**

However, conformity pressures also work in more subtle ways. There are pressures to be practical and economical, which can be inconsistent with innovative, creative thinking. Further, we learn not to be "nosy," not to ask too many questions; but as Simberg (1978, p. 126) noted, "By stifling questioning, we are cutting out the very heart of creativity—curiosity." There also is a subtle

---

[1]Note: "Unconventional" young people—beatniks of the '60s, hippies of the '70s, punkers of the '80s—may be viewed as conforming to different norms.

[2]As we will see in Chapter 4, however, the creative person must take risks and sometimes fail; that's part of being an innovator.

belief that *fantasy* is a waste of time. (Where would creativity be without fantasy?) Moreover, society tells us to have faith in reason and logic, tendencies that can delicately repress imagination and innovation.

Simberg (1978) also noted that, especially in corporate settings, an overemphasis either on cooperation *or* competition can be barriers to creativeness. If high cooperation is stressed, a person must temper his or her creative ideas in order to "fit in," to conform and please others. On the other hand, an overemphasis on competition can orient us toward "beating somebody else to it," rather than toward finding good creative solutions.

Van Gundy (1987) described subtle *social/political* barriers to creative innovation, which include any organizational norms that reinforce conformity, inhibit innovation, discourage "idea people," or otherwise ban rocking the boat. For example:

Attitudes of secrecy

A reluctance to share ideas

The attitude that creative types do not fit in

A fear that innovation may change the uniqueness of an organization

A desire to protect the status quo

A fear that innovation will reduce jobs

As a general guideline, *there is a time to conform, and a time to think independently and creatively.*

EMOTIONAL BLOCKS

Strong
Emotions
Interfere

Particularly
Chronic
Anxieties

Emotional blocks interfere with clear thinking, sometimes by preoccupying and distracting our creative minds, other times by making us "freeze" in our thinking. Simberg (1978) imagined a balance scale with emotions on one side and clear thinking on the other; as one side goes up, the other goes down. Some familiar emotional blocks might be anger, fear, anxiety, hate, or even love. Some are temporary states, caused perhaps by problems with peers, parents, partners, or children, or by pressures and worries at school or work, financial stresses, or poor

"FOR THE LOVE OF TILLIE"
Formerly
"TILLIE'S PUNCTURED ROMANCE"

Emotional states will interfere with creativity. This woman got upset over a simple game of hide-and-seek. (The Museum of Modern Art/Film Stills Archive.)

health. More permanent emotional blocks include such chronic sources of insecurity and anxiety as fear of failure, fear of being different, fear of criticism or ridicule, fear of rejection, fear of supervisors, timidity, or poor self-concepts.

Van Gundy
Called Them
Individual/
Attitudinal
Barriers

Van Gundy's (1987) *individual/attitudinal* barriers will block either the creation of innovations or their adoption and implementation:

> Fear of taking risks
> Fear of uncertainty and ambiguity
> Differences in values and needs
> Personal characteristics that produce conflict

Can Take a
Problem Solving
Approach to
Emotional
Blocks

While this book does not deal in psychotherapy, we should note that moderate amounts of tension and anxiety are normal. In fact, some feelings of urgency or motivation are required for creative thinking and problem solving. However, if emotional blocks are interfering with thinking, it may help to take a creative problem-solving approach to dealing with them. That is, ask "What is the problem?" and "What can I/we do about it?" Chapter 5 will present the *Creative Problem Solving* (CPS) model that also may be used effectively with personal problems.

RESOURCE BARRIERS

Resource
Barriers Not in
Short Supply

Van Gundy (1987) described one last type of organizational block to creative innovation, *resource barriers,* which is just that—a shortage of people, money, time, supplies, or information. Innovation requires such resources, beyond what is needed for routine organizational procedures. Internal conflicts, a type of social/political (or cultural) barrier, are likely if resources are pirated from one department to develop an innovation in another department.

A WHACK ON THE SIDE OF THE HEAD

Von Oech:
Being Creative
= Removing
Mental Blocks

One fine book on stimulating creativity, written for corporate readers, was entitled *A Whack on the Side of the Head* (Von Oech, 1983). The entire book focused on 10 mental blocks of the variety discussed above. It is noteworthy that to Von Oech—a highly successful consultant and author in the area of corporate creativity— stimulating creativity is seen almost entirely as a matter of removing mental blocks. As his book title suggests, it can take a whack on the side of the head to jolt us out of our anti-creative mental blocks.

A Second Right
Answer?

The first of Von Oech's mental blocks, *The Right Answer,* is the usual assumption that there is just one right answer. Not so. We should look for the second right answer, the third right answer, and more. A later "right answer" is likely to be more creative than the first right answer. In Chapter 6 we will see that brainstorming, a creativity technique, is based squarely on deferring judgment until many possible solutions are produced.

This One
Makes Sense

Von Oech's second block, *That's Not Logical,* is based on our culturally-rooted assumption that logical thinking is better than illogical thinking. However, illogical thinking can provide the imaginative play and new perspectives necessary for a creative breakthrough. In contrast to strictly logical thinking, Von Oech listed other possibilities: speculative thinking, fantasy thinking, analogical thinking, divergent thinking, lyrical thinking, mythical thinking, poetic thinking, visual thinking, symbolic thinking, foolish thinking, ambiguous thinking, surreal thinking, and others. Instead of "getting down to brass tacks" we should consider steel tacks, copper tacks, plastic tacks, sailing tacks, income tax, syntax, or contacts.

We Should
Inspect the
Rules We Follow

A third block to creative thinking is *Follow the Rules.* Following rules means thinking of things only as they are. Instead of following the rules, says Von Oech, we should play the revolutionary and challenge rules. He recommended holding "rule-inspecting and rule-discarding" sessions within one's organization. (We might add "tradition-inspecting" and "tradition-discarding" sessions as well.)

Be Practical is his fourth block. Instead of being inhibited by pressures toward practicality, we should ask creativity stimulating "what if" questions, and encourage "what-iffing" in others. Sometimes preposterous "what-iffing" leads to practical ideas. In an example of Von Oech's, an engineer at a large chemical company asked this question: "What if we put gunpowder in our house paint? . . . (When it got old) we could just blow it right off the house!" This led to adding an inert chemicial additive to the paint; when another additive was later applied to the old paint, a reaction would take place and the paint would strip right off.

Avoid Ambiguity is the fifth block. In fact, ambiguity serves as a subtle form of motivation that inspires imaginative ideas. One can pose problems in deliberately ambiguous ways to induce imaginative answers. We will see in Chapter 7 that Gordon's "book titles" or "compressed conflicts" are ambiguous two-word statements that deliberately can be created as a means of provoking new viewpoints. Does the book title "motionless exertion" suggest ideas for physical exercises?

Von Oech's sixth block is *To Err is Wrong,* which we earlier noted is a well-reinforced habit. A fear of making mistakes inhibits trying new things—but creative innovation necessarily requires making errors and even failing. One story claims that while working on the light bulb, Edison tried nearly 2,000 ideas. Edison optimistically reported that he knew 2,000 ways not to build a light bulb! One probably surprising strategy for increasing creative productivity is to deliberately *increase* your failure rate. Creative person Thomas Watson, founder and president of IBM, claimed that "The way to succeed is to double your failure rate" (Von Oech, 1983, p. 93). Observed Von Oech, "Errors (serve) as stepping stones. . . . We learn by our failures. A person's errors are the whacks that lead him or her to think something different (pp. 90–92)."

Ask "What If" Questions

An Explosive Idea!

Never Ambiguity Is Always Helpful

Fear of Making Mistakes

Thomas Edison, Thomas Watson: Mistakes Lead to Success

These political reformers are stymied in their creative thinking because of their strong beliefs that "We Must Follow The Rules," "We Must Be Practical," "We Must Not Be Foolish," and "To Err is Wrong." "Oh, what the heck," said Abe, honestly, "let's just go to the play and see what happens!" (The Museum of Modern Art/Film Stills Archive.)

Play with Ideas   Another block, Von Oech's seventh, is the notion that *Play is Frivolous.* Countless creative innovations and scientific discoveries have been born by playing with ideas. As we will see in Chapter 4, childlike thinking, humor, and playing with ideas are exceedingly common characteristics of creative people. Necessity may be the mother of invention, said Von Oech, but play certainly is the father!

I Know Nothing of This Topic, It's Not My Area   Block number eight is *That's not My Area.* This block is rich with implications for creative thinking and problem solving. Most obviously, this block is an excuse for not even trying to solve a problem because of presumed ignorance. Moreover, such a thinker certainly will not look **Analogical Thinking** for ideas and inspiration in other fields. In fact, many innovations are born by adapting ideas from outside of one's

"Okay, wise guy, what was the name of von Oech's book?" (Wisconsin Center for Film and Theater Research.)

own field—as we will see in Chapter 7 on analogical thinking. Von Oech suggested finding ideas in old science magazines, history, want ads, and "studying a subject on a shallow level" (p. 109). Many innovations come from people outside of an area, or who know little about the given problem situation.

C'Mon Von Oech, Get Serious!

Don't be Foolish, block nine, is another cultural barrier rooted in conformity. Says Von Oech, you occasionally should play the fool, and you certainly should be aware of when you or others are putting down a creative "fool." Prince's (1968) "get fired" technique, in which you propose an idea so totally foolish that your boss will immediately fire you, helps create the playfulness and craziness that can lead to creative ideas.

Self-Squelcher
Will Be
Accurate

Finally, we have the tenth block, the self-squelcher *I'm Not Creative. If you seriously believe this, you will be correct.* It is a self-fulfilling prophecy.

Do you need an occasional whack on the side of the head?

IDEA SQUELCHERS

Ideas (and Ideas
for Idea
Squelchers)
Come from
Somewhere

It is bad enough to be uncreative. It is worse to squelch other people's creative thinking. This list of *idea squelchers* is based on one created by Warren (1974), who modified a list by Clark (1958) in his book *Brainstorming*, plus a few more from the cover of the *Journal of Creative Behavior* (1974, Issue 2), and a couple from Biondi (1980).

You would never make any of these comments, would you?

We've never done it before
We've tried that before
It won't work
We haven't the teacher-student ratio
It's not in the budget
We're not ready for it yet
All right in theory but can you put it
    into practice?
Too academic
Not academic enough
What will the parents think?
Somebody would have suggested it
    before if it were any good
Too modern
Too old fashioned
Let's discuss it at some other time

You've got to be kidding

You don't understand our situation

We're too small for that

We're too big for that

We're too new for that

We have too many projects now

It's been the same for 20 years, so it
    must be good

What bubblehead thought that up?

Won't we be held accountable?

I just know it won't work

Too blue sky

Let's form a committee

Let's put it in writing

We need more lead time

Walk, don't run

You'll never sell it to the union

Don't forget the chain of command

Let's not fight city hall

Be practical

Let's wait and see

I don't see the connection

It won't work in our neighborhood

We can't do it under the regulations

There's no regulations covering it

The Board will faint

That's not our responsibility

That's not our department

Thats not our job

That's not our role

It's low in our priorities

That's trouble

Don't rock the boat
I'll bet some professor suggested that
But we have to be practical
It's not in the plan
It's not in the curriculum
We did all right without it
You can't argue with success
It'll mean more work
It will increase taxes
It's too early
It's too late
It will offend
It doesn't matter
Our people won't accept it
Stay on their good side
Don't step on any toes
Have you checked with . . .
And you stand there saying . . .
You don't understand the problem
You can't teach an old dog new tricks
No adolescent is going to tell me how
    to run this operation

Probably the only positive feature of understanding barriers to creativity, particular external ones, is that it forces you to plan ahead—to anticipate the resistance that may greet your innovative ideas and plans (Van Gundy, 1987).

SUMMARY

We all would be more creative if it were not for blocks and barriers to creative thinking.

Habit and learning, which are necessary for humankind, also are obvious blocks to creative thinking.

Rules and traditions, too, are essential for society, but also inhibit imagination and innovation. Van Gundy's organizational barriers included the status hierarchy, degree of formalization (rule following), and procedural barriers.

Perceptual blocks—mental set, perceptual set, functional fixity—are based in learning. They prevent us from seeing new meanings, relations, applications, and new possibilities generally. Perceptual blocks are related to "jumping to conclusions," prevent us from "seeing the real problem," and prevent us from getting an accurate picture of our world.

Cultural blocks are social influence, expectations, and conformity pressures, which combine with our "fear of being different" to squelch creative thinking. Torrance's fourth-grade slump, and his smaller kindergarten and seventh-grade slumps, are due to conformity pressures and expectations.

Some subtle conformity influences are pressures not to ask questions, a belief that fantasy is useless, and an overemphasis on cooperation or competition (Simberg). Van Gundy described such social/political barriers as attitudes of secrecy, dislike for creative types, and protecting the status quo.

Emotional blocks may be temporary states or more chronic insecurities and fears, particularly fear of failure, ridicule, being different, or taking risks.

One can take a creative problem solving approach to emotional blocks.

Resource barriers are shortages of people, money, supplies, time, or information.

Von Oech's Whack on the Side of the Head approach to increasing creativity amounted to unlocking 10 mental blocks: The Right Answer; That's Not Logical; Follow the

Rules; Be Practical; Avoid Ambiguity; To Err is Wrong; Play is Frivolous; That's Not My Area; Don't be Foolish; and "I'm Not Creative."

Finally, a list of "idea squelchers" furnishes good suggestions for squelching other prople's creativity.

Don't forget: As a general principle, as you proceed down the yellow brick road of life, there is a time to conform and a time to be creative.

Solutions to Puzzles

1. Time flies? You cannot, they fly too fast.
2. The other four wrestlers were women.
3. Try removing S-I-X L-E-T-T-E-R-S.

definitions and theories: what is creativity?

[Scene: Austrian court room. Judge Heinrich Hangum is reading the charges against defendant Sigmund Freud.]

Judge Hangum: Herr Doktor Freud, you bin charged mit using schmutty ideas in your creativity theory und offendink the sensitivities of delicate folks. How do you plead, you guilty rascal?

Sigmund Freud: Not guilty, Herr Judge. I bin writin' und speakin' only die truth!

Judge: But die truth is, you bin sayin' we're bein' creative because we got a big sexy sex drive! You bin guilty as Cain!

Freud: But Herr Judge, dot isn't schmutty! We're bein' creative 'cause our id got sex needs, our superego got a clean conscience, und so our ego—dot's our "self"—puts the sex needs into creative fantasies!

Judge: Schmutty fantasies?

Freud: Nein, nein! Creative idea fantasies—poetry und painting, nice tings like dot.

Judge: Sounds fischy to me! Herr Doktor Freud, are you sure?

Freud: I am not die world's greatest psychoanalyst for nothink, you know.

Judge: I sink I vill give you six months in das schlammer to clean up your theory.

Freud: I sink you love your mama, hate your papa, und so you bin pickin' on defenseless psychoanalysts!

Judge: Make dot a year.

Definitions and Theories Simplify Complex Phenomena

There are many definitions and theories of creativity. Sometimes, the definitions are considered theories, and vice versa. The commonality is that both theories and definitions seek to simplify and explain very complex phenomena. To impose some structure, this chapter will review five categories of definitions of creativity and then

Lombroso:
Creativity
Related to
Insanity

briefly review three traditional theoretical approaches to creativity. For a more extensive review of creativity theory and definitions, the reader might begin with the Rothenberg and Hausman (1976) collection of creativity theories from philosopher Plato, who stressed inspiration from the gods through muses, to behaviorist Skinner, who emphasized the reinforcement of creative responses and analyzing the reinforcement history of creative persons, and brain experts Bogen and Bogen, who look at the link between creativity and brain hemisphere functions. Somewhere in between was Cesare Lombroso, who in 1895 related creativity to insanity—and therefore degeneration of the brain—because both the creative and the insane tend to be original. The more creative reader will appreciate Lombroso's contribution to scientific knowledge.[1] Other fine theory-laden works are Arietti (1976), Treffinger, Isaksen, and Firestein (1982), Sternberg (1988b; especially the chapter by Taylor), and Dacey (1989).

Many
Definitions
and Theories

To set the tone, there are about as many definitions, theories, and ideas about creativity as there are people who have set their ideas on paper. As a few pertinent quotes, Freeman, Butcher and Christie (1968) concluded that ". . . there is no unified psychological theory of creativity" and that we freely use such terms as imagination, ingenuity, innovation, intuition, invention, discovery, and originality interchangeably with "creativity." Folmer (1975) observed ". . . no coherent theory was ever able to be formulated, while opinions on the problem have become frequently incompatible, if not contradictory." Nicholls (1972) adds that ". . . the term creativity is used with something approaching (reckless) abandon by psychologists . . . and people in general." More recently, in discussing various chapters in Sternberg's creativity anthology, Tardif and Sternberg (1988, p. 429) concluded that "Different levels of analysis were used to address the concepts; within levels, different components were put forth; and even when similar components were discussed, differences were seen in how these components are defined and how crucial they were claimed to be for the

---

[1]Lombroso would have loved Rosanne Barr, Steve Martin, Bill Cosby, and Howard Hughes.

larger concept of creativity." (Translation: Gee whiz, everybody's got different ideas about what's important for creativity!)

Creativity Is Complex, Multifaceted

The problem, of course, is the complexity and multifaceted nature of creativity.[2] Psychologist Carl Jung (1959) wrote ". . . the creative aspect of life . . . baffles all attempts at rational formulation." Well, not entirely. Two traits of creative people are attraction to complexity and tolerance for ambiguity, which also seem to characterize anyone who is seriously interested in pursuing this topic.

DEFINITIONS OF CREATIVITY

Four Interrelated P's

It is convenient and conventional to discuss creativity in terms of three *P*s: the creative *person,* the creative *product,* and the creative *process* (e.g., Barron, 1988). As we will shortly see, most definitions focus on one or some combination of these. There also is an indispensable fourth *P,* the creative *press* (environment, climate, "place"; Isaksen, 1987; Mooney, 1963; Taylor, 1988). These Ps are interrelated in the obvious way: Creative products are the outcome of creative processes engaged in by creative people, all of which is supported by a creative environment (press). Torrance (1988, p. 47) relates the creative process, person, product, and press with these words: "I chose a process definition of creativity for research purposes. I thought that if I chose a process as a focus, I could then ask what kind of person one must be to engage in the process successfully, what kinds of environments will facilitate it, and what kinds of products will result from successful operation of the processes" (p. 47).

To the four Ps we add a fifth category of definitions: *mysterious mental happenings.*

---

[2]Complexity of creativity is elaborated in both Chapters 1 and 8.

Creative Person

Creative
Persons Possess
Particular
Traits

In Chapter 4 we will review many recurrent person-
nality and biographical traits of creative people, for example, confidence, energy, risk-taking, humor and a
history of creative activities. Definitions with a person
orientation respond to the question "What is creativity?"
with an answer such as, "Well, a creative person is
someone who . . ." possesses particular traits.

Lombroso's
Signs of
Degeneracy in
Creative People

There are several historically notable and unique definitions of creativity with a distinct person emphasis. For
example, Lombroso's degenerate brain definition (or
theory) could fit here. Naming specific famous persons,
Lombroso (1895) noted that "signs of degeneration in men
of genius" include stuttering, short stature, general ema-
ciation, sickly color (pallor), rickets (leading to club-foot-
edness, lameness, or being hunched-back), baldness,
amnesia/forgetfulness, sterility, and that awful symptom
of brain degeneration—left-handedness. The preceding
was presented for its entertainment value. The characteristics are not related to creativity, except maybe the
left-handedness (Dacey, 1989).

Rank's Creative
Type

Otto Rank (1945) described his *creative type,* also referred to as the *artist* or the *man of will and deed,* as
someone who has a strong, positive, integrated personality and who "is at one with himself . . . what he does,
he does fully and completely in harmony with all his
powers and ideals." His creative type contrasts with his
"average man" and his "conflicted and neurotic man."

Jung's
Psychological
Type

Carl Jung (1933, 1959, 1976), describing the creative
works of novelists and poets, particularly Goethe, identified two types of artistically creative people, the *psychological type* and the *visionary type.* The psychological
type of creation draws from the realm of human consciousness—lessons of life, emotional shocks, and experiences of passion and human crises. The poet's work is
thus an interpretation and illumination of conscious life
that raises the reader to greater clarity and depth of
human insight. Said Jung (1933), novels about love, crime,
the family, or society, along with didactic poetry and
much drama, is of the psychological type. The material
is understandable, based in experience, and fully explains
itself.

**Jung's
Visionary Type**

More interesting and more mystical is his visionary type. "It is a strange something that derives its existence from the hinterland of man's mind. . . . It is a primordial experience which surpasses man's understanding" (Jung, 1933). This "primordial experience" is said to be an activation of one's "archetypes" or "primordial images." According to Jung, "The archetypal image . . . lies buried and dormant in man's unconscious since the dawn of culture . . . they are activated—one might say, 'instinctively'—(in the) visions of artists and seers." The visionary creative person, due to dissatisfaction with current circumstances, is said to reach out to this collective unconscious. "The creative process, in so far as we are able to follow it at all, consists in an unconscious animation of the archetype, and in a development and shaping of this image till the work is completed" (Jung, 1976, p. 125–126).

Thin Evidence!

Is there evidence for this eyebrow-raising ("What's this?") explanation of the creative person? Said Jung, the assumption that an artist has tapped his collective unconscious for an unfathomable idea can be derived only from *a posteriori* analysis of the work of art itself (Jung, 1976). That is, the material seems *not* to be a reflection of the poet's personality, experience, or psychic disposition. However, said Jung, ". . . we cannot doubt that the vision is a genuine, primordial experience, regardless of what reason-mongers may say" (Jung, 1933). The critical reader, presumably a reason-monger, might place Jung's archetypes in the same category as Plato's muses or your nephew's Santa Claus.

**Three-Facet
Theory of
Creativity:
Sternberg**

A more coherent and recent person-based definition (theory) of creativity is Sternberg's (1988a) *three-facet model of creativity*. In a summary statement (p. 126), ". . . creativity is . . . a peculiar intersection between three psychological attributes: intelligence, cognitive style, and personality/motivation. Taken together, these three facets of the mind help us understand what lies behind the creative individual."

1. Intelligence

Intelligence, from Sternberg's information processing and triarchic theory perspective, cannot be summarized briefly. Let's just call it *intelligence,* with an emphasis on verbal ability, fluent thought, knowledge, planning,

"I got primordial archetypes and you-ou don't. I got primordial archetypes and you-ou don't!" gloated Harpo. "They're probably in that stupid hat!" replied Zeppo. (Wisconsin Center for Film and Theater Research.)

problem defining, strategy formulation, mental representation, decisional skill, and a general intellectual balance and integration (see Sternberg, 1988a, 1991).

2. Cognitive Style

The *cognitive style* (or *intellectual style* or *mental self-government*) found in a creative person evolves around low conventionality: a preference for creating one's own rules and doing things one's own way, a liking for problems that are not prestructured, an enjoyment of writing, designing, and creating, and a preference for creative occupations, such as creative writer, scientist, artist, investment banker, or architect. Sternberg included in creative intellectual styles an *anarchic* form of mental self-government, characterized by a potpourri of needs and goals, a random approach to problems, motivation from "muddle" and other inexplicable forces, frequent lack of clear goals, tendencies to simplify, an inability to set priorities, and others. Said Sternberg (1988a, pp. 140–141), "Anarchics have the ability to remove themselves from existing constraints, ways of seeing things, and ways of doing things. . . . Anarchics are not to the tastes of either teachers or parents, because the anarchics go against the existing grain."

3. Personality and Motivation

The *personality/motivation* dimension includes creative traits that duplicate those to be described in Chapter 4, for example, tolerance for ambiguity, flexibility, drive for accomplishment and recognition, perseverence in the face of obstacles, willingness to grow in creative performance, and moderate risk-taking.

Concluded Sternberg, "People are creative by virtue of a combination of intellectual, stylistic, and personality attributes" (p. 145).

Creative Process

Torrance's Definition

Torrance's (1955, 1988) definition of creativity describes a process that resembles steps in the scientific method: "I tried to describe creative thinking as the process of (1) sensing difficulties, problems, gaps in information, missing elements, something askew; (2) making guesses and formulating hypotheses about these deficiencies; (3) evaluating and testing these guesses and hypotheses; (4) possibly revising and retesting them; and finally (5) communicating the results" (1988, p. 47). Torrance's definition is unique in including the entire creative episode, from detecting a problem to presenting the results. We noted earlier that Torrance's process definition implicitly or explicitly includes the creative person (someone who can do this), the creative product (the successful result), and the creative press (the environment that facilitates the process).

Wallas Stages

In Chapter 5 we will look at several proposed sets of stages in creativity, each of which has been described as the creative *process*. For now, we will just mention Wallas' ancient-but-nice 1926 steps consisting of *preparation, incubation, illumination* and *verification*. The terms are almost self-defining, but you may peek at Chapter 5 if you

CPS Model

Combining
Ideas

Koestler:
Bisociation of
Ideas

wish. The "best" set of stages, in the sense of being useful in creatively solving real problems, is the CPS (creative problem solving) model (Chapter 5).

Other process definitions assume that a creative idea is a *combination* of previously unrelated ideas, or looking at it another way, new relationships among ideas. Therefore, the creative process is the process of combining those ideas or perceiving those relationships.

The most eloquent statement of the idea combining definition is found in Arthur Koestler's (1964) *bisociation of ideas* concept: ". . . let me recapitulate the criteria which distinguish bisociative originality from associative routine. . . . The first (is) the previous independence of the mental skills or universe of discourse which are transformed and integrated into the novel synthesis of the creative act. . . . (Creativity is) the amalgamation of two realms as wholes, and the integration of the laws of both realms into a unified code of greater universality. . . . The more unlikely or more 'far-fetched' the (idea combination), the more unexpected and impressive the achievement."

To note a few more notables who endorse idea-combining activities in the creative process:

"It is obvious that invention or discovery, be it in mathematics or anywhere else, takes place by combining ideas" (Hadamard, 1945).

"The ability to relate and to connect, sometimes in odd and yet striking fashion, lies at the very heart of any creative use of the mind, no matter in what field or discipline" (Seidel, 1962).

"The intersection of two ideas for the first time" (Keep, cited by Taylor, 1988).

"Any process by which something new is produced— an idea or an object, including a new form or arrangement of old elements" (Harmon, 1955).

"The integration of facts, impressions, or feelings into a new form" (Porshe, 1955).

"That quality of the mind which allows an individual to juggle scraps of knowledge until they fall into new and more useful patterns" (Read, 1955).

"The creative process is the emergence in action of a novel relational product, growing out of the uniqueness

Many creative ideas are the product of combining previously unrelated ideas. In this historic photo Winchester Arms inventor Wally Boome combined the idea of "big oaf" with the idea of "cannon" to produce the first self-propelled, self-aiming artillery piece that runs on a daily fuel supply of five chickens and 25 pounds of potatoes. "A little rhubarb pie, too," adds Olaf Oaf, carefully taking aim. (The Museum of Modern Art / Film Stills Archive.)

of the individual" (Rogers, unpublished paper cited in Fabun, 1968).

"Creativity is the production of meaning by synthesis" (Allen, 1966).

"Creativity is a marvellous capacity to grasp two mutually distinct realities without going beyond the field of our experience and to draw a spark from their juxtaposition" (Preface to Max Ernst Exhibition. Cited in Fabun, 1968).

Poetry Can Result from Combining Ideas, Experiences

Looking at the creative process as combining ideas is not limited to creating concrete "things." John Livingstone Lowes (1927) analyzed Samuel Taylor Coleridge's writing of *Kubla Khan*. Coleridge had reported that he composed over two hundred lines while in a deep opium sleep, and published it almost without modification. Lowes explained that Coleridge's prior readings and writings filled his mind with the ideas and images that combined into the poetic *Kubla Khan.* As Lowes wrote in dry social science journalese, "Facts which sank at intervals out of conscious recollection drew together beneath the surface through almost chemical affinities of common elements . . . there in the darkness moved phantasms of fishes and animiculae and serpentine forms of his vicarious voyages, thrusting out tentacles of association and interweaving beyond disengagement."

High Intuitive Appeal

Defining creative ideas as new combinations of existing ideas has strong intuitive appeal. For example, virtually any new consumer product, from weed eaters and skate boards to Chinese pizza and glowing golf balls, can easily be dissected into the parts that were combined into the innovative wholes. The same applies to scientific, medical, technological, and sometimes artistic and literary creations.

Creative Combinations Require a Creative Person

However, it is important to realize that defining the creative process as combining ideas, and therefore creative products as new idea combinations, helps only slightly to simplify the nature of "creativity." The fact that a creative chemist has access to chemical elements, or a creative writer to words, cannot explain their adeptness in combining these parts into creative and valuable wholes. Assembling high quality creative combinations normally requires considerable experience, highly-developed technical and stylistic skills, high energy, a lively imagination, and a polished aesthetic taste to know when the idea combination is "good." The final creation is sometimes a simple combination, such as chocolate ants, and sometimes a complex one, such as Coleridge's *Kubla Khan.*

How Can Something Come from Nothing?

Generation, Selection, Preservation of Ideas: Perkins

Generation, selection, and preservation of ideas: Perkins. David Perkins' (1988) explanation of creativity also is based on how a creative person deals with idea combinations. Perkins began by posing the hypothetical question of whether invention is possible, the *ex nihilo* question: How can something come out of nothing? His solution, in brief, includes a process analogous to natural selection: the *generation, selection,* and *preservation* of ideas. Unlike natural selection, the process is not random. The potential "combinatorial explosion" of possibilities is "mindfully directed" by creative people—people who are motivated, have creative "patterns of deployment" or "personal maneuvers of thought," and have raw ability in a discipline. Such people mentally represent and "operate on" traditional boundaries, producing practical innovations (the light bulb) and impractical ones (poetry).[3]

Creative Product

Product and
Process Related

Originality

And Social
Worth

He's a Good
Egg!

Some of the definitions of creativity in the *process* category are a hair-width, or less, from defining the creative *product* and could easily appear in this product section.

Definitions that focus on the creative product invariably emphasize originality, a word sometimes used interchangeably with creativity. And if the person penning the definition thinks a few seconds longer, he or she usually will include some notion of practicality, value or social worth in order to exclude the bizarre, off-the-wall—but unquestionably original—scribblings of a chimpanzee or the babblings of a child, mentally deranged person or politician. Said Briskman (1980, p. 95), "The novelty of a product is clearly only a necessary condition of its creativity, not a sufficient condition; for the man who, in Russell's apt phrase, believes himself to be a poached egg may very well be uttering a novel thought, but few of us, I imagine, would want to say that he was producing a creative one" (Briskman, 1980, p. 95).

Some definitions emphasizing just originality are:

"Creative ability appears simply to be a special class of psychological activity characterized by novelty (Newell, Shaw, & Simon, 1962).

"Creativity may be defined, quite simply, as the ability to bring something new into existence" (Barron, 1969).

Creativity is ". . . the process of bringing something new into birth" (May, 1959).

"Creativity . . . is a noun naming the phenomenon in which a person communicates a new concept (which is the product)" (Rhodes, 1961).

[3]Offended poets are asked to contact Perkins (School of Education, Harvard University), not Davis.

Adding a dash of practicality, value or social worth we get:

"Creativeness, in the best sense of the word, requires two things: an original concept, or 'idea,' and a benefit to someone" (Mason, 1960).

"Creativity is the occurrence of a composition which is both new and valuable (Murray, cited in Fabun, 1968).

"Creativity is the disposition to make and to recognize valuable innovations" (Lasswell, cited in Fabun, 1968).

"The creative process is any thinking process which solves a problem in an original and useful way" (Fox, cited in Fabun, 1968).

"Creativity is defined as the ability to make new combinations of social worth" (Haefele, 1962).

"A creative person, by definition, . . . more or less regularly produces outcomes in one or more fields that appear both original and appropriate" (Perkins, 1988, p. 379).

Barron:
Newness,
Purposefulness,
Fitness

Also emphasizing both originality and worth, Barron (1988, p. 80) wrote that "Creativity is an ability to respond *adaptively* to the needs for new approaches and new products. It is essentially the ability to bring something new into existence purposefully." Expanding further on the purposefulness of innovations, Barron emphasized ". . . their aptness, their validity, their adequacy in meeting a need, and a rather subtle additional property that may be called, simply, *fitness*—esthetic fitness, ecological fitness, optimum form, being "right" as well as original at the moment. The emphasis is on whatever is fresh, novel, unusual, ingenious, clever, and apt."

Creative Press

Press May
Repress
Creativity

A fourth category of definitions or approaches to creativity emphasizes the creative *press,* the social and psychological environment.[4] The environment may repress imagination, creativity, and innovation, as in institutions that seem devoted to the *status quo,* as we described in

---

[4]Mnemonic device: Think of social "pressure."

our cultural barriers section of Chapter 2. And as in cultures where conformity, tradition, duty, obedience, and role obligations are stressed.

Or Support Creativity

We find an emphasis on a favorable creative press in brainstorming, with its defining principle of deferred judgment (no criticism, no evaluation; Chapter 6), in Carl Rogers' (1962) emphasis on psychological safety, and in any classroom or corporate setting where a creative climate encourages creative thinking and innovation. Isaksen (1987, p. 14) mentioned as ". . . necessary conditions for the healthy functioning of the preconscious mental processes which produce creativity: The absence of serious threat to the self, the willingness to risk; . . . (and) openness to the ideas of others."

Also, Responses to Social Needs

Response to social needs. Rhodes (1987) mentioned two other important aspects of the "press" that are important for creativity. First, many creative innovations, particularly inventions, are in response to social needs—the world needed a cotton gin, a telephone, a Xerox machine, good Broadway shows, a heart transplant, and awful-tasting TV dinners (but they're quick). Current needs—safer automobiles, a cure for AIDS, a better TV picture—are motivating near-frantic levels of creative problem solving. Second, for many types of innovations, especially those based in technology, the "press" must offer ". . . a sufficiently advanced stage of culture and a proper technical heritage" (Rhodes, 1987, p. 220).

Society Decides Who and What Is Creative

Society as judge. Society plays another subtle role in creativity. That of deciding who and what is creative. Csikszentmihalyi (1988) noted that the judgment of what is "genuinely creative" does not reside in the object itself. Rather, ". . . the reason we believe that Leonardo or Einstein was creative is that we have read that that is the case" (p. 327). It is the artistic and scientific establishments, in whom we place great trust, that make such judgments. It is thus social agreement that decides what is "creative." Sometimes "society" reduces to one or two art, movie, theatre, or book critics who tell us in their weekly columns what is innovative (and therefore good) and what is of little value. Said Csikszentmihalyi, in regard to the "notoriously fickle realm of the arts," the ". . . critics and viewers who have looked . . . closely at Botticelli's work are just as indispensable to Botticelli's creativity as was the painter himself" (p. 328). In math, physics, and chemistry, the attribution of creativity again is a social process which, as in the case of art, can be relative, fallible, and sometimes reversed by posterity.

So that's why van Gogh died poor. In October, 1989, one of his paintings was offered for sale at 40 million dollars, which sounds high but the frame and little light were included.

Mysterious Mental Happenings

Things That Go
Bump: Shulz

Creativity
Eludes
Understanding:
Jung

Descriptions of creativity in this category come from people who should best understand the process of creation—acknowledged creative geniuses. The main point is that creativity either is inexplicable or just sort of happens. Peanuts cartoonist Shulz, for example, claims that many of his ideas stem from "things that go bump in the night." Jung (1933) noted, "Any reaction to stimulus may be causally explained; but the creative act, which is the absolute antithesis of mere reaction, will forever elude human understanding."

Fabun (1968) provides additional relevant examples: "It is like diving into a pond—then you start to swim. . . . Once the instinct and intuition get into the brush tip, the picture *happens,* if it is to be a picture at all" (D. H. Lawrence).

While D. H. Lawrence credits his brush tip, Gertrude Stein gives most credit to her pen and paper. ". . . think of writing in terms of discovery, which is to say that creation must take place between the pen and the paper, not before in thought or afterwards in a recasting. . . . It will come if it is there and if you will let it come."

"I have no idea whence this tide comes, or where it goes, but when it begins to rise in my heart I know that a story is in the offing" (Dorothy Canfield).

We already noted that Plato credited muses for creative inspiration. Martindale (1975) described other creative people whose creativity mystified even them:

William Blake reported that he wrote one poem ". . . from immediate dictation, 12 or sometimes 20 or 30 lines at a time without premeditation, and even against my will."

Beethoven and Mozart both heard symphonies in their respective heads and had only to scribble out the notes.

Mathematician Poincare reported that after some stiff coffee, ". . . ideas rose in crowds, I felt them collide until pairs interlocked, making a stable combination. By the next morning I had established the existence of a class of Fuchsian functions . . . I had only to write out the results."

Poet A. E. Housman said that, after drinking a few beers, "As I went along, thinking nothing in particular, . . . there would flow into my mind with sudden and unaccountable emotion, sometimes a line or two of verse, sometimes a whole stanza at once."

Poet Rimbaud wrote, "I witness the breaking forth of my thoughts. I watch them, I listen to them."

Socrates: Divine Power

Plato (Cooper, 1961) had Socrates explain this account of the poetic process: "A poet is a light and winged thing, and holy, and never able to compose until he has become inspired, and is beside himself and reason is no longer in him . . . for not by art do they utter these, but by power divine."

Finally, Ghiselin (1963), quoted Mozart's description of unconscious processes in creativity:

Mozart Had Nothing to Do with It, He Said

When I feel well and in a good humor, or when I am taking a drive or walking after a good meal, or in the night when I cannot sleep, thoughts crowd into my mind as easily as you could wish. Whence and how do they come? I do not know and I have nothing to do with it. Those which please me, I keep in my head and hum them; at least others have told me that I do so. Once I have my theme, another melody comes, linking itself to the first one, in accordance to the needs of the composition as a whole.

Much about
Creativity
Remains a
Mystery

The lesson in this series of definitions and analyses is that although we do understand much about creative people and creative processes, much also remains a mystery. Even history's most creative people are confused.

Theories of Creativity

Three
Traditional
Approaches

There are a large number of ideas that are considered "theories of creativity," including most of the definitions and descriptions above. This section will briefly review three traditional approaches, the *psychoanalytic, behavioristic,* and *self-actualization* viewpoints.

Psychoanalytic Approaches

There is not a single, unitary psychoanalytic interpretation, rather, there are several.

Freud: Conflict
Between Libido
and Social
Conscience

Freud. The best-known and least-liked psychoanalytic theory of creativity is that of the great man himself, Sigmund Freud. Freud's approach focuses on the motivation to create. Very briefly, and highly simplified, creative

Sublimation into
Acceptable
Outlet:
Creativity

productivity results from an unconscious conflict between the primitive sexual urges (*libido*) of the *id* and the repressive influences of the social conscience, the *superego.* One cannot freely indulge one's sexual urges, can one. Therefore, the sexual energy is rechanneled (sublimated) into acceptable forms—creative fantasies and products. The id is happy, the superego is happy, and the self (*ego*) has successfully fended off an attack of neurosis stemming from the conflict.

Uncreative
Person
Represses
Fantasies: Freud

Freud concedes that everyone has the innate sexual urges which must be sublimated. However, not everyone is highy or even moderately creative. The solution to this dilemma is that the creative person accepts the libido-stimulated fantasies and elaborates upon them, while the uncreative person represses the fantasies and ideas.

Childlike
Regression

Primary Process
Thinking

Secondary
Process
Thinking

Freud also noted that fantasy and creative thinking include a regression to more childlike modes of thought. In fact, to Freud creativity is a continuation of and substitute for the free play of childhood (Getzels & Jackson, 1962). As a vocabulary lesson, we might note that this regression is to *primary process* thinking, which contrasts with *secondary process* thinking. Primary process thinking, which developmentally occurs before secondary thinking, happens during relaxation. It includes the chaotic realm of dreams, reveries, free associations and fantasies—your basic stuff of creativity. Secondary process thinking is logical, analytic, and oriented toward reality.

A Negative
View

The Freudian view is a rather negative one—creativity is merely the outcome of an unconscious neurotic conflict. Most of us prefer a more positive explanation of the motivation behind creativity—for example, encountering problems or difficulties; innate needs to construct, create, achieve success, impress one's friends, or improve the lot of humanity. The desire for money has stimulated plenty of entrepreneurial creativity. Compton (1952) described the motive to create simply as "The decision to do something when you are irritated."

Kris: Sex Plus
Aggression
Drives Are
"Discharged"

Emphasis on
Preconscious
and Conscious
Activity

Kris. A more contemporary psychoanalyst, Ernst Kris (1952), presented a view that is just a slight modification of Freud's creativity theory. The main distinctions are that (1) creativity is motivated by two main instincts of the *id,* the libido (sex drive) and aggressive instincts; and (2) instead of *unconscious* neurotic conflicts, Kris emphasizes *preconscious* and *conscious* mental activity. Said Kris, "Fantastic, freely wandering thought processes [creativity] tend to discharge . . . libido and aggression. . . ." According to Kris, creative fantasies occur in the preconscious mind. The preconscious mental activity can most easily be understood in terms of idle fantasies and daydreaming which often occur on the fringes of consciousness. The shift of creative ideas from the preconscious to the conscious is felt as a sudden "Eureka!" or illuminating experience, following the preconscious incubation of the problem. As with Freud, Kris also accepts regression to more childlike thought processes—primary process thinking—as part of the preconscious activity.

Psychoanalyst Ernst Kris tells us that aggressive instincts find outlets in creative productivity. "Oh, how I wish our students would have had some crayons!" laments teacher Rose Busch, left. "Maybe they'll do better in first grade," answers the student teacher. (The Museum of Modern Art/Film Stills Archive.)

Freud: Id

Kris: Ego

An important theoretical distinction between Freud and Kris is that, to Freud, creativity is said to "be in the service of the *id*," since creativity unconsciously releases libidinal (id) energy. To Kris however, creativity is said to "be in the service of the ego," since the ego exercises some voluntary control over regression and over the shifting of preconscious ideas to the conscious mind. Your author is uncertain to whom this distinction is important.

Kubie: Preconscious Activity

Conscious End of Continuum: Anchored in Reality

Kubie. A third psychoanalytic theory of creativity is that of Lawrence Kubie (1958). While Kubie ignores ids, egos, libidos, and superegos, like Kris he does emphasize preconscious mental activity. Imagine a continuum of consciousness. At one end is conscious mental life and conscious symbolic processes (e.g., language). With these conscious symbolic processes we communicate, we think, we examine our thinking, we also rearrange our experiences into logical categories. Such conscious processes have their roots in learning and experience. Since these processes are anchored in reality, there is little flexibility or imaginative free play, says Kubie.

Unconscious Is Rigid, Not Creative

At the other end of the continuum are unconscious, symbolic processes. According to Kubie, in the unconscious symbolic meanings are hidden, lost, or repressed and can only be made conscious by special techniques, for example, psychoanalysis, hypnosis, or drugs. This unconscious system of symbols, meanings, and relationships is said to be even more fixed and rigid than the conscious system—not flexible nor creative at all. This rigidity of the unconscious, says Kubie, leads the artist, composer or poet to repeatedly use the same recognizable style and content in his or her works.

Creativity Takes Place in the Preconscious, on the Fringe of Consciousness

Creative activity takes place *between* the conscious and the unconscious, that is, in the *preconscious*. The preconscious is not tied stricty to the everyday pedestrian realities of the conscious mind, nor is it anchored to the even more rigid symbolic relationships of the unconscious. Rather, the preconscious can engage in free play with ideas, meanings and relationships, thereby producing the new and unexpected connections, metaphorical relationships, overlapping meanings, puns, and allegories that we call *creativity*.

Education: Ties Preconscious to Conscious

On education, Kubie says, "The price we pay for traditional educational methods is that they . . . tie our preconscious symbolic processes prematurely to precise [conscious] realities. . . ."

Freud/Kris Theory Misleading: Kubie

On the Freud-Kris explanation of creativity, Kubie says, ". . . the ad hoc postulate that there is a separate and special mechanism known as the sublimation of unconscious processes may not be needed to explain creativity, and may actually be misleading. . . . Neurosis corrupts, mars, distorts and blocks creativity in every field" (Kubie, 1958).

Rugg: Similar to Kubie

Rugg. Finally, Harold Rugg's (1963) formulation of creativity is extremely similar to that of Kubie. The difference, in fact, seems mostly semantic. Rugg emphasized "off-conscious" mental activity or thinking in the "transliminal chamber" which he located midway between the unconscious mind and conscious mental activity. The transliminal chamber was called "the center

Transliminal Chamber: Midway Between Conscious, Unconscious

of creative energy." Here, the mind is free to draw from the vast store of experiences in the unconscious, and to creatively use these in conscious everyday living.

Both Kubie and Rugg thus emphasize the importance of preconscious, fringe-conscious, or off-conscious thinking in creativity. Perhaps this explains why creative people have strong needs for privacy, away from the demands of conscious realities, and why daydreaming and incubation (both of which are forms of preconscious activity) can produce creative inspirations.

Behavioristic and Learning Theories

Learning theorists do not agree either. To review your introductory psychology, traditional learning theory emphasizes the reinforcement (reward) of correct responses and stimulus-stimulus associations. You may recall Skinner's hungry rats who learned to press a bar to earn lunch, and Pavlov's dog who learned the association between bells and food, causing him (the dog) to spit whenever the bell rang. The approach is called *behaviorism* because the focus is on the visible behavior itself, rather than the unseen mental events that control the behavior.

Skinner. The big gun behaviorist, of course, is B. F. Skinner—a highly creative person who creatively argues that there is no such thing as creativity. In his best selling *Beyond Freedom and Dignity* (Skinner, 1971), he argued that we have no *freedom,* since all of our behavior is controlled by those who dispense reinforcements and punishments (parents, teachers, peers, police, and others who enforce laws, traditions, customs, mores, social expectations, etc.). Nor should we accept the *dignity* which comes from personal accomplishment, since again those achievements were determined by our history of rewards and punishments.

Creativity Due
to Genetics,
Environment,
Learning

Now let's examine how he deprives us of our creativeness. Basically, the behavior of a creative person such as a poet is ". . . merely the product of his genetic and environmental history" (Skinner, 1972).[5] The act of composing a poem out of "bits and pieces" is not an act of creativity, since in the experience of the poet he or she ". . . had to learn how to put them together." In behavioristic terms, ". . . the behavior [response] was . . . triggered by the environment [stimulus] . . . [and] . . . the consequences [reward] may strengthen his tendencies to act in the same way again." While creating a poem may indeed require exploration and discovery, these are tied to the history of the poet and to trial-and-error learning activities.

History Plus
Trial-and-Error

Poet Is Unaware
of Source of
Ideas: Skinner

Since the poet is not aware of all of his or her history, he or she does not know where the poetic ideas (behavior) come from. Therefore, the poet erroneously attributes his or her own creations to a creative mind, an unconscious mind, or perhaps ". . . to a muse, . . . whom he has invoked to come and write his poem for him." Even Shakespeare is given little credit for his own works because "Possibly all their parts could be traced by an omniscient scholar to Shakespeare's verbal and nonverbal histories." Shakespeare himself merely put the bits and pieces together in a fashion that produced rewarding consequences.

Shakespeare:
No Creativity
Here Either

Even Shakespeare deserves no dignity.

Maltzman:
Increase
Original
Behavior with
Reinforcement

Maltzman. Moving to a second and related behavioristic theory of creativity, in a well-known article publilshed in a journal with high social status, experimental psychologist Irving Maltzman (1960) argued that we can increase original behavior simply by rewarding it. He also reviewed his own research which proved beyond doubt that when original word associations were rewarded, the frequency of original word associations increased. A scientific study, entitled "The Creative Porpoise," showed that if porpoises were given a dead fish only when they

The Dead Fish
Approach

[5]This section presents many direct quotes from Skinner in order to decrease the suspicion that your author fabricated Skinner's unusual position on creativity. Skinner really said these things.

performed a new, creative stunt—but not when they repeated an old one—they quickly learned to put a lot of
variety and creativity into their act (Pryor, Haag, &
O'Reilly, 1969).

Is Something Amiss?

It is comforting to have this scientific confirmation that
creativity will increase when it is encouraged and rewarded. Something seems amiss however, when porpoises are called *creative* but William Shakespeare is not.

Staats: Complex Stimulus Control

Staats. A third behavioristic analysis of creative
thinking also is quite straightforward. Arthur Staats
(1968) described how S-R psychology can explain the
production of novel, creative behavior through "complex
stimulus control." We begin with the existence of two unrelated stimulus-response (S-R) relationships, each established by previous reinforcement. For example, the
stimulus "Berlin Wall" elicits images of the Berlin Wall
guarded by East German Soldiers. The stimulus of "people
leaving" can elicit the verbal direction "Turn out the
lights when you leave." In the fall of 1989, when East
Germans were first allowed to leave their country, at least
three cartoonists created a cartoon showing exiting East
Germans telling a border guard to "Turn out the lights
when you leave!"

Two Unrelated Stimuli Elicit Novel Response Combination

This approach (theory?) assumes that creative ideas
are new combinations of previously unrelated ideas. The
approach simply describes in stimulus-response language how two previously unrelated stimuli, when encountered together, can elicit a creative response
combination. The description applies, according to Staats
(1968), to any creative act from a child uttering a novel
sentence to a scientist creating a theory.

A Creative Person Has Many Available Mental Associations: Mednick and Mednick

The Mednicks' RAT

Mednick. A fourth and final behavioristic view of creativity focuses upon mental associations. Mental associations—for example, the word *carrot* might elicit
rabbit—are assumed to be learned on a contiguity basis.
That is, carrots and rabbits have been repeatedly experienced together, and so a mental association between
them is formed much as Pavlov's dog Rin-Tin-Tinovich
formed the association between the bell and the Alpo. According to psychologist Sarnoff Mednick (1962; also
Martha Mednick & Andrews, 1967), a highly creative
person is one who possesses a large number of verbal and
non-verbal mental associations which are available for

recombination into creative ideas. A less creative person is one who is able to respond with just a few, highly dominant mental associations. For example, in listing unusual uses for a brick, the low creativity person, with few-but-strong associations, would quickly snap off, "Well, . . . uh . . . you might build a house or a garage with 'em . . . if you had enough. That's all I can think of." Mednick (1967) published the *Remote Associates Test* (RAT; now out of print and therefore omitted from our creativity testing chapter), which was supposed to measure differences in the availability of verbal associations; that is differences in creative ability. The test taker would be given three words (*birthday, surprise, line; shopping, washer, picture*) and was asked to produce a fourth word somehow associated with all three.

Oversimplification The traditional criticism of stimulus-response psychology is that of oversimplification or *reductionism.* Such complex human behavior as hopes, plans, aspirations, neuroses, speech, reading this book, chuckling at the jokes, or solving chemistry problems, writing poetry, or designing a marketing plan theoretically could be "reduced to" principles of Pavlovian (classical) conditioning or Skinnerian (instrumental) conditioning, Much of the complexity of learning and mental life is lost in such oversimplification.

Self-Actualization Approach

Self-Actualization Equals Mental Health

Self-Actualized and Special Talent Creativity

The essence of the *self-actualization* approach to creativity was presented in Chapter 1. The central point was that the creative person also is a self-actualized person— a fully-functioning, mentally healthy, forward-growing human being who is using his or her talents to become what he or she is capable of becoming (Maslow, 1954, 1968; Rogers, 1962). Some refer to this as a *mental health* or *psychological growth* explanation of creativity. To account for creative neurotics (or neurotic creatives) the reader should recall Maslow's distinction between *self-actualized* creativity, the mentally healthy tendency to approach all aspects of one's life in a creative way, and *special talent* creativity, having a strong creative talent in a particular area with or without mental health and self-actualization. The reader also should recall Maslow's 15 characteristics of a self-actualized person summarized in Inset 1.1. (Yes, you should look again at Inset 1.1.)

Rogers: Psychological Safety

Carl Rogers (192) adds a few important conditions for creativity:

1. ***Psychological safety.*** This is the creative atmosphere, a flexible and receptive environment. It is entirely a matter of attitudes.

Internal Locus of Evaluation

2. ***Internal locus of evaluation.*** This refers to personal characteristics of self-confidence and independence, a tendency to make one's own judgments, and a willingness to accept responsibility for one's successes and failures.

Playfulness

3. ***A willingness to toy with ideas, to play with new possibilities.***

Openness to Experience: External and Internal

4. ***Openness to experience.*** This includes a receptiveness to new ideas and an attraction to new interests and experiences in the external world. It also includes a willingness to acknowledge internal wants, needs and habits, some of which may be of questionable social acceptability. For example, a creative male is more willing to accept traditionally feminine interests or behaviors, such as petting a cat, making baby formula, or baking a cake (Bem, 1974).

From Rogers' humanistic point of view, one stimulates creativity by creating a psychologically safe environment, modeling openness to experience and an internal locus of control, and encouraging students to play with possibilities.

SUMMARY

Definitions and theories try to clarify complex phenomena. There are many definitions and theories of creativity, due to its complexity.

Most definitions focus on the creative person, the creative product, the creative process, or the creative press (environment).

Person definitions emphasize characteristics of creative people. Lombroso noted that the creative and the insane both are original, and that creative people showed signs of mental degeneration. Contrasted with his average man and neurotic man, Rank's creative type is basically self-actualized.

Jung's visionary type of creative person, who contrasts with the psychological type, is said to get ideas from archetypes, the collective unconscious.

Sternberg's three-facet model included three dimensions of the creative person—intelligence, cognitive style, and personality/motivation.

Process approaches to creativity include Torrance's definition (sensing problems, forming and testing hypotheses, communicating the results); stage approaches such as Wallas' preparation, incubation, illumination, and verification and the CPS model; Koestler's notion of bisociation of ideas; and numerous one-sentence definitions based on combining ideas.

Lowes argued that Coleridge's drug-induced writing of *Kubla Khan* was a matter of combining ideas and images.

Perkins emphasized the generation, selection, and preservation of idea combinations by people who are motivated, have creative thought patterns, and high ability in an area.

Product definitions emphasize originality, usually combined with value or social worth.

The fourth P is the creative press, the environment, which can support or repress creativity. Further, much creativity is in response to social needs; society also judges who and what is "creative."

A category of definitions entitled mysterious mental happenings emphasized reports by creative people of inexplicable mental activities that resulted in creative ideas and products.

Freud's psychoanalytic theory focused on an unconscious conflict between the libido (sex drive) and the superego (social conscience), which is resolved in creative fantasies and products. It is a negative view of motivation to create. In the plus column, he stressed regression to childlike modes of thought (primary process thinking).

Similar to Freud, Ernst Kris stressed the neurosis-preventing discharge of both libidinal and aggressive energy in creative fantasies. However, Kris emphasized preconscious and conscious mental activity.

Kubie argued that a neurotic conflict always is bad for your creative health. Like Kris, however, he proposed that the free play of creative thinking takes place in preconscious mental activity, between conscious and unconscious processes.

Rugg similarly located creative thinking between our conscious and unconscious minds, in an area he called the transliminal chamber.

Learning theories emphasize reinforcement of correct responses and stimulus-stimulus associations. Leader Skinner claimed that creativity, like freedom and dignity, does not exist. Creative acts are said to be explainable in terms of genetics and one's experiential history. We are reinforced for combining bits and pieces into creative wholes, says Skinner.

S-R psychologist Maltzman simply proposed that originality, like any other behavior, may be strengthened by reinforcement, a position confirmed by cooperative porpoises.

In his S-R approach to explaining creative idea combinations, Staats argued that two stimuli, encountered together for the first time, would elicit a novel (creative) combination of responses (ideas).

Sarnoff and Martha Mednick suggested that creative people have large repertoires of mental associations that are available for combination into creative ideas. Less creative people possess only a few, dominant associations to stimuli.

Learning theory approaches to complex behavior are considered oversimplified and reductionistic.

Carl Rogers and Abraham Maslow see creativity as self-actualization, which stresses mental health. Maslow makes the important distinction between self-actualized creativity and special talent creativity. Rogers emphasizes psychological safety, internal locus of evaluation, playfulness, and openness to experience.

4

the creative person: flexible, funny, and full of energy

[Scene: Living room of eccentric inventor Alexander Graham Schwartz, recent developer of the automatic talking chicken. TV cameramen have set up microphones, cameras and floodlights. ABC News correspondent Barbara Walters enters and sits down, facing Mr. Schwartz. The floodlights are turned on and the director counts "3, 2, 1!" and points to Ms. Walters.]

Barbara Walters: (Smiling) Mr. Schwartz, is it true that you are stark raving mad? A lunatic inventor in the true traditional sense?

Alexander Graham Schwartz: Mad? Not completely. But sometimes I think funny—I play with ideas, turn things upside down and inside out. I push ideas together and take them apart. Sometimes I look at a problem like I was four-years old—maybe from Mars. Right now I'm working on invisible tennis balls for players who keep saying, "I sure didn't see that one!"

Walters: Hmmm, I see. Tell me Mr. Schwartz, what else is it about creative people that makes them different from others?

Schwartz: It takes energy, a sense of adventure, and the confidence to stick your neck out and do something different—maybe wild and crazy. You can make a real fool of yourself, you know. How many people would go on national television to talk about talking chickens and invisible tennis balls?

Walters: I see your point. Tell me, should everyone try to be a little crazier—a little more creative—or is it just for you eccentric inventors?

Schwartz: (Jumps up, pretends to shoot down Red Barron) Eccentric? Who's eccentric? Yes, everyone should think about being creative. Most people have creative talents that never see the light of night!

Walters: That's very interesting, Mr. Schwartz. Now about those chickens, do they really talk or are you just a ventriloquist?

Schwartz: They talk, absolutely! No hanky-panky here. I start them off as chicks
with vowels—long "e," short "a," that sort of thing. Then we get to
consonants and whole words. For most, their first sentence is "Wake up,
you handsome devil you!" These are for people who can't stand all that
cock-a-doodle-do stuff at 5 o'clock in the morning.

Walters: And now, Mr. Schwartz, just one more question. Would you tell me and
our viewers at home just how you would like to be remembered?

Schwartz: As somebody with a little humor, a little independence, a little
imagination, and who isn't afraid to talk to a chicken.

What Makes a Creative Person Creative?

They Have Much in Common

Will Help Us Recognize Creative People

Psychologists and educators have taken many long looks at creative people in a continuing effort to understand the sorts of characteristics that underly and contribute to creativeness. The purpose of this chapter is to examine commonalities—characteristics that have recurred again and again in studies of creative people. Dozens of research studies, buttressed by informed opinions, point to one conclusion: *Creative people may be nonconformist, but they certainly have a lot in common.*

An awareness of characteristics of creativity will help us understand creative people and how they think. It also will help us recognize creative children and adults. We will not become perfect in our recognition of creative talent, however. Consider these examples of creative persons who were *not* recognized by their teachers, professors, or supervisors:

Albert Einstein was four years old before
he could speak and seven before he
could read.

As a boy Thomas Edison was told by his
teachers that he was too stupid to
learn anything.

Werner von Braun flunked ninth-grade
algebra.

Fred Waring was once rejected from high
school chorus.

Winston Churchill failed the sixth grade.

Leo Tolstoy flunked out of college.

Louis Pasteur was rated mediocre in chemistry when he attended the Royal College.

Harrison Ford (Indiana Jones) flunked out of Ripon College in Wisconsin.

F. W. Woolworth got a job in a dry goods store when he was 21, but his employers would not let him wait on customers because he "didn't have enough sense."

Walt Disney was fired by a newspaper editor because he had "no good ideas."

Caruso's music teacher told him, "You can't sing, you have no voice at all!"

Abraham Lincoln entered the Black Hawk War as a Captain and came out as a private.

Louisa May Alcott was told by an editor that she could never write anything that had popular appeal.

Creative Talent: Can Be Subtle, Complex

Such historical facts definitely are amusing. They also raise our awareness of the complexity and subtlety of creative talent.

PERSONALITY TRAITS, ABILITIES, BIOGRAPHICAL TRAITS

Personality, Cognitive Abilities, Biographical Traits

Distinction Sometimes Blurred

There are three types of characteristics that combine to produce creativeness: *personality traits, cognitive abilities* (including information processing styles), and *biographical traits* (experiences). The distinction between affect (personality), cognition (abilities), and learning (biographical traits, experiences) is an ancient one. However, in creative people the three categories interweave quite tightly, and some traits could fit in one category as easily as another. For example, *humor, independence, originality,* and *perceptiveness* could be viewed as personality traits, cognitive abilities, or both.

Similarities and Differences

Commonalities Across Different Areas

There are then, commonalities among creative persons in different areas. A creative scientific researcher, a creative artist, and a creative business entrepreneur—

But Also Wide Variation Between and Within Areas

by virtue of being creative—will have many personality traits and abilities in common. However, as one might guess, there also is wide variation in personality patterns, abilities, and experiences not only between persons in different areas, but among persons within the same area (e.g., two artists).

High Creatives May Not Be Well Adjusted

It also is true that some persons with great creative talent (Maslow's special talent creativity) will not be particularly well-adjusted in the self-actualization sense, while others will. As we will see later, some of the most highly creative people are fair-to-middling in neuroses or schizophrenia.

Creative in Own Area, Not Others

Most special talent creative people are creative in their own area but not in another; for example, a creative chemist may be a very uncreative artist, writer, or cook.

Except for Gifted Few

A few gifted personages have been creative in many areas—Leonardo Da Vinci, Thomas Jefferson, Benjamin Franklin (best known for trying to electrocute himself with a kite), Howard Hughes, and Orson Welles.

CREATIVITY AND INTELLIGENCE: THE THRESHOLD CONCEPT

Creativity and Intelligence Are Separate

Before turning to personality, cognitive, and biographical traits, let's look at a long-standing issue in creativity: the relationship between creativity and intelligence. On one hand, creativity and intelligence are recognized as two separate constructs. Landmark research by Getzels and Jackson (1962) and Wallach and Kogan (1965) identified and contrasted highly intelligent versus highly creative students, confirming that the two traits are indeed not the same. Further, developers of creativity tests take pride in demonstrating negligible correlations between scores on their creativity test and IQ scores. Their purpose is to establish that their test measures creativity, and not just components of intelligence (e.g., verbal ability, logical thinking, decision making).

But Creativity and Intelligence Also Are Related

Research Evidence

On the other hand, it also is agreed that creativity and intelligence are very clearly related. For example, Walberg (1988) reviewed biographical information about more than 282 eminent men (e.g., Mozart, Newton, Lincoln, Martin Luther, Goethe, Napoleon, Washington, Rembrandt, Da Vinci, Beethoven, Dickens, Galileo, Darwin) whose intelligence (IQ) had been estimated in an earlier study by Cox and Terman (Cox, 1926). Walberg concluded, "There is no doubt that IQ and (creative) eminence are linked." Walberg also compared high school students who won competitive awards in science or art with control students who were not award winners. Said Walberg (1988, p. 356), "They (the award winners) indicated they were brighter than their friends and quicker to understand." In Simontons's (1988) review of factors contributing to creativity, he concluded that " . . . creative individuals are noticeably more intelligent than average (p. 399)."

Intuitive Evidence

There also is persuasive intuitive evidence of a correlation between creativity and intelligence. No major creative accomplishments of worldwide significance have emerged from the legions of our mentally retarded citizens. Also, as children grow older, they become smarter. They also produce better quality poetry, art work, and science projects, and they score higher on most tests of creativity, especially divergent thinking tests. There is a good argument for a moderate relationship between creativity and intelligence.

Threshold Concept

Above a Base Level, No Relationship

The increasingly accepted resolution to this apparent inconsistency (creativity *is* versus *is not* related to intelligence) lies in the *threshold* concept. The cornerstone research behind this breakthrough was Donald MacKinnon's (1961, 1978a) studies of creative architects at the University of California at Berkeley. MacKinnon's creative architects scored higher on intelligence tests than did undergraduate students. However, when the architects were rank-ordered according to peer-rated degree of creativity, the correlation between their IQ scores and their creativity was nil ($-.08$). This research illustrated that *a base level of intellectual ability is essential for creative productivity; above that threshold, however, there is virtually no relationship between measured intelligence and creativity.*

Moderate
Relationship
Over Wide
Range of
Intelligence

Threshold: IQ
= About 120

Other Traits
Important

Barron (1961), based on his own and others' research, similarly reported correlations of about .40 between creativity and IQ scores—a moderate relationship—over the total range of intelligence. However, above the threshold IQ of 120, intelligence was a small factor in one's creativeness. Walberg (1988), based on his study of deceased eminent persons, also concluded that the linkage between intelligence and (creative) eminence is by no means tight: "The brightest . . . are not necessarily the best" (p. 355). Walberg further noted that research on contemporary writers, scientists, and those adolescents who won art or science awards suggests that outstanding performance requires a base level of moderately superior intelligence. However, higher levels of intelligence is less important that the presence of other psychological traits and conditions (Walberg, 1988). These critical traits will be reviewed in our *personality* section.

Rehash

In sum, creativity and intelligence are separate constructs. A highly intelligent person may or may not be highly creative, and vice versa. At the same time, over the wide range of intelligence there is a moderate correlation. The threshold concept assumes a minimal required level of intelligence (about IQ = 120), above which there is little correlation between intelligence and creativity.

PERSONALITY TRAITS

12 Core Traits?

There are many, many lists of personality characteristics of creative people. Some good sources are books and articles by Barron (1961, 1969, 1978, 1988), MacKinnon (1976, 1978a, 1978b), Torrance (1962, 1979, 1981a, 1984a, 1984b, 1987a, 1988), Lingeman (1982), Walberg (1988; Walberg & Herbig, 1991), Simonton (1988),

Creative people are independent. "I don't care how you sit when you read the paper," said this innovative thinker. (Wisconsin Center for Film and Theater Research.)

Perkins (1988), Sternberg (1988a), and Tardiff and Sternberg (1988). Oh yes, and research by Davis (1975; Davis & Bull, 1978; Davis & Subkoviak, 1978) and Rimm (Davis & Rimm, 1982; Rimm & Davis, 1976, 1980, 1983). An interminable list of characteristics extracted from these sources has been sorted into just 12 (count 'em) major categories (see Table 4.1). Creative people tend to be (or have):

1. Aware of their own creativeness
2. Original
3. Independent
4. Risk taking
5. Energetic
6. Curious
7. Sense of humor
8. Attracted to complexity and novelty

9. **Artistic**
10. **Open-minded**
11. **Needs for privacy, alone time**
12. **Perceptive**

Table 4.1

Personality Characteristics of Creativeness

Aware of Creativeness
    Value originality and creativity
    Value own creativity

Original
    Imaginative
    Full of ideas
    Flexible in ideas and thought
    Is a "what if?" person
    Resourceful
    Non-conforming
    Unconventional in behavior
    Challenges assumptions
    Enjoys pretending
    Constructs
    Builds and rebuilds
    Finds ways of doing things differently
    Radical
    Bored by routine

Independent
    Individualistic
    Internally controlled, inner directed
    Sets own rules
    Self-aware
    Self-confident
    Self-sufficient
    Self-accepting
    Unconcerned with impressing others
    Uninhibited
    May dress differently
    May not fit environment
    May resist societal demands
    Dissatisfied with the status quo
    May experience conflict between self-confidence and self-criticism
    May need to maintain distance from and avoid contact with peers

Risk Taking
    Does not mind consequences of being different
    Not afraid to try something new
    Willing to cope with hostility
    Willing to cope with failure
    Rejects limits imposed by others
    Optimistic
    Courageous

Energetic
  Adventurous
  Sensation seeking
  Seeks interesting situations
  Enthusiastic
  Alert
  Spontaneous
  Industrious
  Persistent
  Persevering
  Impulsive
  Unwilling to give up
  Driving absorption
  Drive for accomplishment and recognition
  High commitment
  High intrinsic motivation
  High need for competence in meeting challenges
  Ambitious
  Thorough
  Goes beyond assigned tasks
  Strives for distant goals
  Task-oriented
  Excitable, enjoys telling about discoveries / inventions

Curious
  Questioning
  Experimenting
  Inquisitive
  Wide interests
  Open to new experiences and growth

Humorous
  Playful
  Plays with ideas
  Childlike freshness in thinking

Attracted to Complexity
  Attracted to novelty
  Attracted to the mysterious, asymmetrical
  Is a complex person
  Tolerant of ambiguity
  Tolerant of disorder
  Tolerant of incongruity
  Tends to believe in psychical phenomena, flying saucers

Artistic
  Artistic Interests
  Aesthetic Interests

Open-Minded
  Receptive to new ideas
  Receptive to other viewpoints
  Open to new experiences and growth
  Liberal
  Altruistic

Needs Alone Time
    Reflective
    Introspective
    Internally preoccupied
    Sensitive
    Likes to work by himself or herself
    May be withdrawn

Perceptive
    Intuitive
    Sees relationships
    Uses all senses in observing

Not All Traits
Apply to All
Creative People

Of course, not all traits will apply to all creative persons. There simply are too many forms of creativity and creative people to make such a generalization. Particularly, there definitely is a subtype of artistic/poetic creative people who are shy and withdrawn—not at all high in the confidence, energy, and humor that characterize the stereotyped creative nut.

Awareness of
Creativity

Aware of creativeness. Most highly creative people are quite aware of their creativeness. They are in the habit of doing things creatively and they like being creative. Walberg's (1988; Walberg & Herbig, 1990) high school students who had won awards in art or science were consciously interested in creativity and they were confident of their own creativity. Said Walberg (1988, p. 356), "The creative groups felt more creative, imaginative, curious, and expressive and . . . felt that it is important to be creative." These award winners attached great importance to money, but when choosing the "best characteristic to develop in life" they selected "creativity" more often than "wealth and power."

Creativity
Consciousness:
Extremely
Important

Creativity consciousness is an important and common trait among creative people. It is the number one trait to develop to become more creative.

Now Write This
One Down!

Originality. In a memorable comment stemming from their review of commonly cited traits of creative people, Tardiff and Sternberg (1988) noted that *originality* and a good *imagination* " . . . are commonly said to be associated with creative individuals (p. 434)." This is like saying comedians are reputed to be funny and thieves lean toward dishonesty.[1] Originality—a term sometimes used

---

1. The comment was more intelligent in context. They stressed the important of four traits: relatively high intelligence, originality, articulateness and verbal fluency, and a good imagination.

interchangeably with *creativity* (see any dictionary)—is obviously a core characteristic of creativity. We noted earlier that "originality" is both a creative ability and a personality trait, in the sense being unconventional, flexible, habitually looking for new ways of doing things, and being a "what if?" person.

Independence, Risk-Taking

Independence, risk-taking. The creative person must be high in independence and self-confidence, and must be more willing than the average to take a creative risk. These are essential traits. The innovative person must dare to differ, make changes, stand out, challenge traditions, make a few waves, and bend a few rules. We noted in Chapter 3 that creative people tend to have an internal locus of evaluation, rather than being swayed too easily by external influences and opinions. Because of their independence and innovativeness, creative people expose themselves to (a) failure, (b) criticism, (c) embarrassment, (d) the distinct possibility of making idiots of themselves, or (e) all of the above.

Willingness to Fail

High Energy

High energy. Creative people typically have a high energy level—a certain enthusiastic zest and a habit of spontaneous action. The creative person may get caught up in seemingly simple problems, perhaps working well into the night on an exciting project. "Driving absorption," "high commitment," "passionate interest," and "unwilling to give up" are phrases used to describe the energy and motivation of highly creative persons. The creative artist, writer, researcher, business person, engineer, or advertising executive becomes totally immersed in his or her ideas and creations, literally unable to rest until the work is complete. According to Taylor (1988, p. 99), "One fellow scientist described his colleague by saying that the only way one could stop him from working on his problem would be to shoot him."

Driving Absorption

C'mon Guys, Stop It!

As stated by Author Schawlow, Nobel prize winner in physics, "The labor of love is important. The successful scientists are often not the most talented, but the ones who are just impelled by curiosity—they've got to know what the answer is" (Amabile, 1987, p. 224). Amabile (1987) reported that General Motors' most successful locomotive was designed by a small team of scientists and technicians who had been told four times to "cease and desist from building a locomotive" (p. 224).

Thrill Seeking

A related motivational trait has been called *sensation seeking, arousal seeking,* or *thrill-seeking* (Farley, 1986), which combines traits of high energy, adventurousness, and risk-taking. A personality test called the *Sensation Seeking Scale* (Zuckerman, 1975) is a better measure of creative tendencies than some creativity tests, according to a study by Davis, Peterson, and Farley (1973). In their research with college students, creative individuals were much more likely than the average to say "yes" they would like to:

> Take up skiing
> Ride motorcycles
> Parachute from an airplane
> Try mountain climbing
> Be hypnotized
> Work in a foreign country
> Explore strange cities without a guide

they preferred:

> Camping to a good motel
> To jump right into a cold pool instead of
>   dipping a toe first
> Bright colors in loud modern art over
>   subdued traditional paintings

and they liked:

Phew!

> Some body odors

Positive and
Negative Thrill-
Seeking

Farley (1986) emphasized that, due to favorable or unfavorable social circumstances, the drive for thrill-seeking may be satisfied in constructive creative outlets or in destructive delinquent ways. There is thus a potential for creative achievement among our delinquent population.

Curiosity

Wide Interests,
Unusual
Hobbies

Curiosity. The creative person also has strong curiosity, a childlike sense of wonder and intrigue. He or she may have a history of taking things apart to see how they work, exploring attics, libraries, or museums, and have a generally strong urge to understand the world about him or her. The curiosity produces wide interests, unusual hobbies, and an experimenting nature. More than one creative person has muddled college graduation requirements by taking intriguing courses that do not meet graduation requirements.

Is the creative couple carrying the traits of originality, self-confidence, risk-taking and sensation seeking too far? "I do," said the groom. "They both do," added the bridesmaid, "and who's flying this thing, anyway?" The Museum of Modern Art / Film Stils Archive.)

High curiosity is a classic creative trait.

Humor. An especially frequent creative trait is a good sense of humor, which is first cousin to the ability to take a fresh, childlike, and playful approach to a problem. Many discoveries, inventions, problem solutions, and artistic creations are the result of "fooling around" with ideas, playing with strange possibilities, or turning things upside down or backward. A favorite quote is that "The creative adult is essentially a perpetual child—the tragedy is that most of us grow up" (Fabun, 1968, p. 5). Both Sigmund Freud and Carl Rogers (Chapter 3) agreed that regression to a more childlike, fanciful, playful state of mind is an important feature of creative thinking and creative thinkers.

Attraction to complexity and novelty. The creative person is attracted to novelty, complexity, incongruity, and the mysterious, a proclivity that may reflect the creative person's own complexity. One test, the *Barron-Welsh Art Scale* (Welsh & Barron, 1963; see Chapter 8), has repeatedly shown that creative persons prefer smudgy, complex, asymmetrical drawings over simple and balanced ones (Barron, 1969).

Martindale (1975) made a relevant observation related to novelty:

> Confronted with novelty, whether in design, music, or ideas, creative people get excited and involved, while less creative people turn suspicious or even hostile. Given a new solution to a problem, imaginative students . . . get enthused, suggest other ideas, and overlook defects or problems with the plan. Less creative students do the opposite. They find fault with the solution, and start analyzing its defects rather than exploring its potential.

Sternberg (1988a) reviewed the subtle but crucial role of *tolerance for ambiguity* in creativity, dubbing it " . . . almost a *sin qua non* of creative performance" (p. 143), an observation also made by Barron (1968), MacKinnon (1978b), Vernon (1970), and Dacey (1989). Creative ideas

Margin notes:

Good Humor Person

Are You a Perceptual Child?

Attracted to Novelty, Complexity, the Mysterious

Enthusiasm Instead of Fault-Finding

Tolerance for Ambiguity: Necessary in Elaboration, Development of Ideas usually require some amount of elaboration and development, in accord with the two-stage model described in Chapter 3. Therefore, the creative person necessarily must work with ideas that are incomplete and ambiguous. In such circumstances relevant facts are missing, rules are unclear, and "correct" procedures are unavailable (MacKinnon, 1978b). Whether writing a novel, creating a work of art, or solving an engineering problem the ideas will evolve from the original "insight" or "big idea" through a series of modifications, approximations, and improvements—which requires coping with uncertainty and ambiguity. "To be creative, one must be willing and able to tolerate at least some ambiguity in order fully to manifest one's creativity" (Sternberg, 1988a, p. 143).

Stronger Believers in ESP, Flying Saucers, Ghosts

Attraction to complexity includes a probably surprising twist: Creative persons tend to be stronger believers in such psychical and mysterious matters as extrasensory perception (ESP), mental telepathy, precognition, astral projection (out-of-body experience), flying saucers, and spirits and ghosts (Davis, Peterson, & Farley, 1973; Schuldberg et al., 1988). They also are more likely to have psychical experiences (Torrance, 1962). Many creative persons have reported mystical experiences, for example, Mark Twain. Another example is the late Orson Welles, creator of the 1938 radio show *The War of the Worlds,* which scared the daylights out of millions of Americans, and the movie *Citizen Kane,* usually rated the best movie ever made. Welles frequently demonstrated his psychical abilities on TV shows; but he also was an accomplished magician, suspiciously enough.

Livlier Imagination?

Or Slightly Strange?

There are at least two possible explanations for this belief in paranormal happenings. First, such beliefs may simply reflect the creative person's livelier imagination and openness to fantastic possibilities. Another possibility is that such beliefs reflect a slight psychopathology, which will be described in a few pages.[2]

Artistic

Aesthetic Interests

Artistic, aesthetic interests. The creative person usually will rate himself or herself high in being "artistic," whether or not he or she can draw. The creative person thus tends to be more conscious of artistic considerations

---

2. Of course, a third possibility is that creative people understand mystical things that escape the rest of us.

and also has aesthetic interests—interests in music and dance concerts, plays, art galleries, photo exhibits, antique shows, Masterpiece Theatre, a good sunset, scenic views from the freeway, and so forth. On the *How Do You Think* test (Davis, 1991a; Chapter 8), an inventory for assessing creative personality traits, a high self-rating of "artistic" is one of the single best items on the test (Davis & Subkoviak, 1978).

An obvious reason for above-average artistic and aesthetic interests is that creative people are more likely to be, or to have been, involved in artistic and aesthetic enterprises—music, dance, theatre, art, handicrafts, or others.

Open-Mindedness

Open-minded. We have emphasized that creativity consciousness and creative attitudes are absolutely essential affective characteristics of creative people. Open-mindedness is a prime creative attitude. It includes receptiveness to new ideas and a willingness to look at a problem or situation from other points of view. It includes not fearing the new, different, or unknown, and not making up your mind in advance (Dacey, 1989). Open-mindedness includes a dash of adventurousness. It also leads to personal growth (Barron, 1988; Tardif & Sternberg, 1988; Walberg, 1988; Walberg & Herbig, 1991).

The reader is encouraged to look again at Von Oech's 10 whack-in-the-side-of-the-head guides in Chapter 2. Barriers to creativity—such as looking for just one right answer, being practical and logical, and avoiding ambiguity, frivolity, mistakes, and foolishness—are quite inconsistent with creative open-mindedness.

Idealistic, Altruistic

If we stretch the definition of "open-minded" a bit, and keep in mind Maslow's characteristics of self-actualization (Chapter 1, Inset 1.1), we might squeeze the traits of *idealistic* and *altruistic* to this open-mindedness category. Self-actualized creativity includes accepting oneself and others, having deep feelings of brotherhood and benevolence, and being democratic and unprejudiced. We're talking real open-mindedness here.

Need Some Privacy, Alone Time

Needs for alone time. Creative children and adults need some privacy and alone time. The urge to create demands time for thinking, for reflection, for solving problems, for creating. Creative children and adults may prefer to work alone, which reflects their creative independence.

Perceptiveness

Or "Aesthetic
Sense:" Tardif
& Sternberg

Perceptive. Creative people possess a certain perceptiveness and intuitiveness that enables them to see relationships and make "mental leaps." Tardif and Sternberg (1988) described this trait as an "aesthetic ability" which comes into play in defining and solving problems. According to Tardif and Sternberg, "The one characteristic that seems to prevail among creative people . . . is what seems almost to be an aesthetic ability that allows such individuals to recognize 'good' problems in their field and apply themselves to these problems while ignoring others. . . . this aesthetic sense is clearly a pervasive feature of creative persons" (p. 435).

Difficult to
Explain (But
Easy to Name)

Tardif and Sternberg were at a loss to explain this "aesthetic ability," suggesting that it may be a combination of cognitive abilities and thinking styles, or perhaps a personality or motivational trait, or perhaps something entirely separate. Of course, just naming it "perceptiveness" and "intuitiveness" in this section does not explain this mysterious capability either.

NEGATIVE CREATIVE TRAITS

Negative Traits
Can Be
Upsetting

So far, the creative person looks pretty good—intelligent, independent, energetic, good sense of humor, artistic, open-minded, perceptive, etc. However, creative children, adolescents, and adults may show some habits and dispositions that can upset a normal supervisor, parent, teacher, and other students and colleagues as well. Torrance (1962, 1981a), Smith (1966), and Domino (1970) suggested the items below as not-uncommon characteristics of creative students. Most of these "negative traits" are directly related to creative students' general unconventionality, combined with their self-confidence, independence, curiosity, humor, interest in novelty, and persistence. Some are likely to cause personal or social adjustment problems:

> Tends to question laws, rules, authority
>   in general
> Indifferent to common conventions and
>   courtesies

Stubborn, uncooperative, resists domination

Argues that the rest of the parade is out of step

May not participate in class activities

Argumentative, cynical, sarcastic, rebellious

Demanding, assertive, autocratic

Low interest in details

Sloppy, careless, disorganized with unimportant matters

Self-centered, intolerant, tactless

Capricious

Temperamental, moody

Emotional, withdrawn, aloof, uncommunicative

Forgetful, absentminded, mind wanders, watches windows

Overactive physically or mentally

Won't join scouts

Rechannel
Energy

And Patience

When stubborn Sammy or independent Elissa show some of these upsetting characteristics, the teacher might consider the possibility that the symptoms are part of a larger picture of energetic creativeness that may need rechanneling into constructive outlets. In the business or professional setting: patience and understanding.

THE BERKELEY STUDIES

Most Extensive
Studies of
Creative People

Architects,
Writers,
Mathematicians

Tests,
Inventories,
Observations

The single most extensive examination of traits of creative people took place at the University of California, Berkeley, in the 1950s. Psychologists Frank Barron (1969, 1978, 1988), Donald MacKinnon (1976, 1978a), and others studied nationally recognized creative architects, writers, and men and women mathematicians. The names were selected by nominations from faculty in Berkeley's Departments of Architecture, English, and Mathematics. The creative persons were observed informally over a three-day weekend and also took intelligence tests and a variety of personality tests and self-descriptive inventories

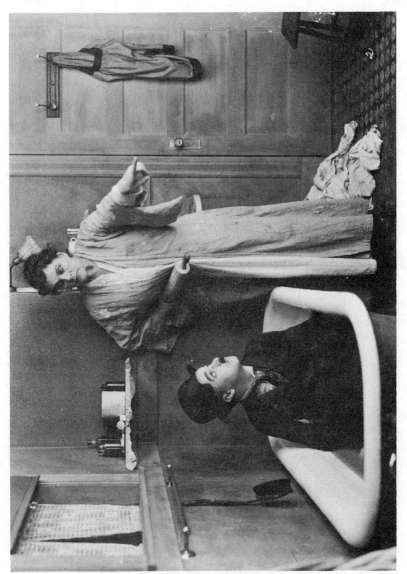

Creative people may forget unimportant details. (The Museum of Modern Art / Film Stills Archive.)

(e.g., the *Minnesota Multiphasic Personality Inventory,* MMPI; *California Psychological Inventory; Adjective Check List; Myers-Briggs Type Indicator*). Barron also went to Ireland to study innovators in business management, using many of the same tests. Many of the personality traits described in this chapter originated from or were confirmed by this research. For example, their creative people tended to be original, imaginative, independent, verbally fluent, flexible, energetic, productive, artistic, emotional, unconventional, nonconforming, and had aesthetic interests and wide interests generally.

Creativity and Mental Disturbance

Self-Centered, Moody

Creative Writers: High in MMPI Psychopathology

Also High in Ego Strength: Sicker and Healthier

The Berkeley group also uncovered an interesting trend among high-level creative people, reminiscent of Maslow's sometimes-disturbed *special talent* creative persons (Chapter 1). The research indicated that some traits of these very talented people would not be considered mentally healthy. Compared with representative women mathematicians, creative women mathematicians were more likely to be self-centered, rebellious, and have fluctuating moods, and they tended to be undependable, irresponsible, and/or inconsiderate. Looking at successful creative writers, ". . . the *average* creative writer, in fact, is in the upper 15 percent of the general population on *all* measures of psychopathology furnished by this test!" (MMPI; Barron, 1965, p. 62): *hypochondriasis, depression, hysteria, psychopathic deviation, paranoia, psychasthenia, schizophrenia,* and *hypomania.* Critically, they also scored high on *ego strength,* a measure of mental health and stability. Barron (1969) summed up his findings with, ". . . they are both sicker and healthier psychologically than people in general . . . they are more troubled psychologically, but they also have far greater resources with which to deal with their troubles."

Creative College Students Higher in Psychopathology

This interesting tendency of highly creative people to show mental disorders has a long history (see, e.g., Jamison, 1989; Schuldberg et al., 1988). Noted Schuldberg et al., " . . . research has noted affective disorders, schizophrenia, unconventional or antisocial behavior, and alcohol and substance abuse in eminent and creative individuals and sometimes in their relatives" (p. 648). The research of Schuldberg *et al.* showed that normal (?) garden-variety male and female college students who scored high on a creative personality inventory (*How Do You Think,* HDYT; Davis, 1975, 1991a) also scored high on a combined measure of psychopathology: *perceptual aberration* (e.g., ordinary sounds are reported as sometimes uncomfortable) and *magical ideation* (having superstitious and supernatural beliefs). Shields (1988) found that the best group of items in the HDYT creativity test were those that measured belief in paranormal phenomena (ESP, precognition, flying saucers, etc.), which relates closely to Schuldberg's magical ideation.

Walberg: Some Eminent Men Introverted or Neurotic

In Walberg's (1988; Walberg & Herbig, 1991) study of historically eminent people described earlier, the *majority* showed traits that reflect "psychological wholesomeness": Ethical, sensitive, solid, magnetic, optimistic, and popular. However, said Walberg, about a quarter to a third showed definite introversion or neuroses. In a recent TV interview, the business manager of Yves St. Laurent said that, despite his fame and success, the genius of fashion design actually is withdrawn and somewhat neurotic.

Observed Barron (1965), "Mad as a hatter" is a term of high praise when applied to creative people.

BIOGRAPHICAL CHARACTERISTICS

Not-So-Subtle Traits: History of Creative Activities

Recurrent biographical traits of creative people may be of two sorts: *Subtle* and *not-so-subtle.* Not-so-subtle biographical factors are simply the person's history of creative activities. It is hardly surprising that, beginning in childhood, most creative people accumulate a history of building and making things, artistic and handicraft interests, involvement in music, dance, or theater, creative writing, scientific interests, unusual hobbies (such as collecting spider webs, horse bones, or atypical music, or juggling, inventing gadgets or games, or doing Charlie Chaplin impressions), or other creative activities that grow from the energetic originality.

If the person has been creative in the past, there is an eminently strong likelihood that he or she will continue to be creative in the future.

Subtle Traits: More Surprising

Owning a Cat

Imaginary Playmate

Subtle biographical correlates of creativity include background facts that are a bit more surprising. Schaefer (1969, 1970) found that creative high school students were more likely to have friends younger and older than themselves, rather than the same age. The creatives also were more likely to have lived in more than one state and may have traveled outside the USA. High school girls who were creative writers were more likely to personally own a cat. Definitely subtle. Schaefer, confirmed in studies reviewed by Somers and Yawkey (1984), also found that creative students more often reported having an imaginary childhood playmate. Said Somers and Yawkey, imaginary companions contribute to creativity be developing originality and elaboration and by fostering sensitivity in relationships.

Perfect Predictors of Creativity?

In your author's experience, two biographical traits each are 100 percent accurate as predictive of creativeness: having had an imaginary playmate and/or participation in theatre. Persons who claim one or the other (or both) invariably show the typical creative personality traits described in this chapter. They also will report present or past involvement in creative activities.

Handedness and Birth Order

Handedness and birth order are two traits that occasionally are mentioned as possibly related to creativity, with left-handed people and first-born or only children usually suggested as more creative.

Only Children and First-Born Higher Achievers

Birth-order effect. The birth-order effect has been studied for some years. Only children and first-born children tend to be more studious, higher achievers, and are more likely to be National Merit scholars. As adults they are likely to be better educated and have higher-level careers (Hilgard, Atkinson, & Atkinson, 1979). For example, most U.S. presidents are first or only children; about 93 percent of astronauts are first or only children.

An actual photograph of an imaginary playmate. Can you guess whose playmate he was? (Wisconsin Center for Film and Theater Research.)

Only Children Especially Well Adjusted, Higher Achievers

Only children tend to be even more secure, better adjusted, and higher achievers than even first-borns (Hetherington & Parke, 1979). The youngest child—the "baby of the family"—tends to be more secure, confident, and popular than the first born, and also tends to be a relatively high achiever.

Better Prenatal
Environment

Younger Child
More Emotional

Environmental
Explanation

Space will not permit a detailed elaboration of the proposed causes of the birth-order effect. Briefly, one early genetic-based argument was that first-borns somehow have a more favorable prenatal environment, resulting in less "fetal stress." An explanation that combines genetic and social factors is that later born children experience repeated and unexpected intrusions by the older, 3–4 year old sibling, resulting in an altered brain limbic system that makes the younger child more sensitive, anxious, and withdrawn. The current emphasis is on social/environmental causes of the birth-order effect. First born and only children receive more attention, are read to more, and receive more educational encouragement and assistance. They may develop a learning style that aids their informal and formal education.

First-Borns
More Anxious,
Conforming?

Research
Support

Regarding the relationship of birth order to creativity, ideas and research findings go both ways. For example, Hetherington and Parke (1979) concluded that first and only borns were more anxious, conforming, worried about failure, and passive—definitely uncreative traits. Eisenman's (1964) research with 20 art students seemed to confirm that, sure enough, first-borns were *less* creative than middle or youngest children. Staffieri (1970) reported similar findings.

First-Borns
More Creative,
Independent?

Research
Support Here,
Too

On the other hand is the argument that first-borns are *more* creative than later borns, which would be consistent with the tendency for first-borns to become more independent from the mothers when the next child arrived, and with the well-confirmed trend toward higher achievement generally (Simonton, 1988). Lichtenwalner and Maxwell (1969) administered divergent thinking tests, a common form of creativity test (e.g., "list unusual uses for a brick"; see Chapter 8), to preschool children. First and only born children produced higher ideational fluency scores.

Research:
"Only" Children
More Creative
Than Others

Runco and Bahleda (1986) administered divergent thinking tests to 234 fifth-, sixth-, seventh-, and eighth-grade children with IQ scores ranging from 97 to 165. Their results supported Lichtenwalner and Maxwell's findings. Sort of. "Only" children produced the highest divergent thinking scores—but there were no significant differences among the first-born, second-born, and third-and-later-born groups. Runco and Bahleda (1986) and Lichtenwalner and Maxwell (1969) suggested that only-born children develop greater autonomy, which underlies their higher creativity.

Conclusion: Inconclusive Information

The conclusion one should draw from this discussion is that, at the time of this writing, research relating birth-order to creativity is inconclusive.

Ditto for Handedness

Handedness and creativity. If the reader's tolerance for ambiguity is not yet too strained, he or she can deal with the fact that the same inconclusive results apply to handedness.

Left-Handers: Better Access to Both Halves of Brain?

There has been speculation that left-handers are more creative. The main—but weak—evidence is that many historically creative people were left-handed, for example, Leonardo Da Vinci, Michelangelo, and Benjamin Franklin. The argument is that left-handed people, most of whom in fact are ambidextrous, have better access to both hemispheres of their brains. That is, with normal right-handed people the left side of the brain controls speech, writing, sequential, and analytical functions; the right side controls spatial, wholistic, intuitive, and creative functions (Al-Sabaty & Davis, 1989; Springer & Deutsch, 1985). The left-handed person's more integrated access to both hemispheres should aid creative thinking and problem solving; at least that's the logic.

Left-Handed Architects

Other Research: No Relationship

Peterson and Lansky (1980), in fact, discovered that in a sample of 17 architecture faculty, five were left-handed (29.4 percent), and two more were left-handed as children but were "cured," for a total of 7 of 17 or 41.2 percent. Dacey (1989) reported that 65 percent of the students in a major art school were left-handed. These figures are substantially above the universe-wide average of 10 percent left-handedness. On the other hand (sorry), with a group of 100 20-year olds Katz (1980) found absolutely no relationship between handedness and scores on three different creativity tests.

The association of left-handedness with creativity, as with birth order, remains inconclusive.

CREATIVE ABILITIES

Cognitive vs.
Affective Traits

In addition to personality (or affective) traits and bio-graphical characteristics, there also are *cognitive* abilities that are important for creative thinking—abilities that are well-developed and often-used by creative people. Such abilities are partly genetic and partly learned. Long-time creativity expert Frank Barron (1988) listed just six "ingredients" of creativity that intermix affective and cognitive traits:

Barron's Six
Ingredients

1. Recognizing patterns
2. Making connections
3. Taking risks
4. Challenging assumptions
5. Taking advantage of chance
6. Seeing in new ways

Many Abilities
Relate to
Creativity

These penetrate to the core of creative thinking and productivity. However, there are many more intellectual and stylistic abilities that contribute in one way or another to creative potential. Actually, it would be difficult to isolate mental abilities that have absolutely nothing to do with creativeness. It also is true, as already noted twice in this chapter, that some traits in the "personality" list could be considered cognitive "abilities" (originality, humor, perceptiveness).

Abilities that seem especially important to creativity appear in Table 4.2. Most have appeared elsewhere in the creativity literature, for example, in Torrance (e.g., 1962, 1979, 1984, 1987, 1988) or Tardif and Sternberg (1988).

Table 4.2
Creative Abilities

Fluency	Able to predict outcomes, consequences
Flexibility	
Originality	Analysis
Elaboration	Synthesis
Transformation	Evaluation
Sensitivity to Problems	Logical Thinking
Able to define problems	Able to regress
Visualization, imagination	Intuition
Analogical/Metaphorical Thinking	Concentration

Fluency is the ability to produce many ideas, verbal or nonverbal, for an open-ended problem or question. Pseudonyms include *associational fluency* and *ideational fluency*.

Flexibility is the ability to take different approaches to a problem, think of ideas in different categories, or view a problem from different perspectives.

Originality is just that—uniqueness, nonconformity in thought and action. Dictionary synonyms include *creativity, novelty,* and *innovativeness.*

Elaboration is the important ability to add details to an idea, which includes developing, embellishing, improving, and implementing the idea.[3]

Transformation = Perceptual Change

Transformation is a subtle term that could be used interchangeably with *creative thinking* itself. Every creative idea involves a transformation—changing one object or idea into another by modifying, combining, or substituting. Transformation is "seeing" new meanings, implications, or applications or adopting something to a new use. For nearly four decades creativity legend J. P. Guilford (e.g., 1986) emphasized the significance of transformation abilities for creative thinking. We will see in Chapter 5 that *perceptual change*—looking at one thing and seeing another—is a central creative process which is approximately identical in meaning to *transformation.*

Sensitivity to problems reflects the ability to find problems, detect difficulties, detect missing information, and ask good questions.

Involves Logical Thinking

Problem defining is an important and complex ability that includes at least the abilities to (1) identify the "real" problem, (2) isolate important aspects of a problem (and unimportant aspects), (3) clarify and simplify a problem, (4) identify subproblems, (5) propose alternative problem definitions, and (6) define a problem more broadly. Items 5 and 6 open the door to a wider variety of problem solutions. Note that one's logical thinking ability would be involved throughout "problem defining" as described here.

---

3. Fluency, flexibility, originality, and elaboration are four scores derived from the popular *Torrance Tests of Creative Thinking* (Chapter 8). They are important and well-known creative abilities, but not the only creative abilities.

Note also that both *sensitivity to problems* and *problem defining* seem to require a certain *perceptiveness* and *intuitiveness,* described earlier as personality traits. Once again the distinction between "abilities" and "personality traits" is clearly blurred.

Visualization is the ability to fantasize, to "see" things in the "mind's eye," to mentally manipulate images and ideas. The term is used interchangeably with *imagination* itself and is considered to be an absolutely essential creative ability.

Analogical/metaphorical thinking is the ability to borrow ideas from one context and use them in another, borrow a problem solution from a related problem, or otherwise "see a connection" between one situation and another. Analogical thiinking is sufficiently important to justify a relatively substantial chapter in this book (Chapter 7).[4]

Predicting outcomes or consequences is the ability to foresee the results of different solution alternatives and actions. It is related to *evaluation* ability.

Analysis is the ability to separate details, break down a whole into its parts.

Synthesis is the ability to see relationships, to combine parts into a workable, perhaps creative whole.

Evaluation is the important ability to separate the relevant from the irrelevant, to think critically, to evaluate the "goodness" or appropriateness of an idea, product, or solution.[5]

Logical thinking is the ability to make reasonable decisions and deduce reasonable conclusions. It permeates all aspects of creative thinking and problem solving and, logically, would be part of every other ability in this list.

---

4. While "analogy" and "metaphor" have slightly different meanings, they seem to be used interchangeably in the creativity literature. Typically, creative ideas that stem from "seeing a similarity" or "making a connection" are analogical ("Hey, that bird's nest gives me an idea for a new sandwich!"). A metaphor is the application of a term to describe something to which it does not literally apply, e.g., "the curtain of night" or "God is a fortress." Creative people tend not to worry much about picky distinctions. E.g., was Darwin's use of a branching tree diagram to help explain natural selection a metaphor or an analogy? Does it make any difference? See Gruber and S. N. Davis (1988) for more about metaphorical thinking than you ever wanted to know.

5. The reader with a background in education might recognize *analysis, synthesis,* and *evaluation* as higher-order thinking skills in Bloom's taxonomy of educational objectives, cognitive domain.

The *ability to regress* includes a facility for "thinking like a child," whose mind is less cluttered by habits, traditions, rules, conformity pressures, etc.—the barriers we explored in Chapter 2. The ability to regress is related to playfulness and humor.

Intuition is a little-understood capability to make "mental leaps" or "intuitive leaps," to see relationships based upon little, perhaps insufficient information, to "read between the lines." It relates to *perceptiveness,* described earlier in the personality list.

Concentration is the ability to focus one's attention. It relates to the task-orientation or even "driving absorption" of creatively productive people.

Information Processing Traits

Information Processing Characteristics

A list of dynamic information processing characteristics related to creative thinking, modified from Tardif and Sternberg (1988), and which they extracted from numerous chapters in the Sternberg (1988b) book, appears in Table 4.3. Because these seem self-defining, and in fact overlap with the personality traits and cognitive abilities in Tables 4.1 and 4.2, we will bypass a tedious definition of each.

Table 4.3
Information Processing Traits
(Adapted from Tardiff & Sternberg, 1988)

Uses existing knowledge as basis for new ideas
Avoids perceptual sets and entrenched ways of thinking
Questions norms and assumptions
Builds new structures, instead of using existing structures
Uses wide categories, sees "forest" instead of "trees"
Thinks metaphorically
Thinks logically
Makes independent judgments
Alert to novelty and gaps in knowledge
Copes well with novelty
Finds order in chaos
Uses internal visualization
May prefer nonverbal communication
Flexible and skilled in decision making

CULTIVATING A MORE CREATIVE PERSONALITY

Creativity Tied
to Personality

Attitudes Can
Be Changed and
Abilities
Strengthened

This chapter and Chapter 1 should make it clear that creativity, both the general self-actualized creativity and special-talent creativity, is tied closely to personality. Based upon outcomes of creativity training programs and courses (e.g., Davis & Bull, 1978; Edwards, 1968; Torrance, 1987b), there is every reason to believe that attitudes and personality can be changed to produce a more flexible, creative, and self-actualized person. Creative abilities, too, may be strengthened with practice and exercise (Chapter 11).

Environmental
Influences on
Eminence:
Walberg

One source of evidence for environmental (learning) influences on creativity, including both affective and cognitive components, comes from Walberg's (1988) study of historically eminent people. Many were exposed to stimulating family, educational, and cultural conditions during childhood. More than half were encouraged in their educational and professional development by parents, and a large majority were encouraged by teachers and other adults at an early age. A full 60 percent were exposed to eminent persons during childhood.

Confidence and
Creativity
Increase
Together

Be More
Adventurous

Polish Your Wit

Many of the traits listed in this chapter probably can be changed in a more creative direction—if a person is motivated to do so. Increases in creativeness are frequently accompanied by increases in self-confidence and independence (Parnes, 1978); it is a chicken-egg problem as to which causes which. One also might consciously try to cultivate curiosity and wide interests, and cultivate artistic and aesthetic interests by attending concerts and plays, and visiting art galleries, museums, and scientific exhibitions. One's adventurousness might be exercised by exploring new places and trying new activities. Most likely, even one's sense of humor can be sharpened.

Do Something
Creative!

Of critical importance, becoming involved in creative activities in guaranteed to increase one's creativity consciousness, strengthen some creative abilities, and increase creative productivity.

SUMMARY

Studies of creative people indicate that despite their unconventionality and individualism, they have a lot of traits in common.

Studying characteristics of creativity will help us recognize and understand creative people.

Three types of characteristics are personality traits, cognitive abilities (including information processing styles), and biographical characteristics. The distinction between personality traits and cognitive abilities sometimes is blurred.

There are common traits among creative people in different areas (e.g., art, science), but also large differences even among creative persons in the same area. Some will be well-adjusted (self-actualized); others will be neurotic or slightly psychotic.

Most special talent creative people are creative only in their own area.

Over the wide range of intelligence, creativity and intelligence are moderately related. The threshold concept states that above an IQ of about 120 there is no relationship. Other factors—personality, particularly—become determiners of creative productivity.

A long list of personality traits mentioned by numerous sources was reduced to 12: aware of own creativeness ("creativity consciousness"), original, independent, risk taking, energetic (even thrill-seeking), curious, good sense of humor, attracted to complexity and novelty (including a belief in paranormal phenomena), artistic (including aesthetic interests), open-minded, a need for alone time, and perceptive. Not all traits apply to all creative people, of course.

"Negative" traits, so called because they may cause personal or social problems, include indifference to conventions, stubbornness, uncooperativeness, resistance to domination, not participating in class activities, argumentativeness, a low interest in details, and being demanding, disorganized, self-centered, temperamental, too emotional, absentminded, overactive, and others.

Much information on the creative personality was derived from research by Frank Barron and Donald MacKinnon at Berkeley, where they studied creative architects, writers, and mathematicians. Many showed neuroses or psychoses, especially the creative writers. However, the writers also scored high on MMPI ego strength, indicating they were psychologically "sicker and healthier" than the average. Mental disturbance in highly creative people is not unusual.

Non-subtle biographical traits include one's background of creative interests, hobbies, and activities. Subtle biographical traits include much traveling, owning a cat, and having an imaginary childhood playmate. Having had an imaginary playmate and participation in theatre appear to be perfect predictors of creativeness.

Speculations that birth order and handedness each are associated with creativity remain unconfirmed. Research is inconsistent.

Creativity expert Barron listed six "ingredients" of creativity: recognizing patterns, making connections, taking risks, challenging assumptions, taking advantage of chance, and seeing in new ways, which mix personality (affective) and cognitive traits.

Many abilities contribute to creativity. Some seemingly important creative abilities include fluency, flexibility, originality, elaboration, transformation, sensitivity to problems, problem defining, visualization, analogical/metaphorical thinking, predicting outcomes, analysis, synthesis, evaluation, logical thinking, ability to regress, intuition, and concentration.

Creative thinking also involves patterns of information processing, such as using existing knowledge as a basis for new ideas, avoiding perceptual sets, questioning norms and assumptions, using wide categories, being alert to novelty and gaps in knowledge, coping well with novelty, "finding order in chaos," using internal visualization, skill in decision making, and others.

Relevant attitudes and personality traits can be changed in a more creative direction; creative abilities can be exercised. Especially, involvement in creative activities is recommended.

5

the creative process: steps and stages and perceptual changes

[Scene: Office of Marvin J. Mogul, tycoon Hollywood movie producer. Mogul is in a heated debate with creative script writer Woody Allen.]

Marvin J. Mogul: Look Woody, time is money! We gotta' have that scene written by tomorrow noon—at the latest!

Woody Allen: So I'm writing, I'm writing, I'm writing! I'm not a faucet, you know! You want hot jokes? Cold jokes?

Mogul: If you're workin' so hard, how come every time I see you you're starin' out the window? You're not workin', you're starin'.

Woody: It's called incubating! I'm incubating! If you were a writer, you'd know. You can't write unless you incubate. Every writer incubates!

Mogul: Woody, you're not gettin' paid to hatch baby ducks, you're paid to write. Please pick up your pen and put some words on the paper. Please?

Woody: Didja' ever hear about muses? Shakespeare had muses, Hemmingway had muses, I got muses! An' I can't rush my muses! I gotta' stare out the window, incubate, and let my muses do their work! When my muses get ready they'll give me some funny stuff—believe me!

Mogul: Muses? Muses? First it's baby ducks and now you're subcontracting to mythical spirits! Please Woody, for me, put the pen in your hand. Now here's some nice clean paper . . .

Woody: OK, OK! Tell you what. I'll do some rough outlines . . . invent a few characters, maybe write a few jokes. You like Jewish jokes? No Jewish jokes. What about mugger jokes or maybe a few George Bush jokes . . .

Mogul: No script?

Woody: No script. This is called preparing. I'm studying the problem, thinking about what we need, kicking around a few possibilities. Writers prepare all the time. It gives the incubator something to work with. It's like an Italian cook fondling his noodles and garlic . . . he prepares, getting ready to attack.

Mogul: What happened to your muses?

Woody: They don't like Italian food. Now please lemme' alone Marv. I gotta' stare.

Creative Process: Steps and Stages

Perceptual Change

Techniques

The phrase *creative process* is used several different ways. First, it can refer to a sequence of *steps* or *stages* through which the creative person proceeds in clarifying a problem, working on it, and producing a solution that resolves the difficulty. Second, it can refer to the relatively rapid *perceptual change* or *transformation* that takes place when a new idea or problem solution is suddenly produced or detected. Third, the creative process can refer to the *techniques* and strategies that creative people use, sometimes consciously and sometimes unconsciously, to produce the new idea combination, relationships, meanings, perceptions and transformations.

Later: Analogical Thinking

Other Techniques

This chapter will first examine the creative process as a set of steps or stages and then as a change in perception. Chapter 6 will focus on that most common and effective creative thinking technique, analogical and metaphorical thinking—"seeing a connection" between one situation and another, as when cockleburrs inspired inventor George De Mestral to create Velcro, or a cartoonist sees a connection between David and Goliath and steroid testing and writes, "Bad news David, the Philistines want to check you for steroids!" Chapter 7 will review other techniques of creative thinking, primarily "standard" techniques that are used by many creative people and are taught in many creativity courses, texts, and workshops, for example, *brainstorming*.

One Process or Many?

Same Process?

Many Processes?

By way of introduction, in discussing the complexity of creativity in Chapter 1 we noted that intelligent, creative people claim that the creative process is basically the same in art, science, business, and elsewhere. Other intelligent, creative people argue that there is no one creative process, and there may be as many creative processes as there are creative people. The truth depends upon which aspect of the creative process one looks at.

Combining Ideas

Analogical Thinking

Common Stages

At a fairly global level, most new creations are combinations of previously unrelated ideas, and so one can view the creative process as combining Idea #1 with Idea #2 to produce novel Idea #3. Common creative techniques, particularly analogical thinking and modifying existing products, can be used by creative thinkers in any topic area to produce novel Idea #3.[1] There also is a similarity in the steps or stages through which an artist, scientist, business person, or other problem solver proceeds in defining, clarifying, and solving a problem.

Common Global Processes

Idiosyncratic Abilities, Experiences, Thinking Styles

Different Media, Different Problems Require Different Processes

However, despite commonalities in such global processes as (1) combining ideas, (2) using similar idea-finding techniques, and (3) proceeding through similar steps, there still are unique and idiosyncratic experiences, abilities, perceptions, thinking styles, and strategies that influence the creative processes of each creative person. Further, the particular area or media within which one creates—math, chemistry, biology, painting, architecture, poetry, music, theatre, etc.—logically will demand thinking with different concepts and with different problem solving techniques. Even within a given media, specific types of problems will require different "processes"—writing comedy or designing a garage will require different processes than writing obituaries or designing a shopping center. Therefore, in some global ways the creative process may indeed "be the same" in different areas and among people with different creative specialities; however, the creative process also must be different according to the media in general, the requirements of the creative task, and the idiosyncracies of every creative individual.

1. Modifying the important attributes of an existing product is an effective and not uncommon idea-finding technique. In Chapter 7 it is called *attribute listing*.

CREATIVE PROCESS: INSIGHT, CHANCE, OR HARD WORK?

We also mentioned in Chapter 1 that different opinions exist regarding whether creativity is "building on an initial insight" or whether it is the result of systematic planning and hard work—with sudden "insights" and chance discoveries playing no significant role.

These views are not inconsistent. A creative problem solution may be born instantly in an "Aha!" (insight) experience, inspired perhaps by the chance encounter of a needed idea or solution. A creative product also may result from months or years of systematic planning, hard work, and trial-and-error experimentation—perhaps based on an earlier "Aha!" or insight that was a chance occurrance. For example, in Hollywood one busy street passes through a tunnel under a hill. The illusion of height created in the Harold Lloyd movie *Safety Last* was discovered by chance—in a sudden insight—when a fence was trimmed out of a picture taken from that hilltop. The movie scenes themselves, of course, required months of planning, development, and hard work.

STEPS AND STAGES

Necessary
Steps: Clarifying
the Problem,
Working on It,
Finding a
Solution

Solving a problem or "doing something creative" necessarily involves the three steps already casually mentioned—clarifying the problem, working on it, and finding a good solution. More formal sets of stages are elaborations of these. For example, Torrance's (1988) definition of creativity that we saw in Chapter 3 describes a stepwise process of:

Torrance
Definition

1. Sensing a problem or gap in information
2. Forming ideas or hypotheses
3. Testing and modifying the hypotheses
4. Communicating the results

"Do I think 'chance' plays a role in creativity? No, of course not. It's all hard work. I don't believe in taking chances." (The Museum of Modern Art/Film Stills Archives.)

A similar but less well-known model is Kingsley and Garry's (1957) steps:

Kingsley and
Garry Steps

1. A difficulty is felt
2. The problem is clarified and defined
3. A search for clues is made
4. Various suggestions appear and are tried out
5. A suggested solution is accepted (or the thinker gives up)
6. The solution is tested

John Dewey's
Two Steps

John Dewey (1933), writing on the nature of thinking, compressed the Torrance and Kingsley/Garry steps into just two, with no apparent loss of information. First, there appears a state of doubt, perplexity, or mental difficulty in which the thinking originates; followed by an act of searching, hunting, or inquiring to find material that will resolve the doubt, and settle and dispose of the perplexity.

THE WALLAS MODEL

Since 1926:
Graham Wallas

The most traditional analysis of stages in the creative process was originated by Wallas in 1926. The fact that the model has survived over a half-century of scrutiny certainly says something about the appeal of the model. There are four steps.

Preparation

Preparation. Preparation includes just that—exploring and clarifying the situation, perhaps looking for the "real" problem, thinking about requirements for a good solution, gathering and reviewing relevant data, becoming acquainted with innuendos, implications and perhaps unsuccessful solutions, itemizing available materials and resources, and so on. Gordon (1961) called this "making the strange familiar," an important creative activity.

Incubation:
Fringe
Conscious
Activity

Incubation. One entire issue of the *Journal of Creative Behavior* (Issue 1, 1979) was devoted to untangling the mysteries of *incubation.* Success was limited. According to Wallas (1926), and as we saw in the theories of Kubie and Rugg (Chapter 2), incubation may best be viewed as a period of preconscious, fringe-conscious, off-conscious or perhaps even unconscious mental activity that takes place while the thinker is (perhaps deliberately) jogging, watching TV, playing golf, eating pizza, walking along a lakeshore, or even sleeping. In Wallas' own words, "The incubation stage covers two different things, of which the first is the negative fact that during incubation we do not voluntarily or consciously think on a particular problem, and the second is the positive fact that a series of unconscious and involuntary (or foreconscious and forevoluntary) mental events may take place during that period . . . the period of abstention may be spent either in conscious mental work on other problems, or in a relaxation from all conscious mental work."

Guilford: Some People More Reflective Than Others

Guilford (1979) suggested that incubation takes place during reflection, a pause in action, and that some people are simply more reflective than others.

Illumination: "Eureka!"

Illumination. The "Aha!" or "Eureka!" experience. Basically, there is a sudden change in perception, a new idea combination, or a transformation that produces a solution that appears to meet the requirements of the problem. There usually is a good feeling, even excitement.

Verification

Verification. Verification is checking the solution (what else), in case your Eureka turns out to be a vacuous idea.

Resemble Scientific Method

Stages Not Invariant

Like other sets of stages, the Wallas stages resemble steps in the scientific method of stating the problem, proposing hypotheses, planning and conducting research, and evaluating the results. Note also that the Wallas stages are not an invariant sequence. Some stages may be skipped or the thinker may backtrack to an earlier stage. For example, the process of defining and clarifying the problem (preparation) often leads directly to a good, illuminating idea. Or if the verification confirms that the idea won't work or is not acceptable, the thinker will recycle back to the preparation or incubation stage.

An Information Processing Theory of Incubation

Levels of Processing Theory

Developments in cognitive psychology suggest another way to interpret the less-than-conscious incubation process. *Levels of processing theory* (Norman, 1976) focuses on the common human ability to consciously attend to one, and only one, main activity (such as talking, listening, watching, or thinking), yet conduct several other activities at the same time. For example, while talking you also can walk, chew gum, drive a car, or notice leaves rustling in the wind. These other activities are said to be processed at lower levels of consciousness.

Low Level (Fringe Conscious) Activity: Matching Input Against Schemas

More specifically, or more theoretically, the familiar and expected activities and events are said to be "matched" against internal representations (or *schemas*) of these activities and events. If there is a match, these events are "accounted for" and further processing at a higher, conscious level is unnecessary. The events are dealt with completely at a fringe-conscious or even unconscious level. However, if something unexpected or novel occurs—stepping in dog stuff, biting a grain of sand, or seeing a horse in the road or a parrot in a tree—the matter cannot be handled at the lower, unconscious level. That is, the novel event does not match existing schemas; it therefore is passed to higher processing levels where, by definition, it receives one's full attention.

With No Match, Input Gets Full Attention

Incubation: With Fringe Conscious Solution—Full Attention

It is conceivable that incubation involves similar information processing activities. "Getting away from the problem" essentially means that one's high-level, conscious attention is directed toward other matters—watching TV, playing golf, eating pizza, etc. However, perhaps one's fringe-conscious or unconscious processing activities occasionally review a particular problem and possible solutions. When something novel occurs—namely, a good solution—the matter instantly gets passed to higher levels of processing. That is, it gets your full attention. Psychologically, you experience it as a sudden "Eureka!" experience.

Similar to Psychoanalytic Primary, Secondary Processes

This level of processing interpretation of incubation is similar to Kris' psychoanalytic description of creative thinking (Chapter 3): Preconscious primary process fantasy activity is followed by a "Eureka!" and conscious secondary process logical thinking.

THE CREATIVE PROBLEM SOLVING MODEL

CPS Model: It
Works

It is difficult to say enough about the Creative Problem Solving (CPS) model, a remarkable set of five stages that is virtually guaranteed to help you solve or find ideas for any type of personal or professional problem. As a bit of background, the strategy originally was formulated by Alex Osborn (1963), creator of brainstorming, founder of the Creative Education Foundation (CEF), and co-founder of Batten, Barton, Dursten and Osborn, the highly successful New York advertising agency. Sidney Parnes, a bright and creative person who followed Osborn as President of CEF, has invested approximately 30 years thinking about the creative process and teaching creativity in workshops, institutes, and college courses. His best shot at "What is the creative process?" and "How can we teach creativity?" is (you guessed it) the CPS

Parnes: Magic
Of Your Mind

model. Parnes' inspiring (1981) book, *The Magic of Your Mind,* explains how using the CPS model can improve your life (remember the self-actualization emphasis in Chapter 1?). His book and the CPS model are highly recommended.

CPS Advocates:
Treffinger,
Firestien,
Isaksen

Creativity leaders Treffinger, Isaksen, and Firestien (1982; Isaksen & Treffinger, 1985) also understand the remarkable potential of this model as a teachable and effective creative problem solving strategy.[2] These authors have refined the use of the CPS model in some insightful ways that will be described later in this section.

Inset 5.1.
Discovering Problems and Challenges

Actually, there is one crucial stage in the CPS model that takes place *before* the five steps of fact-finding, problem-finding, idea-finding, solution-finding, and acceptance-finding: finding a problem, opportunity or challenge to which to apply this dynamite model. Instead of passively waiting for a problem to bang on the door and demand a creative solution, we can

---

2. The author wishes to express his gratitude to these three for the coffee mug and necktie.

take a more active, high-initiative approach to improving our lives by looking for nuisances, challenges, or things that you would like to see happen—difficulties that seem to cry out "Help! Help! Get the CPS model, quick!"

To help you discover challenges and opportunities and generally increase your problem sensitivity, Parnes (1981) itemized a list of prodding questions, some of which are itemized below. Do these suggest topics for one-person CPS sessions?

> What would you like to get out of life?
> What are your goals, as yet unfilled?
> What would you like to accomplish, to achieve?
> What would you like to have?
> What would you like to do?
> What would you like to do better?
> What would you like to happen?
> In what ways are you inefficient?
> What would you like to organize in a better way?
> What ideas would you like to get going?
> What relationship would you like to improve?
> What would you like to get others to do?
> What takes too long?
> What is wasted?
> What barriers or bottlenecks exist?
> What do you wish you had more time for?
> What do you wish you had more money for?
> What makes you angry, tense, or anxious?
> What do you complain about?

Now what is this superlative set of stages?

Five Steps
Guide Creative
Problem Solving

Divergent Then
Convergent
Thinking At
Each Step

The five stages are *fact-finding, problem-finding, idea-finding, solution-finding* (evaluation), and *acceptance-finding* (implementation). The steps guide the creative process; that is, they tell you want to do at each immediate step in order to eventually produce one or more creative, workable solutions. A unique feature is that each step first involves a *divergent* thinking phase, in which lots of ideas (facts, problem definitions, ideas, evaluation criteria, implementation strategies) are generated, then a second *convergent* phase, in which only the most promising ideas are selected for further exploration. Figure 5.1 illustrates the divergent/convergent nature of each step.

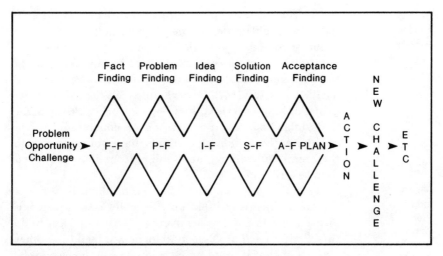

Figure 5.1. The creative problem solving (CPS) model.

Fact Finding

The first stage, *fact-finding,* involves "listing all you know about the problem or challenge" (Parnes, 1981) ". . . to help you explore all the information, impressions, observations, feelings, and questions that you have about a mess on which you've decided to work" (Isaksen & Treffinger, 1985). Parnes recommends the use of *who, what, when, where, why* and *how* questions. That is:

Who Did What When, Where, Why, and How?

Who is or should be involved?
What is or is not happening?
When does this or should this happen?
Where does or doesn't this occur?
Why does it or doesn't it happen?
How does it or doesn't it occur?

Fact-Finding Similar to Preparation Stage

The CPS fact-finding stage clearly parallels the preparation stage in the Wallas model. As an example, let's say the problem is thinking of ways to stimulate creativity in a classroom room or business organization. An individual or group first would list all of the facts they could think of relating to training creative thinking and perhaps to the nature of creativity and creative abilities. The *who, what, when, where, why* and *how* questions aid thinking in this step. The list of ideas is then convergently narrowed to a smaller number of facts that might be especially productive.

Problem-
Finding:
IWWMW?

What Is The
"Real"
Problem?

Ask "Why?":
Broadens
Problem
Definition

Idea-Finding:
Use Deferred
Judgment

Solution Finding
Is Idea
Evaluation

Common
Criteria

The second stage, *problem-finding,* involves listing alternative problem definitions. One principle of creative problem solving is that the definition of a problem will determine the nature of the solutions. In this step, it helps to begin each statement with "In what ways might we (or I) . . ." (IWWMW). For example, IWWMW find divergent thinking exercises, find books, workbooks or other materials, find resource persons or consultants, learn about creativity training methods, have someone else do the creativity training, have the persons involved teach themselves, and so on.

It may help to ask what the *real* problem is: What is the main objective? What do you really want to accomplish? Also, in most cases asking "*Why* do I want to do this?" after each problem statement will lead to another statement that is more broad and general. For example, asking "Why do I want to find divergent thinking exercises?" leads to the answer "In order to strengthen creative attitudes and abilities," which suggests the broader problem statement "IWWMW strengthen creative attitudes and abilities?" And asking "Why do I want to strengthen creative attitudes and abilities?" leads to "In order to improve creative potential and self-actualization," leading to the more general "IWWMW improve creative potential and self-actualization," and so on.

One or more of the most fruitful definitions is selected for the third stage, *idea finding.* This is the divergent-thinking, brainstorming stage. Ideas are freely listed, without criticism or evaluation, for each of the problem definitions accepted in the second stage.

The fourth stage, *solution finding,* should have been named *idea evaluation.* In three related steps, (1) criteria for evaluation are listed, (2) the ideas are evaluated, and (3) one or more of the best ideas are selected. In general, evaluation criteria might include:

Will it work?
Is it legal?
Are the materials and technology
    available?
Are the costs acceptable?
Will the public accept it?
Will higher-level administrators accept
    it?
Would grandmother approve?[3]

3. Another list of evaluation criteria appears in Chapter 7.

"I've told you for the last time, Mildred, IWWMW doesn't mean 'I'll wipe my white mitts wherever I want'!" (The Museum of Modern Art / Film Stills Archive.)

Criteria: Screen
Ideas

Relating specifically to the problem of teaching creativity, some criteria might be: Will the strategy strengthen important creative abilities? Will it teach creative attitudes and awarenesses; that is, will it work? Will it cost too much? Will it take too long? Are materials available? Will others accept the idea? Will the participants enjoy the experience? Will they cooperate? And so on. The list may be convergently reduced to the most relevant criteria. As Isaksen and Treffinger (1985) point out, the ". . . criteria are used to screen, select, and support options for which you will eventually be developing a plan of action."

Evaluation
Matrix

Take Another's
Perspective

Sometimes, an evaluation matrix can be helpful, with possible solutions listed on the vertical axis and the criteria across the top (see Figure 5.2). Each idea is rated according to each criteria, perhaps on a 1 to 5 scale, with the ratings entered in the cells. The scores would be totaled to find the "best" idea(s). Parnes (1981) suggested that you also can evaluate ideas by taking the perspective of another person and imagining how the idea looks to them; or else visualizing others reactions as you tell them about the idea.

List Good and
Bad Points

Another evaluation device is to make a list of what is *good* and what is *bad* about each idea. This approach helps prevent prematurely discarding an idea that has some good qualities or prematurely accepting an idea that has some serious faults.

Acceptance-
Finding: Action
Plan

Finally, *acceptance-finding* (idea implementation) amounts to thinking of ". . . ways to get the best ideas into action" (Parnes, 1981), that is, "The result of your acceptance-finding efforts will be a plan of action . . . a plan containing specific steps to be taken" (Isaksen & Treffinger, 1985).

Sources of
Assistance,
Resistance

Difficulties:
Areas of
Concern

To help formulate an action plan, Isaksen and Treffinger suggest that for each implementation idea, one can itemize sources of *assistance* (people, things, activities, locations) and sources of *resistance* (people, things, activities, locations). Also, one can ask "What are some difficulties that might arise?" and "What is the worst imaginable thing that could happen?" These two questions lead to a list of "areas of concern" plus ideas for "How to prevent it" and "How to respond if it happens."

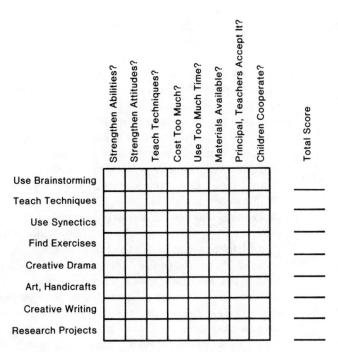

Figure 5.2. Example of an Evaluation Matrix. The problem was, "How can we teach creativity?" Each idea is rated on a 1 (low) to 5 (high) scale according to each criterion. Total scores are then tallied.

Convergent
Techniques:
Treffinger

Hits!

Hot Spots

Treffinger, Isaksen and Firestien (1982) noted that training in creative problem solving always emphasizes *divergent* techniques. They outlined some *convergent* techniques that can be used in any of the five CPS steps to aid in finding "good" facts, problem definitions, ideas, evaluation criteria (and solutions), and implementation strategies for further exploration. Especially interesting are their *hits* and *hot spots.* Hits are ideas that strike the problem solvers as important breakthroughs—directions to be pursued further because they could form the basis for a good problem solution. Groups of related hits are called hot spots. Hot spots are thus "a collection of hits that center around a specific issue or relate to a similar aspect of the problem." The hot spot is given a label that paraphrases the essential meaning of this group of hits and thus "suggests the strongest aspect of the hot spot." In the convergent part of each CPS step, think of hits and hot spots as good leads to good solutions.

Steps Should Be Habitual, Automatic

In his book *The Magic of Your Mind,* Parnes (1981) leads the reader through problem after problem with the goal of making the five steps habitual and automatic. That is, when encountering a problem, challenge, or opportunity one quickly would review relevant facts, identify various interpretations of the problem, generate solutions, evaluate the ideas, and speculate on how the solution(s) might be implemented and accepted.

Useful in Classroom, Corporation

Other Sequences of Steps May Help

In the classroom or corporation, Parnes' CPS stages may be used to guide a creative thinking session that (1) teaches an effective creative problem solving strategy, (2) improves understanding of the creative process, (3) exposes learners to a rousing creative-thinking experience, and (4) solves a problem. Incidentally, while chatting with Parnes over 1½ hot fudge sundaes (yes, Parnes ordered 1½ hot fudge sundaes), he mentioned that people tend to use the five stages too rigidly. On a sticky napkin he diagrammed a star-shaped model enclosed in a circle, emphasizing that—if it helps the creative process—one may flexibly move directly from any one step to any other. Rub a little chocolate on Figure 5.3 and you will get the full flavor of his suggestion. Actually, a little-known fact is that Osborn (1963) had Stages 1 and 2 reversed in the first place, with *problem-finding* preceding *fact-finding.*

A TWO-STAGE ANALYSIS

Two-Stage Model: Big Idea, Elaboration

Stripped to its essentials, creating something in art, science, business, or any other area involves two fairly clear steps: the *big idea* stage and an *elaboration* stage. The big idea stage is a period of fantasy in which the creative person looks for a new, exciting idea or problem solution. After the idea is found, perhaps using analogical thinking or some other creative thinking technique, the elaboration stage requires idea development, elaboration, and implementation. That is, the artist must assemble the materials, do preliminary sketches, and create the final work; the novelist must create characters and plot and write the story; the research scientist or business person must organize the details and carry out the work necessary to implement the big idea.

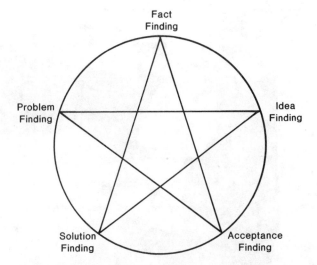

Figure 5.3. An alternative conception of the CPS model emphasizing that one may flexibly move from any stage to any other.

<table>
<tr><td>Von Oech: First
Stage is Right
Brain Thinking</td><td>Von Oech (1983) suggested that the first stage includes creative activity—for example, fantasy, imagination, and synthetic and analogical thinking. When a creative idea</td></tr>
</table>

Von Oech: First Stage is Right Brain Thinking

Second Stage: Left Brain Thinking

Creativity Also Needed in Second Stage

Von Oech (1983) suggested that the first stage includes creative activity—for example, fantasy, imagination, and synthetic and analogical thinking. When a creative idea is found, the activities of logical thinking, analyzing, and sequential planning are needed to develop and implement the idea. Actually, continued creative thinking and problem solving is needed in the elaboration and development stage as well as in the initial fantasy stage. Consider, for example, the elaboration and development of the plot for a novel or a research idea; much imagination and creativity are needed after the big idea is found.

THE CREATIVE PROCESS AS A CHANGE IN PERCEPTION

New Relationship, Meaning, Transformation, Idea Combination

The process of creation frequently involves a dramatic and usually instantaneous *change in perception*. There suddenly is a new way of looking at something, a *transformation,* a relationship that was not there before. One perceives new idea combinations, new implications, new meanings, or new applications. This phenomenon occurs whether the illumination is a simple modification of a

Figure 5.4. Mysterious picture. Can you find the one main picture? Ten other meaningful pictures? What else can you see? (Sidney J. Parnes, Ruth B. Noller and Angelo Biondi, excerpted from *Guide to Creative Action.* Copyright © 1976 Charles Scribner's Sons. Reprinted with the permission of Charles Scribner's Sons.)

cookie recipe, perhaps substituting mint candies for chocolate chips, or an unfathomably complex discovery in mathematics, physics, medicine, or astronomy.

Visual Puzzles Illustrate Perceptual Change

One simple way to illustrate this sudden perceptual change is with visual puzzles. For example, look at Figure 5.4. There is one main, meaningful figure that was created, in fact, from a photograph. After you find this figure, try to locate (1) a flying pig, (2) an Al Capp Li'l Abner character with a snaggle lower tooth, (3) a woman with her hair in a bun reclining on a sofa (she is in white). If you can find these easy (?) ones, look for (4) the Road Runner, (5) Harry Belafonte, (6) Popeye, (7) Blackbeard the Pirate, (8) a side profile of Jesus, (9) right next to Jesus a lady in a boufant hairdo, and (10) E. T. You will find yourself exclaiming, "Oh, there it is!" or "Now I see it!" The solutions are outlined at the end of this chapter.

Perceptual Transformation is Mysterious, Lies at Core of Creative Inspiration

We do not understand this sudden perceptual change or transformation very well. It is the mental activity underlying the creative insight itself; it is the very birth of creative inspiration. In some cases the perceptual transformation may take place while viewing or thinking about

Creativity frequently involves a change in perception. "My perceptions change all the time," agrees Ben. "I think I need an alignment." (The Museum of Modern Art / Film Stills Archive.)

one or two objects or ideas, and then mentally modifying them, combining them, or otherwise detecting a new meaning or relationship. For example, one of Harold Lloyd's movie makers experienced an abrupt perceptual change when the hilltop view of the Hollywood street was suddenly "seen" as an illusion of great height. A writer may "see" an intriguing story take shape as the result of a visit to San Salvador, Beirut, or Baghdad in early 1991. A product developer suddenly may "see" a new product, a new use for a material, or new marketing possibilities while flipping through the Yellow Pages. Inventor Mestral "saw" a new line of fastening devices while plucking cockleburrs from his hunting dog. The perceptual change or transformation process appears to be partly, if not largely, involuntary.

Playful
Perceptions May
Aid Perceptual
Change Ability

One book entitled *Playful Perception* (Leff, 1984) seeks to teach creative thinking by helping the reader to perceive the environment in creative, interesting, entertaining, and unusual—make that *weird*—ways. Leff

Awareness
Plans

describes the use of *awareness plans,* essentially "mental recipes" that require a person to select certain items in the environment and perform certain operations on them. Such plans are intended to stimulate insight and curiosity, help us learn to influence our feelings and our views of the world, treat things in life in a constructive and enlightened fashion, relate to others in creatively cooperative ways, and generally use our "powers of attention and imagination . . . (to open) doorways to expanded awareness on a variety of fronts." While some exercises are designed for fun and fantasy, others are intended to elicit beneficial changes for the world.

Exercises

You probably will not be able to resist trying some of the following exercises (adapted from Leff, 1984).

Try seeing and thinking about everything around you as if it were alive. (Is the light bulb a visitor from space? The trash can a helpless, hungry creature?)

Think of past and future reincarnations of things around you. (In its next life, will that garbage can be a Sears trash compactor?)

Think of alternative meanings and interpretations of common things and events. (Is the clerk's "May I help you?" a religious invocation? A four-word poem? A secret password? Is a volleyball game a new dance?)

Reverse things, events and causation from what you normally assume they are. (Articles in garbage may be seen as valuable treasures, expensive jewelry as junk. Bicycles cause kids feet to turn in circles.)

View the world from the perspective of an animal or an object. (How does the big dog look to a visiting cat? What if you are the room you are in, and the things in the room are part of you.)

See everything as edible, and imagine how it would taste?

"OK, stick 'em up, stick!" said the sheriff, who had just read the book *Playful Perception*. "I know you're the one who did the stick up! Where did you stick the loot! I hope you like stickin' around, 'cause you're gonna' be stuck in our jail for a long time!" (Wisconsin Center for Film and Theater Research.)

Look at objects as the tops of things, and imagine what the underground portion looks like.

Visually search your environment for things that are beautiful or aesthetically interesting.

Look for things you normally would not notice.

Look for boring things, and then think of something interesting about them.

Imagine the likely past and future of different objects.

Think about cultural values implied by things in your environment.

Think about what you can learn from whatever you encounter.

These kinds of exercises should indeed strengthen one's ability to make perceptual changes and transformations.

SUMMARY

The "creative process" can refer to sets of stages, the perceptual transformation that occurs during creativity, or to techniques and strategies.

Opinions differ regarding whether there are one or many creative processes. Idea combining, progressing through a sequence of steps, and the using idea-finding techniques, particularly analogical thinking, are global processes that are common across areas.

However, the creative processes of each creative person are influenced by experiences, abilities, thinking styles, and the requirements of different media and specific problems.

Insight, chance, and hard work are not inconsistent views of creative productivity. All have a role and are often interrelated.

Three intuitively necessary stages are clarifying the problem, working on it, and finding a solution.

Torrance's definition of creativity included steps of sensing a problem, forming hypotheses, testing the hypotheses, and communicating the results. Kingsley and Garry's similar steps included sensing a difficulty, clarifying the problem, searching for clues, trying out suggestions, and accepting a solution.

Dewey reduced problem solving steps to just two: a state of perplexity followed by searching for material to dispose of the difficulty.

The classic Wallas model included preparation, incubation, illumination, and verification. The stages do not necessarily occur in exactly that order.

Guilford suggested that incubation takes place during reflection, and that some people are more reflective than others.

Levels of processing theory suggests that incubation may involve fringe-conscious "low level" mental activity. If a good solution is encountered, it is passed to higher, conscious levels of processing.

The Osborn/Parnes CPS model included five steps of fact-finding, problem-finding, idea-finding, solution-finding (idea evaluation), and acceptance-finding (implementation). Each step involves first a divergent then a convergent thinking phase.

The CPS model represents both a creative process and a highly effective way to teach creative problem solving.

Fact-finding is aided by asking who, what, when, where, why, and how questions.

Problem-finding involves listing IWWMW questions, looking for the "real" problem, and asking "Why?" after each problem statement.

Idea-finding requires deferred judgment, the main brainstorming principle.

Solution finding includes listing evaluation criteria, evaluating the ideas, and selecting the best idea(s). An evaluation matrix may be used. One also can take another's perspective on the problem, or list what is good and what is bad about each idea.

Acceptance-finding results in an action plan.

Treffinger recommended looking for sources of assistance and resistance. His convergent techniques included finding hits, seemingly important ideas, and hot spots, which are groups of related hits.

Parnes recommends practicing the CPS model until the five steps become habitual and automatic. Said Parnes, the steps can be used in any order, if it helps.

A two-stage analysis of creative problem solving included a big idea stage, followed by an elaboration stage. Creativity is involved in both stages.

Perceptual change or transformation is a mysterious but core process that underlies insight and creative inspiration. It can be demonstrated with visual puzzles, in which new meanings, transformations, and idea combinations suddenly are "seen."

Leff's book *Playful Perception* provides many exercises, or action plans, for perceiving the environment in new and creative ways.

Solutions to Visual Puzzle.

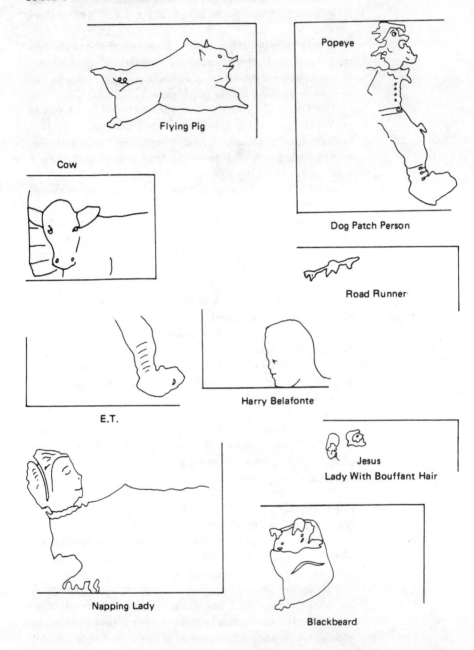

Flying Pig

Cow

Popeye

Dog Patch Person

Road Runner

E.T.

Harry Belafonte

Jesus

Lady With Bouffant Hair

Napping Lady

Blackbeard

6

creative inspiration through analogical thinking

[Scene: Mountain top cave in eastern country. Rich but simple Americans, John and Mary Simple, are seeking the meaning of life from bearded guru Swami Ci-Alli, seated in lotus position.]

John: Tell me Swami Ci-Alli, what is the meaning of life?

Swami: (Somberly) Life is a hamburger.

John: It is? I mean, what is life all about?

Mary: He's speaking metaphorically, John. He means that the total sandwich is made of what you put into it. Am I right Swami?

Swami: You see through mist with eyes of magic fog lamp.

John: Oh, okay. But what should I do in this world? What is the best life?

Swami: An arrow can only fly straight.

John: Huh?

Mary: It's metaphorical again, John. I think he means that you should get out more, maybe take up archery.

Swami: Not quite, madam. I mean that a ball can only bounce.

Mary: Well, there's my bowling ball that doesn't . . .

John: Maybe he means that I am what I am and I should do what I do best. Right, Swami?

Swami: Your thoughts are a razor cutting through the beard of reality.

Mary: And what else Swami Ci-Alli? I mean, this was an expensive trip.

Swami: You must sail the oceans of the unknown and discover islands of truth.

John: Wait a minute. Sir Isaac Newton said that hundreds of years ago!

Swami: If you want originality, you must toss your own metaphorical salad.

Mary: Let's get out of here, my feet are beef in a meat grinder, dough under a rolling pin, blasphemers on the inquisitors' rack, . . .

John: Oh cut it out!

Most Creative
Ideas Stem from
Analogical,
Metaphorical
Thinking

We Make a
Connection

One cannot overstate the importance of analogical and metaphorical thinking in creativity.[1] It is simply and absolutely true that many—perhaps the large majority—of our creative ideas and problem solutions are born in analogical and metaphorical thinking. *When we think analogically or metaphorically, we take ideas from one context and apply them in a new context,* producing the new idea combination, new transformation, new theoretical perspective, or more colorful literary passage. We "make a connection" between our current problem and a similar or related situation.

"Was Inspired
By"

Bronowski,
Koestler Agree

Analogical and metaphorical thinking is extremely common in all areas of creativity and creative problem solving. The frequent comments "was inspired by" and "is based upon" indicate that ideas for a specific creation were suggested by or borrowed from another source by the particular composer, novelist, movie maker, artist, architect, decorator, designer, scientist, engineer, new product developer, business entrepreneur, or other creative person. Said historian Jacob Bronowski (1961), "The discoveries of science, the works of art, are explorations—more, are explosions—of (seeing) a hidden likeness." Philosopher Arthur Koestler (1964) observed that the creative thinker finds such metaphoric and analogical connections while ordinary individuals do not.

CATS Inspired
by T. S. Eliot
Poetry

Perhaps a first example is in order. The brilliantly creative and successful Broadway musical *CATS* was "based on" *Old Possum's Book of Practical Cats,* a book of poems by T. S. Eliot. The *CATS* playbill read:

> Most of the poems comprising *Old Possum's Book of Practical Cats* have been set to music complete and in their originally published form . . . However, some of our lyrics, notably *The Marching Song of the Pollicle Dogs* and the story of *Grizzabella,* were discovered among the unpublished writings of Eliot. The prologue is based on

---

1. As we noted earlier, in the creativity literature the distinction between *analogy* and *metaphor* is blurred to the point where the terms are used nearly (not completely) interchangeably.

Ideas come from somewhere. The design for this automobile was inspired by a door hinge. "Hey fellas," yelled the exasperated inventor, "Could you pull ahead? I gotta' slam my frame!" (Wisconsin Center for Film and Theater Research.)

ideas and incorporates lines from another unpublished poem entitled *Pollicle Dogs and Jellicle Cats.* Growltiger's aria is taken from an Italian translation of *Practical Cats. Memory* includes lines from and is suggested by *Rhapsody on a Windy Night,* and other poems of the *Prufrock* period. All other words in the show are taken from the Collected Poems.

May Be Sudden

Is analogical thinking important in high-level creative accomplishments? Do creative ideas come from nowhere?

Sometimes an analogical connection will burst forth suddenly and unpredictably. That is, a sudden "insight" may be a matter of instantly "making a connection."

May Take Painstaking Search

Other times the creative person will deliberately and painstakingly search for suitable analogical relationships, as when a professional advertiser looks for a good strategy for promoting a client's product or an architect searches his or her books and magazines for ideas for a creative home or building.

A time-honored example of a suddenly-occurring creative visual analogy is Friedrich August von Kekule's report of his discovery of the ring structure of benzene. After days of thinking about the problem:

Tasty Tail: Benzene Ring

I turned my chair to the fire and dozed. Again the atoms were gamboling before my eye. This time the smaller groups kept modestly to the background. My mental eye, rendered more acute by repeated visions of this kind, could now distinguish larger structures, of manifold conformation; long rows, sometimes more closely fitted together; all twining and twisting in snakelike motion. But look! What was that? One of the snakes had seized hold of its own tail, and the form whirled mockingly before my eyes. As if by a flash of lightening I awoke . . . (Rothenberg, 1979, pp. 395–396).

Is "Borrowing" Ideas Ethical and Virtuous?

In the following pages of examples, the reader will see that analogical and metaphorical thinking is exceedingly common in creative innovation. It is both an explanatory creative *process*; it also is a learnable creative thinking *technique.*

When Is "Borrowing" Actually Stealing?

But where, one might ask, does stealing and plagiarism end and "true" originality begin? Young and idealistic creative persons may worry about this issue more than experienced and successful ones, who realize that (1) ideas come from somewhere, (2) the analogical use of ideas is common, effective, and usually quite legitimate, and (3) seeing analogical and metaphorical connections is quite a creative thing to do.

Analogical Thinking Common, Usually Legitimate

Sometimes the analogy or metaphor poses no ethical questions at all, as when:

Kekule used the circular snake as an analogical inspiration for the benzine ring.

Bohr used the solar system as a model for the structure of the atom.

Darwin found inspiration for his theory of natural selection in selective cattle breeding.

A fourth-grader says, "Hey, let's turn the classroom into a carnival for parents' night!"

A movie maker or writer of Broadway plays uses any number of historical events, Biblical events, or comic book characters for inspiration (e.g., *Jesus Christ Superstar, Evita, Superman, Batman*).

A novelist, mystery writer, or playwright finds inspiration in real events, myths, news stories, or children's stories, as Truman Capote, Ernest Hemmingway, Agatha Christie, Shakespeare, and many others have done.

In the business and corporate world, for promoting your business, borrowing and modifying other successful (e.g., marketing) strategies generally is good problem solving. We will see many more examples of analogically, and ethically, "borrowing" ideas in later sections.

Happy Bird Day?

Of course, if you literally "lift" someone else's work, for example, a scientific theory or a contemporary musical composition, change a few details and then claim it for your own, quite obviously that is stealing. To avoid copyright infringement, one publisher of American folk tunes changed the title of *Happy Birthday* to *"Happy Bird Day"* and published exactly the original melody. Lyrics were changed to bird words.

Grey Areas
There are, however, "grey areas," as when a TV movie plot is based directly on, say, an Agatha Christie or other novel without crediting the source; an artist too-closely copies the techniques and ideas of another; or 17 companies create their own version of the *Weed Eater.* One must reach one's own conclusions regarding the originality and ethics of creations that may appear too-directly influenced by a successful predecessor.

EXAMPLES OF ANALOGICAL THINKING IN CREATIVE INNOVATION

Two-Stage Model

Analogical Thinking in Big Idea Stage
Before we look at how analogical and metaphorical thinking is used to find new ideas, it is important to recall the two-stage model of the creative process described in Chapter 5. Again, this is not a theory of how creative problem solving takes place, it is a statement of fact. Stage 1 is the *Big Idea* stage in which the main idea for the artistic creation, invention or problem solution is found. Stage 2 is the *Elaboration* and development stage in which the Big Idea is implemented. In the following examples analogical and metaphorical thinking takes place most clearly in the Big Idea stage—finding that new idea for a creative problem solution, composition, invention, theory, and so on. After the Big Idea is found, of course, it must be developed and implemented, which may or may not involve additional analogical or metaphorical thinking.

Music

Much Music Based Upon Earlier Melodies
The author would not even hint that all music written by all composers is analogically borrowed from earlier melodies. Some compositions inexplicably pop into the

heads of classic and contemporary composers, with roots somewhere in their immense mental store of musical experiences and potential musical combinations. Other compositions are the product of laboriously experimenting with ideas—manipulating, modifying and revising until something good is created. However, there are many instances in which the Big Idea for a composition clearly is borrowed from an earlier piece, consciously and deliberately.

Liszt

Tchaikowsky

Cesar Cui

Brahms, Beethoven

Franz Liszt composed 15 Hungarian Rhapsodies, cleverly titled "Hungarian Rhapsody Number 1," "Hungarian Rhapsody Number 2," "Hungarian Rhapsody Number 3," and so on. All 15 " . . . were built upon traditional songs or dance airs of the romantic gypsies of Hungary" (Thompson, 1942). Franz had good company. Peter Tchaikowsky also based his *Marche Slav* on a folk tune, the same tune used by Cesar A. Cui for his *Orientale*, which accounts for the " . . . striking similarity between this melody (*Orientale*) and that of *Marche Slav*" (Thompson, 1942). And more: "The waltzes of Brahms like those of Beethoven have for their inspiration the old German 'Landler' or peasant dance . . ." (Thompson, 1942).

Aaron Copeland

Aaron Copeland's *Appalachian Spring* symphony was based upon a Quaker folk tune entitled *Simple Gifts*. His bouncy *Hoe Down* from *Rodeo* seems more of an arrangement of a traditional American hoe down than an original composition. However, to keep Copeland's creative genius in its mystical perspective, in a 1984 television interview Copeland mentioned that when his music came alive in his head, he has no choice but to find a pencil and paper and start writing.

Broadway Show Based on a Painting

The Broadway musical *Sunday Afternoon in the Park with George* was inspired by Georges Seurat's famous painting *Sunday Afternoon on the Isle of La Grand Jatte*.

Barry Manilow

Oh Say, Can You Serve Me Another Pint of Ale?

In the popular music category, daughter Sonja Davis was one day playing Chopin's *Prelude in C Minor.* She stopped in mid-melody to announce, "Hey, this is Barry Manilow's *'Could It Be Magic'!*" A check of the Manilow album cover credited these composers, "Barry Manilow, Adrienne Anderson, and F. Chopin." Another long-time hit, Francis Scott Key's *Star Spangled Banner,* is based upon an English drinking song.

A Common,
Creative
Composing
Strategy

The Big Ideas for these and many other popular songs and classical pieces were borrowed from earlier, usually simpler tunes. This is not plagiarism, it is a common analogical creative thinking process used by uncommonly creative people.

Cartoons

Many Cartoons
Analogically
Based

Many newspaper cartoons, both political cartoons and cartoon-strip "funnies," are good examples of analogical thinking in creativity. While all cartoons are not necessarily inspired by related sources, many of them are. If you watch, the best cartoons usually are analogical in nature, with ideas from an unrelated context combined with a current political event or with regular cartoon-strip characters to create a surprising and funny combination.

Sources of
Inspiration

Note the several types of idea sources for the cartoons on the following pages—news events, political events, Hollywood and TV movies, popular TV commercials, a popular song, and children's stories. It is not unusual to see political and other cartoons based upon, for example, movies such as *Jaws, Shogun, Star Wars,* or *Rambo;* mythology such as *Dracula* and *Frankenstein;* or classic literature such as *Robin Hood, Dr. Jekyl and Mr. Hyde,* the *Wizard of Oz,* or *Alice in Wonderland.* Cartoon strips such as *Frank and Earnest, Zippy,* and *The Wizard of Id* regularly incorporate current news and political events into their cartoon setting. (Where did the title "Wizard of Id" come from?)

Art Buchwald:
Master of
Humorous
Metaphors

Tax Fantasies

Political humorist Art Buchwald often uses analogical and metaphorical thinking in his syndicated column in order to poke fun at political events and politicians. One April 15 column on tax fantasies, inspired by books on sex fantasies, appears in Inset 6.1. Even within the larger tax fantasy metaphor, Buchwald metaphorically borrowed ideas from "fat sheriff" commercials and from *Cinderella.*

THE FAR SIDE   By Gary Larson

Moses as a kid

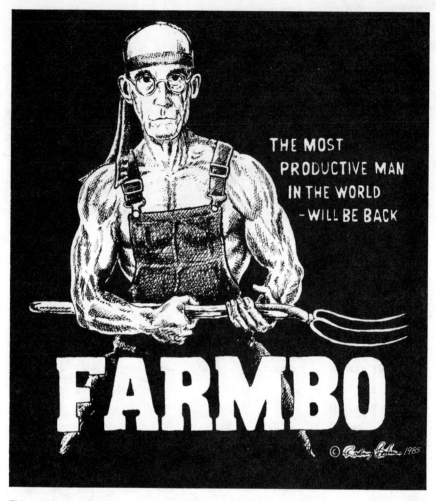

This poster borrowed one idea from RAMBO and another from the classic painting *American Gothic*. (Reprinted by permission of Rodney Bohner.)

© by and permission of News American Syndicate.

BLOOM COUNTY

By Berke Breathed

Reprinted by permission of the Atlanta Constitution.

Joe Heller, Green Bay Press Gazette, Copyright 1988, reprinted with permission. All rights reserved.

Inset 6.1
Erotica for April 15 May Ease the Pain*

Columnist and political humorist Art Buchwald is a master of deliberate metaphorical thinking—transferring ideas from one situation to another situation. The outcome is always funny. Well, usually. The two fantasies reproduced here actually are metaphors within a metaphor—within the "tax fantasy" metaphor ideas are borrowed from the 1970's "fat sheriff" Dodge commercial and from the Cinderella fairytale. Reprinted with permission by the Los Angeles Times.

By ART BUCHWALD

WASHINGTON—Many magazines have been doing articles on sex fantasies. It's amazing how many men and women will talk about them if their names are not used for publication. But it's rare to have anyone admit that they have tax fantasies. After prying and cajoling, I finally got several people of both sexes to tell me their favorite tax fantasies.

L. D., a 30-year-old car salesman, writes: "I have this tax fantasy, maybe two, three times a week. I'm called down to the IRS office for an audit. The agent tells me to bring down all my receipts and records.

"He looks like a fat sheriff in a TV commercial sitting behind his desk smoking a large cigar. I tell him I have been meticulous about my deductions, and he'll find everything in order.

"He chuckles and says, 'That's what they all say. Why don't you make it easy on both of us and tell us exactly how much you've cheated Uncle Sam out of this time?'

"I say, 'It's all here. Every cent I deducted has been verified and accounted for.'

" 'Okay,' he says, taking out his mini-calculator. 'If you want to play rough, I can play rough.' He starts hitting the calculator with his fat fingers. It takes three hours. He goes over the figures again and again. He can't find one thing wrong with my tax return. His face is red. 'There has to be something here,' he says.

"After the fourth time he realizes that the return is perfect. He looks at me, opens the top drawer of his desk and excuses himself to go to the men's room. I wait in my chair. Suddenly I hear a gunshot from the washroom. An aide says, 'Don't feel bad. For him it was the only honorable way out.' "

T. R. IS A 21-year-old career woman who has worked her way up in the stockroom of a very cheap department store. Her boss is known as the "wicked stepmother." Every April there is a ball given by the store before the spring clearance sales.

The stepmother says T. R. can't go to the ball until she counts all the glass slippers that are still unsold from a previous Cinderella promotion which never got off the ground.

As T. R. is counting the boxes, a Fairy Godmother arrives with a new dress from Bergdorf Goodman and a diamond ring borrowed from Elizabeth Taylor. T. R. goes to the ball and meets a handsome prince. He falls in love with her, but at the stroke of midnight she has to leave. She loses her glass slipper. After a futile search he finally finds T. R. in the stockroom and tries the slipper on her foot. It fits.

He confesses he's really not a prince but actually works for H & R Block, the tax consultants. He explains to her that if they get married they could save $345 a year on their income tax. Overcome with the thought of the tax loophole, she says yes, and they live happily ever after.

*Reprinted with permission of Art Buchwald.

Infantry, with Air Support, Overruns Pork and Beans!

See how it works? Could you write a picnic episode, describing in battlefield terms the difficulties with ants and their allies the bees? Could you describe how to bake cookies using the language of a hospital operating room? Could you use the language of a cat stalking a mouse to describe a clever salesperson trying to sell someone an expensive color TV set? Try it.

Your Turn

If that exercise worked, perhaps you are ready for more. Think about the idea sources in the top section of Insert 6.2. Imagine how some of them might be used in either a political cartoon or a brief written satire involving the topics at the bottom of the page. Go ahead and try a few. You probably will surprise yourself?

Science and Invention

Gordon: Examples of Analogical Thinking

Gutenberg: Movable Type

Gordon (1974b), champion of the analogical basis of creativity, described a number of instances of analogical thinking in science and invention. For example, it seems that Gutenberg (1398–1468), inventor of movable printing type, was not too crazy about hand-engraving an entire page of text on a single slab of smooth wood. The analogy of coin-making, in which plain discs are stamped by a coin punch, suggested separate metal letters that could

Inset 6.2
Now Imagine You Are a Cartoonist or Columnist: Exercise in Analogical Thinking

Look at the "scenarios"—the characters, their vocabulary, the setting, their goals or problems—in the top section below. See if you can create an original cartoon by metaphorically applying the ideas to one of the topics in the bottom section. Sometimes there will be an easy fit, for example, just using the caption "Coke is it!" under a drug scene. Go ahead, sketch your ideas. If you prefer, try a short written spoof like the Art Buchwald column on pages 131–132.

ORIGINAL SCENARIO—SOURCE OF CHARACTERS AND IDEAS

Alice in Wonderland (Queen of Hearts, Mad Hatter, March Hare, Mushroom that makes you grow)

Snow White (seven dwarfs, Prince Charming, Wicked Queen with "Mirror, Mirror on the Wall," poisoned apple)

Cinderella (ugly step-sisters, wicked step-mother, magic coach)

Goldilocks and the Three Bears

Three Little Pigs and the Wolf (straw, wood, and brick houses)

Sleeping Beauty (awakened by kiss from handsome prince)

Rapunzel, who let down hair for prince to climb

Little Red Riding Hood, the Wolf, basket of goodies, Grandmother

Kissing a frog, who turns into a prince

Tom Tom The Pipers Son, Stole a Pig and Away He Run

Robin Hood, who steals from the rich to give to the poor

Star Wars Characters (Luke Skywalker, Princess Leia, Darth Vader, Ben Kenobi, Yoda, Ewoks, Walking Machines)

E. T., who wants to phone home and go home

Sasquatch (Yeti, Big Foot); Loch Ness Monster (Nessie)

A McDonalds commercial, with Ronald McDonald

"Coke Is It" commercial

Superman, Batman

Bible (Moses, Noah, Daniel in lion's den, Adam and Eve)

Weather forecast, with weather map showing storms, sunny skies

SITUATIONS IN WHICH TO USE CHARACTERS AND IDEAS

Star Wars space defense system

Summit talks between U.S. President and Russian leader

China becoming more capitalistic, less communistic

Political revolutions in Central American country (pick one)

Revisions in Federal Income Tax that still favor the rich

Local School Board

Growing drug abuse problem

News about fertility pills leading to multiple births

News about unsafe automobiles

News about federal spending or the growing national debt

News about Japanese car imports

News about Kuwait oil fires

News about AIDS continuing to spread despite public awareness campaigns

Other current news events?

---

be rearranged and reused again and again. A wine press suggested his printing press.

Bissel's Oil Pump

Watt: All Aboard for Tea

Galvani's Battery: Hopping Good Idea!

In the 1850s George B. Bissel grew very tired of inefficiently gathering oil out of shallow wells with buckets or else sopping it up with blankets and then wringing them out. He borrowed ideas from a brine pump at a salt plant to design a similar pump for raising oil. James Watt's (1736–1819) steam engine was inspired by the jangling lid of his mother's tea kettle. The wife of Luigi Galvani (1737–1798) placed a steel knife on a tin plate, accidentally touching a frog's leg that suddenly twitched. Galvani deduced that electricity had been created by the joining of two dissimilar metals and promptly invented the battery. His young son deduced that the leg was not yet dead and promptly smacked it with a cleaver.

Brunel's Underwater Tunnel

Sir Marc Isambard Brunel (1769–1849) was wrestling with the problem of efficiently constructing underwater tunnels. He happened to observe a shipworm constructing a tube for itself as it moved forward through a timber, which suggested a short steel cylinder that could be pushed forward as tunnel work progressed. Were it not for that worm, New York's Holland and Lincoln tunnels would be filled with water today.

Morse: Relay Stations

Samuel Morse's (1791–1872) first telegraph messages became weak after just a few miles. Stagecoach relay stations, where fresh horses were added, metaphorically suggested relay stations at appropriate distances where more power could be added to the fading signal. The development of Elias Howe's sewing machine was aided when Howe put the eye in the point of the needle, which was suggested by weaving shuttles. Howe's sewing machine principle was applied by the Singer Company to a leather stitching machine for making shoes.

Howe's Sewing Machine Needle

Darwin's Natural Selection

Charles Darwin observed that animal breeders could selectively breed for characteristics that improved the market value of their animals. This observation suggested that a similar process could happen in natural selection in nature.

Whitney's Cotton Gin Based on Unsuccessful Cat

Eli Whitney claims that he developed his cotton gin after watching a pussycat trying to catch a chicken through a fence. The cat missed, coming up with a pawful of feathers. Hundreds of paws on his cotton gin reach through a tight fence and pull cotton away from the seeds.

Pasteur: Fermenting Flesh?

Wine grapes, which ferment only when crushed, suggested to Louis Pasteur that human flesh would not putrefy unless an open wound allowed putrefying agents to get in. An experiment confirmed this novel idea, which advanced medical understanding of infections and the use of Band-Aids to prevent them.

Westinghouse Air Brake

George Westinghouse, after surviving a head-on train crash, learned of a Swiss rock drill that was powered by an air hose 3,000 feet from the compressor. He immediately designed the Westinghouse air brake, powered the length of the train by compressed air. Scotsman Dunlop's first tire was not only inspired by the flexibility of a garden hose, it *was* a piece of garden hose wrapped around a wheel.

Dunlop's Tire First Used on Grass

One autumn, inventor George De Mestral was walking with his hunting dog through a field that was booby-trapped with cockleburrs, most of which ended up on the dog. During the extraction process he examined the structure of the burrs and determined to replicate its ferocious cling in a commercial product. After hundreds of attempts and dollars, and several years' work, velcro was born.

Many ideas have their roots in analogical thinking. This person's barber was inspired by a blender. "I think I liked punk better," said Mr. Punchbach. (The Museum of Modern Art/Film Stills Archive.)

Duryea's
Carburetor

Wing Flaps from
a Buzzard

Rapid Fir Razor

Charles Duryea, looking for a better way to squirt gas into engine cylinders, used the analogy of his wife's perfume atomizer to develop a spray injection carburetor. The Wright brothers did not have a carburation problem, but they needed to be able to turn their plane. The solution came from a buzzard who twisted the back of its wing slightly downward to increase air pressure in order to turn. Tying a buzzard to each wing did not work, but movable wing flaps did. The Schick injector razor, invented by an army person, was inspired by the loading mechanism of the repeating rifle.

These are a handful of the many discoveries and inventions "inspired by" or "based upon" some analogically related object, process or idea.

Literature, Movie-Making, TV

Shakespeare's Sources

Big Idea Clear, But Elaboration Mysterious

Scholars in university English departments sometimes do source studies to identify the metaphorical sources of ideas and inspirations underlying the works of noteworthy authors and playwrights. We will go right to the top by examining the idea sources of the greatest playwright of all time, William Shakespeare. Table 6.1 presents a shortened version of a complete list of Shakespeare's plays and their idea sources that appears in the World Book Encyclopedia. The left column lists some of his better known plays, the right column identifies the source from which he apparently derived the characters, settings and main plots. While the Big Idea for each play has been traced, the character development, dramatic conflicts, humor, and so on are creative beyond description. As mentioned earlier, it is the elaboration and development stage of creativity that appears to be the most mysterious and intriguing process, and one that sets Shakespeare apart from mortal bards.[2]

Movies, Novels, Plays Have Metaphorical Sources

Shakespeare is not alone in borrowing ideas for characters, settings and plots, of course. Many movies, novels, TV dramas, and broadway plays continue to be inspired by or based upon recognizable events and idea sources. The following is a small sample:

Contemporary Events

From *contemporary events: All the President's Men* (from Watergate); *In Cold Blood* (a midwest murder); *High Noon* (inspired by senate investigations of organized crime in Hollywood); *Killing Fields* (Cambodian holocaust).

---

2. Example of "seeing a connection" in humor: Did you know that Shakespeare's mother was an Avon lady?

Table 6.1
Idea Sources of Shakespeare
(Abridged from the World Book Encyclopedia)

Play	Source
Taming of the Shrew	Taming of the Shrew (unknown English playwright)
Romeo and Juliet	Romeo and Juliet (poem by Arthur Brooke)
Merchant of Venice	Il Pecorone (short story by Giovanni Fiorentino)
Julius Caesar	A tragedy from Plutarch's Lives
Much Ado About Nothing	Orlando Fusioso (comedy by Ludovico Ariosto)
Twelfth Night	Farewell to the Military Profession (short story by Barnabe Riche)
Hamlet	Hamlet (play by unknown English author) and Histoires Tragiques (Francois Belleforest)
All's Well that Ends Well	The Palace of Pleasure (short story by unknown author)
Othello	Promos and Cassandra (play by George Whetstone)
King Lear	The Union of Two Noble and Illustrious Families of Lancaster and York (by Edward Hall, historian) and Holinshed's Chronicles (16th century history book)
Macbeth	Holinshed's Chronicles
Antony and Cleopatra	Plutarch's Lives

History   *History: The Longest Day, From Here to Eternity, Tora Tora Tora, Voyage of the Damned* (all from World War II events); *Gone With the Wind, Red Badge of Courage* (Civil War); *I Claudius, Cleopatra, Ben Hur, Salamis* (Roman, Egyptian, Greek history); *Les Misrables.*

Biographies   *Biographies: Citizen Kane* (life of San Francisco newspaperman William Randolph Hearst), *El Cid* (legendary Spanish hero); *Edison, the Man; Patton; The Miracle Worker* (Helen Keller); *Elephant Man* (story of John Merrick); *Elvira Madigan* (last woman hanged in England); *Ghandi; Bird Man of Alcatraz; Three Faces of Eve; I'll Cry Tomorrow* (Lillian Roth).

Bible   The *Bible: Ten Commandments, David the King, Jesus of Nazareth, Jesus Christ Superstar.*

Classic, Contemporary Literature   *Classic and Contemporary Literature: The Old Man and the Sea, Of Mice and Men, Dr. Jekyl and Mr. Hyde, Ivanhoe, David Copperfield, Alice in Wonderland, Wizard of Oz, Jane Eyre, Tess, For Whom the Bell Tolls, Tale of Two Cities, Superman, Batman.*

Mythology, Legend   *Mythology and Legend:* Frankenstein and Dracula movies, including *Love at First Bite; American Werewolf in London; I Was a Teenage Werewolf; Three Musketeers.*

Shakespeare Has Been Moonlighting   The successful TV show *Moonlighting* based a St. Patrick's day show on a leprechan looking for a pot of gold; a Christmas show included numerous Christmas themes, including a baby and three detectives named King ("Three Kings"); Shakespeare inspired at least two *Moonlighting* episodes (e.g., *Taming of the Shrew*).

Can you think of other movies inspired by specific sources?

Acting

Lady Blue Is Dirty Harriet   Actors and Actresses must develop their stage and screen personalities which often, perhaps always, are borrowed from character types they know. Again, ideas come from somewhere. In a newspaper interview, the star of the 1985 TV detective series *Lady Blue*, Jamie Rose, said "My inspiration for the character is Clint Eastwood's 'Dirty Harry.' In my mind, she (my character, Katy Mahoney) is Dirty Harriet." The article reported, "Ms.

Rose, 26, had the prop master furnish her with a fake .357 magnum pistol with a four-inch barrel, then rented a VCR and all four 'Dirty Harry' movies. 'I hooked up the video to my hotel room TV and kind of shot along with Clint— again and again.' "

Other actors and actresses will borrow the stage personalities of, for example, Marilyn Monroe, James Cagney, and others. Watch for them on TV.

Architecture, Clothes Design

Other Countries,
Other Times

Magazines:
Sources Of
Metaphorical
Inspiration

These two unrelated topics are lumped together because they both can make use of the same analogical strategy for finding ideas. Want to design a creative home? Ideas for a unique wardrobe? Try thinking about other countries and other times. Visit a museum, look at pictures in history books, or flip through encyclopedias. Do you think you could find a few hundred inspirations from Mexico, the orient, Holland, Greece, Ancient Egypt, Peru, Africa, Switzerland, America's pilgrims, Atlanta in 1855, Disneyland, New Orleans, the roaring 1920's, rural America, other places and times? Of course you could. Professional designers have stacks of books and magazines filled with ideas waiting to be modified and applied. The castles at Disneyland and Disney World were inspired by the Neuschwanstein castle near Fussen, West Germany. Frank Lloyd Wright used Viennese, Japanese, and Aztec designs in his architecture. Frank was reasonably successful.

ANALOGICAL THINKING IN PROBLEM SOLVING

Creativity in All
Steps of
Problem Solving

Unless you have a clearly convergent problem with one and only one correct answer (for example, an arithmetic problem, "Where's my dog?" or "Who's picture is on the fifty?"), creativity can be involved in every step of problem solving. The CPS model in Chapter 5 illustrated how creativity can help clarify a problem (fact-finding stage), define the problem (problem-finding), list solution alternatives (idea-finding), evaluate ideas (solution-finding), and implement the solution(s) (acceptance-finding).

Analogical Thinking in Idea Finding

The most obvious use of analogical thinking in the CPS model is in the idea-finding process. Consider a problem such as "How can we get more parents to the school play?" One could find ideas by asking questions that stimulate analogical thinking, such as:

Stimulating Questions

What else is like this?
What have others done?
What could we copy?
What has worked before?
What would professionals do?

Deliberate, Spontaneous Analogical Ideas

Such questions elicit deliberate analogical thinking. Analogical ideas also will occur spontaneously—"Say, Benedict Arnold High School got free newspaper and radio advertising. John Wilkes Booth High held a raffle with the admission ticket—community businesses donated tons of prizes!"

Osborn's Checklist

Incidentally, two of the above five questions appear in Osborn's checklist "73 List Spurring Questions" (Chapter 7). That checklist encourages analogical thinking for finding ideas and problem solutions.

SYNECTICS METHODS

Analogy-Based Techniques Bring Together Different Elements

The word *synectics* is from the Greek *syn*, meaning "together," along with *-ectics*, which was arbitrarily selected (Prince, 1982). Synectics is "the joining together of different and apparently irrelevant elements" (Gordon & Poze, 1980a, 1980b). The synectics methods are conscious, analogy-based and metaphor-based techniques for bringing together these different elements. The originator of the synectics methods is William J. J. Gordon, former school teacher, horse handler, salvage diver, ambulance driver, ski instructor, sailing schooner master, college lecturer, and pig breeder. The outcome of the pig project was " . . . a lot of bone and not much bacon, but they were the fastest pigs in the East" (Alexander, 1978).

Gordon: Well-Rounded Person!

Fast Pigs

Patents, Creative Writing Awards

Familiar
Inventions

Currently, Gordon and his colleagues hold more than 200 patents and their creative writing, published in the *New Yorker* and *Atlantic Monthly,* won them the O. Henry Short Story Award and the Science Fiction Award. A few examples of synectics inventions are Pringles Potato Chips, a trash compactor, an electric knife, a space suit closure device for NASA, a space feeding system, the space-saver Kleenex box, disposable diapers, a disposable baby bottle with formula, an ice cube maker, a jet marine engine, a Ford truck frame suspension system, an accelerated wound-healing system, operating table covers, Sunoco's dial-your-own-octane gas pump, and the presumably similar automatic liquor dispenser.

Made Creativity
Techniques
Conscious,
Teachable

For Adults

For Children

Gordon's early experience with creative thinking groups helped him to identify analogical thinking strategies that creative people use spontaneously. He clarified these strategies, making them conscious and teachable in a form for adults (e.g., Gordon, 1961; Prince, 1968) and for children. Said Gordon (Gordon & Poze, 1980b), "Everyone, to some degree or another, consciously or unconsciously uses analogies to solve problems. The purpose of . . . synectics is to give you a way to use analogies that will make your problem-solving process more effective." In agreement, former synectics colleague George Prince (1968) observed that the procedures " . . . help you think unhabitually." Gordon's workbooks and exercise books *Making It Strange* (Gordon, 1974a), *New Art of the Possible* (Gordon & Poze, 1980b), *Metaphorical Way of Learning and Knowing* (Gordon & Poze, 1971), *Teaching is Listening* (Gordon & Poze, 1972a), and *Strange and Familiar* (Gordon & Poze, 1972b) give children first-hand experience with the fascinating synectics problem-solving methods of *direct analogy, personal analogy, fantasy analogy,* and *symbolic analogy.* Gordon's strategies inspired some of the exercises in Stanish's fine workbooks *Sunflowering* (Stanish, 1977), *Hippogriff Feathers* (Stanish, 1981), and *Hearthstone Traveler* (Stanish, 1988).

Have You
Sunflowered
Lately?

Direct Analogy

With the *direct analogy* method, the problem solver is asked to think of ways that related problems have been solved. While analogies of any sort are welcome, those from nature are especially encouraged. How have animals, birds, flowers, insects, worms, snakes, and so on solved similar problems? Gordon and Poze (1980b), for example, speculate that civilization itself progressed when individuals made analogical connections—seeing that this situation is like that situation. Imagine a starving cave person unsuccessfully trying to spear fish with a sharp stick. There are fish all over the place, but cave person cannot stab enough to feed family and friends. Cave person sees a small swarm of flies become entrapped in a spider's web. Aha! Cave person makes an analogical connection, dashes back to the group, dumps the neighbor out of a hammock and uses the hammock to net fish by the dozens. Another primitive has trouble keeping his pants up, and a snake wrapped around a rock suggested the first belt (Gordon & Poze, 1972b). When his socks kept falling down, a little garter snake suggested a similar solution.

Gordon himself was part of an emergency group faced with removing a sunken ship that blocked the Tripoli habor during WW II. An army colonel imagined his mother vigorously raking away at dirt lumps in her garden, which suggested blasting the offending ship to smithereens and then "raking" it level just as mother did. It worked.

In one synectics problem solving session the problem was to package potato chips compactly and without breaking them. Wet leaves—which pack snugly together without breaking—metaphorically led to Pringles Potato Chips. Magnesium-impregnated bandages that accelerate the healing of wounds came from the analogy of a broken electrical wire (Gordon & Poze, 1980b).

Virtually any sort of problem can be attacked with the direct analogy method. For example, in a creativity workshop for retired people many expressed concern for their personal safety. With the direct analogy approach the problem became: How do animals, plants, birds, etc., protect themselves, and how can these ideas help the elderly?[3] The idea list included spray cans of skunk scent, slip-on fangs and claws, a compressed air can that screams when activated, a snake-faced mask that scares the bejeebers out of potential muggers, an electronic device that secretly "yells" for the police, traveling only in groups, and camouflauge or disguises, for example, wearing a police uniform.

Personal Analogy

What Thoughts Run Through Your Bubble Gum Head?

Imagine you are a piece of bubble gum. You are sitting quietly in your box with your bubble gum friends on the shelf of a candy store. A little boy walks in, places five cents on the counter and points at you. How do you feel? What are your thoughts? You notice that the little boy's nose is running and he sniffles a lot. How do you feel about your immediate future?

For New Perceptions, Become Part of the Problem

Oily Example

With the *personal analogy* method the thinker achieves new perspectives on a problem by imaginatively becoming part of that problem. What would you be like if you were a dazzling dinner for important friends? Or a really efficient floor mop? If you were a check book, how could you avoid becoming lost? In one synectics problem solving session, the group members (intelligent adults) imagined themselves to be rapidly multiplying viruses, tiny and crowded, in order to shed light on the problem of getting an accurate sample of oil-saturated rock from under a reservoir. Said one person, "I feel I am a very successful virus. With the way these other guys feel, I can sit back and relax, enjoy life and play a guitar. One is going to take care of reproducing and one killing. Why should I worry?" Responded another, "I resent his playing his guitar while I'm panicky!" (Gordon, 1961)

3. The author is indebted to Jean Romaniuk for suggesting this problem.

"There I was, learning to swim with the personal analogy method. I imagined I was a frog and . . ." (The Museum of Modern Art / Film Stills Archive.)

Remember
Einstein's
"Mental
Experiments"?

As we will see in Chapter 7, Einstein used the personal analogy method when he imagined himself on a speed-of-light trip through space, leading to the theory of relativity.

Imagining yourself to be a problem object or process should stimulate an inside view of the situation, and some new ideas while you are there.

Fantasy Analogy

Wild Wish
Fulfillment

Space Suit
Closure

With the *fantasy analogy* approach the problem solver thinks of fantastic, far-fetched, perhaps ideal solutions that can lead to creative yet practical ideas. Gordon (1961) saw this method as a sort of Freudian wish-fulfillment. In one of his sessions the task was to invent an air-tight zipper for space suits. In response to the question, "How do we in our wildest fantasies desire the closure to operate?" (Gordon, 1961, p. 49), group members imagined two rows of insects clasping hands on command to draw the closure tight. This fantasy led to a workable device.

Get Fired
Technique

Also Solved
Miner
Unemployment
Problem

An almost tongue-in-cheek strategy that appears to be a variation of the fantasy analogy method was called the *Get Fired Technique.* As described by synectics thinker George Prince (1968, p. 73), "The idea you develop must be so outrageous and such a violation of common sense and company policy that when you present it to your boss he will immediately fire you." In the example accompanying this quote the problem was to "Devise a liquid cake icing that will firm up when released from a can." The get-fired idea was: "I am going to hire out-of-work West Virginia coal miners—very small ones—and put one in each can. When the person presses the valve, the miner goes to work!" The craziness stimulates the playfulness that facilitates creative thinking (Prince, 1968).

Problems That
Solved
Themselves

Use in the
School

The fantasy analogy method includes looking for ideal or perfect solutions, such as having the problem solve itself. Years ago some creative people probably asked: "How can we make a carriage propel itself (Prince, 1982)? How can we make a refrigerator defrost itself? How can we create a fabric that irons itself? How can we make an

In the
Corporation

oven clean itself? How can we make a forgotten iron shut itself off? How can we create a magic drain that will make bones and waste disappear" (Prince, 1982)? Plug-in engine diagnosers probably came from, "How can we make the motor tell us what's wrong?" Teachers might pose such questions as: "How can we get the School Board to want to give us a new basketball floor? How can we get the hallways to keep themselves free of litter? How can we get delinquents to want to be honest citizens?" People in business can ask: "How can we make the product double its own sales? How can we have employees raise their own morale? What will the ideal kitchen (bathroom, family room, garage) be like in the future? How can we make a perfect location find us?"

Working
Backward from
an Ideal Goal

This strategy of looking for perfect, fantastic solutions builds upon the time-tested problem solving method of working backward from an ideal goal. Thinking of what you ideally want, then figuring out how to reach that goal is an effective and creative way to solve problems.

Symbolic Analogy

Compressed
Conflict

Stimulates Ideas

A fourth synectics technique is called *symbolic analogy;* other names are *compressed conflict* or *book titles.* Your dictionary will call them *oxymorons.* The strategy is to think of a two-word phrase or "book title" that seems self-contradictory, such as "careful haste" or "gentle toughness." The compressed conflict would be related to a particular problem, and would stimulate ideas. For example, the phrase "careful haste" might be used by educators or fire fighters to stimulate ideas for quickly and safely evacuating a large school building. "Gentle toughness" might stimulate ideas for designing automobile tires, durable fabrics, or long-distance bicycles.

Window
Breaking Is
Impetuous Idea

Electric Eel
Invents Ice Cube
Maker!

In one zany synectics session the problem of designing an ice cube maker led to the problem restatement "How (can we) make an ice tray disappear after ice is made." This definition suggested the analogy of a boy breaking a window—after which he disappears (Prince, 1968). Book titles for boy-breaks-window included *healthful destruction, right wrongness, intelligent mistake,* and *rational impetuousness.* Speculating on examples of rational impetuousness led to an electric eel, which rationally defends itself by impetuously shocking enemies, and from the eel to a material that would shrink at about 20 degrees fahrenheit and release the ice cubes.

Gordon and Poze (1980b) present some practice problems to help you create and use paradoxes:

Imagine you wish to design a new safety pin that cannot stick the user or open accidentally; it also must be removable and reusable and cost under 5 cents. What are some two-word paradoxes? What are examples of these paradoxes? Do the examples suggest some creative problem solutions?

Imagine you have a littering problem in your school or company, even though there are plenty of trash barrels around. What are some book titles? What examples do the book titles suggest? Do the examples suggest some creative solutions?

An exercise from a synectics workbook, *Teaching is Listening* by Gordon and Poze (1972a), includes a direct analogy, a personal analogy, and illustrates how a symbolic analogy can stimulate ideas:

1. What animal typifies your concept of freedom? (Direct analogy)
2. Put yourself in the place of the animal you have chosen. Be the thing! Describe what makes you feel and act with so much freedom. (Personal analogy)
3. Sum up your description of the animal you chose by listing the "free" and "unfree" parts of your animal life.

   Free: _____

   Unfree: _____

4. Express each of these parts of your life in a single word. Put together these two words and refine them into a poetic, compressed conflict phrase.

   _____   _____

   _____   _____

   _____   _____

5. Circle the phrase you like best. Write an essay about freedom. Use any material you may have developed in this exercise.

Teaching Synectics Thinking

The Synectics Methods: Information on Techniques, Process, Importance of Analogical Thinking

For older students and adults, the synectics methods themselves can be material for lessons on (a) creative thinking techniques, (b) the nature of the creative process, and (c) the importance of analogical thinking in creativity. For students of all ages, including professional adults, Gordon and his colleagues have published workbooks and text books filled with exercises aimed at strengthening skills of analogical thinking, and aimed at helping the reader understand the creative power of analogical thinking. The following are similar to exercises in Gordon (1974a) and Gordon and Poze (1971, 1972a, 1972b, 1980b), Stanish (1977), and Davis (1985).

Exercises

What animal is like a bass fiddle? Why?

A hamburger is like a _____ because _____ .

How is a jar of paste like a school bell?

Which is the toughest, a turtle or a big stone? Why?

Which is stronger, a brick wall or a young tree? Why?

Which is heaviest, a boulder or a sad heart? Why?

What color is sadness? Why?

In what way can coolness be seen?

In what ways can softness be heard?

In what ways can noise be seen?

In what ways can a nice smell be felt?

What is another sound like a door slamming?

What is another sound like a dog's bark?

How is life like a flashlight battery?

Which grows faster, your self-confidence or an oak tree?

What could have given a cave dweller the idea for a spear? What was the connection?

What animal might have suggested the
bow and arrow? Explain the connection.

A parachute is like what animal? Why?

Why is a calendar like a mirror?

What would it be like to be inside a
lemon?

If you were a pencil, how would it feel to
get sharpened? To get chewed on? To
get worn down to a stub?

When you are happy you are like a ___ .

When you are busy you are like a ___ .

How is a roadmap like a saxophone?

How is a good person like a good pizza?

What is similar to looking down from a
high bridge?

How is a rabbit like a TV set?

How is an iceberg like a creative idea?

If a classroom were a lawn, what would
the weeds be? How do the weeds affect
the rest of the class?

It Is Important,
Convinced?

Analogical and metaphorical thinking lie at the core
of much creativity. Further, it may be possible to directly
teach analogical thinking strategies, such as the synectics methods, or to indirectly strengthen skills of analogical thinking with practice and exercise.

SUMMARY

Most creative ideas are in some way born in analogical
or metaphorical thinking. One sees a similarity or "makes
a connection" between the present situation or problem
and a related situation. The credits "was inspired by" and
"is based upon" imply an analogical or metaphoric source
for the artistic, literary, scientific, or technological innovation.

The analogical connection may appear suddenly, as in
an "insight," or require a painstaking search.

Borrowing and transferring ideas usually is a genuine
and legitimate creative process, not plagiarism. However, there are ambiguous cases.

Analogical and metaphorical thinking appear most obviously in the "big idea" stage of the two-stage model described in Chapter 5.

Many classical and contemporary music composers have used existing tunes as the basis of their compositions (e.g., Tchaikovsky, Copeland, Barry Manilow).

The apparently funniest political cartoons and cartoon strips are analogically based upon popular movies, well-known TV advertisements, children's stories, news events, and others.

Examples of analogical thinking in science and invention included Gutenberg's movable type and printing press, the battery, the steam engine, a strategy for building underwater tunnels, the cotton gin, the air brake, and others.

Shakespeare's Big Ideas apparently came from identifiable sources. Countless movies and TV shows have been "inspired by" contemporary and historical events, biographies, the Bible, classic and contemporary literature, mythology and legend, and in the case of *Moonlighting,* even holidays.

Actors and actresses may analogically pattern their characters after personality types they know.

Ideas for architecture and clothes design may be borrowed from other countries and other times.

In problem solving one can use analogical thinking to stimulate ideas by asking such questions as: What else is like this? What have others done? What could we copy?

Synectics methods are deliberate analogical thinking techniques developed by William J. J. Gordon. He made some spontaneous (unconscious) techniques conscious and teachable.

With direct analogy the thinker looks for ways that related problems have been solved, especially in nature.

With personal analogy one achieves new perspectives by becoming part of the problem.

Fantasy analogy is a wild wish-fulfillment approach, including looking for ideal or perfection solutions. Prince's "get fired" technique seems a variation of fantasy analogy.

Symbolic analogy is using two-word compressed conflicts to stimulate ideas.

Teaching the synectics methods themselves helps the learner to understand creative thinking techniques, the nature of the creative process, and the importance of analogical thinking. Exercises may strengthen analogical thinking abilities.

Analogical and metaphorical thinking are extremely important in creativity.

7

techniques of creative thinking: increasing your idea-finding capability

[*Scene: Tavern on Sunset Boulevard in Hollywood, Comedian Norm Crosby is sipping his Pflatz Light when Sam Straightman approaches.*]

Sam Straightman: Say, aren't you Norm Crosby? Can I buy you a beer?

Norm Crosby: Make it a Pflatz Light. An' 'tanks for the jester of good will.

Straightman: Have you hosted the Johnny Carson show lately?

Crosby: Actuary, I'll be doin' the show all next week while Johnny's on vacation in Panguitch, Utah. I 'tink he's watchin' barber poles or somethin'.

Straightman: That's about it in Panguitch. Do you like doing the show?

Crosby: I'm always happy to hold him out. I have a very great affliction for Johnny.

Straightman: Say Norm, where does you creativity come from?

Crosby: I'm glad you asked. Creativity is very impotent. Everybody in show business is highly creative. I'm very enameled of the topic.

Straightman: And where do you get all of your ideas?

Crosby: Sometimes I don't know—I just get inspiraled. But I also got personal creative techniques that I use with deliberate porpoise. All creative people got personal creative thinkin' techniques.

Straightman: You mean your technique of using funny malapropisms?

Crosby: (Sneezes!) Excuse me! I 'tink I got a defection in my androids. Now, what was your question?

Straightman: Norm, you're such a clone!

Techniques for
Creating New
Perceptions,
New
Combinations

In Chapter 5 we examined the creative process in two ways, as a series of steps one may take in solving a problem creatively and as a sudden perceptual transformation. Chapter 6 continued our analysis of the creative process with a look at the most common process, often a deliberate technique, of analogical and metaphorical thinking. This chapter extends the technique orientation of Chapter 6 by reviewing other creative thinking strategies that creative people use to find ideas and problem solutions—strategies that create the new perceptions and idea combinations.

Using
Techniques Is
a Creative
Process

Relative to traditional literature, it is novel to categorize creativity techniques as *processes* of creativity. However, in reading this and the preceding chapter on analogical and metaphorical thinking, it should be obvious that following a conscious procedure that leads to creative ideas certainly is a creative process.

This Chapter:
Personal,
Standard,
Techniques

The chapter is divided into two main sections. First, *personal* creative thinking techniques are individual strategies that are developed and used by every creatively productive person. Second, *standard* techniques are strategies that are taught in many creativity books, courses, and workshops. It is important to emphasize that *in every case,* the particular standard technique originated as some creative person's personal technique for producing ideas and solving problems. The strategy was made conscious, knowable, and teachable.

PERSONAL CREATIVE THINKING TECHNIQUES

Used by All
Creative People

Majority of
Personal
Techniques Are
Analogical

Personal techniques are methods that are developed and used by all creative people, regardless of the subject or content of his or her creations. The topic lies right at the core of such central creativity questions as "Where do ideas come from?" and "What is the nature of internal creative processes?" The reader will detect that the majority of personal creative thinking techniques involve analogical thinking—borrowing, transferring, and modifying ideas and problem solutions.

Examples
Everywhere

Modifications,
Combinations

Idea Sources

After you become sensitive to this notion of personal creative thinking techniques, you will see them continually. For example, while looking at a movie, TV show, paperback book, political cartoon, or new consumer product or while listening to a new hit tune you may understand where the creative person found the idea. The particular innovation might be recognized as a "spin-off" or modification of an earlier idea, a combination of several familiar ideas, or the innovator may have analogically based the idea on a news event, an historical event, or an earlier melody, book, movie, etc.

Einstein: Mental
Experiments

As an example in the science area, Einstein used what he called "mental experiments" to stimulate new perspectives and ideas. For example, in what seems to be a personal analogy, Einstein once imagined himself as a tiny being riding through space on a ray of light, which led to his general theory of relativity.

Disassembling
Picasso

In art we find recurrent subjects and styles with every creatively productive painter, reflecting his or her personal creative thinking techniques. Picasso, for example, deliberately disassembled faces and other elements and put them back together in more original arrangements. He also used analogical and metaphorical thinking, most obviously in his African, Harlequin, blue, and pink (rose) periods during which his paintings were based upon particular themes.

Degas:
Ballerinas

Gauguin: South
Pacific

Seurat:
Pointillism

Sounds Like
Morse Code

Is Lautrec's
Technique Too
Loose?
Utrillo: On the
Street

DaVinci: Faces
for Supper

Edward Degas borrowed the beauty and grace of ballerinas, and sometimes thoroughbred horses, for his famous painting style. Renoir is noted for his soft, pastel, frilly and flowery female subjects and still lifes. Paul Gauguin found ideas in South Pacific natives and settings, again and again. Georges Seurat used a "dot" painting style (pointillism), usually featuring people, water and sailboats. Van Gogh's unique style—dashes instead of dots—was admitted to be influenced by his friend George Seurat. The unique style of Toulouse-Lautrec's heavily outlined, tall, and cartoonlike subjects in evening dress also is familiar. Maurice Utrillo used simple street scenes, devoid of humans. Even Leonardo da Vinci reportedly wandered Italian streets, sketchbook in hand, to find interesting faces for his painting *The Last Supper*. Throughout the history of art, ideas for paintings have been taken from mythology, the Bible, or historical events.

Ideas come from somewhere, and techniques are used to pry them loose from that somewhere.

Professional comedians also use personal creative-thinking techniques, both for their unique type of humor and for their original delivery style. As illustrated, more or less, at the outset of this chapter Norm Crosby uses funny malapropisms. Don Rickles insults people, using the same insults again and again ("Shut up dummy, you're makin' a fool of yourself!").

Joan Rivers and Rodney Dangerfield both continually put themselves down. Rivers claims that when she was a child she was so ugly her father sent a picture of her to Riply's *Believe it or Not.* They sent it back with a note "We don't believe it!" Dangerfield's most famous line is "I don't get no respect," always accompanied by sweating and straightening his tie. When he was born the doctor told his mother "I did everything I could, but he's gonna' be okay!" Said Dangerfield, "I had to share my sand box with two cats. They kept tryin' to cover me up! Once I called this girl for a date, she said 'Sure, come on over, there's nobody home.' So I went over an' nobody was home! Last week my psychiatrist said I was crazy. I told him I wanted a second opinion an' he said, 'Okay, I think you're ugly too!' "

A new generation of women comics use the shock value of brash sex and earthy language for their laughs. Nope, no examples; see cable TV after 9:00 P.M.

Among the most successful Hollywood motion pictures produced were the *Star Wars* Series—based partly upon an effective personal creative thinking technique used by movie maker George Lucas. While writing the script for the original *Star Wars,* Lucas read books on mythology. Said Lucas in a *Time* magazine interview, "I wanted Star Wars to have an epic quality, and so I went back to the epics." Thus we find a young man who must prove his manhood to himself and to his father; he rescues a fair maiden in distress; he has an older and wiser mentor (actually two, Ben Kenobi and Yoda); and he battles with a villain, Darth Vader. Many western movies have been built around the same epic principles.

All creative people develop personal styles and idea-finding techniques. This creative chap operates his handle with a distinctive creative flair. "I can do it with my left foot up, too," says Charlie. (The Museum of Modern Art/Film Stills Archive.)

Creative People Use, Are Aware of Techniques

The list of personal creative thinking techniques could be endless. It is likely that all creatively productive people are fully aware of at least some of their idea-finding techniques and creativity styles.

Developing Personal Creative Thinking Techniques

There are several ways to encourage the development of personal creative thinking techniques. First, the learner should understand some of the techniques that are used by even extraordinarily creative people to "find" ideas.

Modification,
Combination
Legitimate
Creativity

This demystifies creativity and helps to convince new innovators that they also can build upon, modify, and combine existing ideas without feeling uncreative.

Second, some recurrent creativity and problem solving techniques may be learned. For example, some techniques are:

Creative
Problem Solving
Techniques

1. Deliberately looking for analogically related ideas, for example, from history books, travel books, magazines, encyclopedias, catalogs, the Yellow Pages, or other sources (see Chapter 6).
2. Reviewing the successful styles or idea sources used by others (e.g., in art, music, advertising, journalism, creative writing, speaking, or performing).
3. Adapting solutions from similar types of problems.
4. Modifying, combining, and improving present ideas.
5. Starting with the goal and working backward to deduce what is required to reach that goal.
6. Beginning with an "ideal" or "perfect" solution, such as having the problem solve itself, and again working backward to design a creative solution.
7. Asking yourself how the problem will be solved 25, 100, or 200 years in the future.

Standard
Techniques
Can Become
Personal
Techniques

Of course, the standard techniques in this chapter and the analogy-based idea sources and strategies of Chapter 6, including the synectics methods (direct analogy, personal analogy, fantasy analogy, and symbolic analogy), should be added to the list. Such techniques become "personal" techniques when, if they work for a given individual, they become his or her own ways of finding ideas and solving problems.

Active
Involvement

Third, since personal creative thinking techniques develop (1) in the course of doing creative things or (2) from instruction by people who use and understand such techniques, it is important to become actively involved in creative activities. In school these might include art, photography, creative writing, theatre, journalism, independent science projects, or other activities involving creative thinking and problem solving. In the corporation, practicing creativity can take innumerable forms—thinking of and implementing ideas to increase efficiency, employee morale, or production; reducing waste, costs, and overhead; designing new products, new processes, new methods, new procedures, new marketing techniques, new automation systems, new uses for computers; and so on.

Visitors also can teach personal creative thinking techniques. For example, in the school a "visiting professional" program can help students understand the creative processes of a successful artist, writer, scientist, or business entrepreneur. In the corporation it can be very enlightening to hear about creativity and idea-finding techniques either from persons who are themselves creatively productive, or from consultants acquainted with blocks to creativity and techniques for sparking new viewpoints, perceptions, analogies, and idea combinations.

Visiting Professionals

Consultants

A tremendous benefit of visiting creative talent is that these people serve as models—successful examples of creative personalities and creative minds to whom many people are rarely exposed.

Creative Models

STANDARD CREATIVE THINKING TECHNIQUES

There are several well-known methods for producing new ideas and new idea combinations which, as we mentioned, are taught in most university and professional creativity training courses. The strategies also may be taught to high school students, junior high students, and even elementary students. It is important to emphasize that the techniques are intended to *supplement*—not replace—one's intuitive idea supply. When you have a sticky problem and run out of ideas, one or more of these techniques will help.

Taught in University, Professional Creativity Courses

Learnable by Students

We might note the distinction between *intuitive* creativity and *forced* creativity. Intuitive creativity, as the name suggests, refers to the unpredictable inspirations that may or may not appear when and where you need them. There is nothing wrong with inspiration, intuition, and spontaneous creative thought; they solve problems and keep the topic of creativity interesting. With forced creativity, a person or group consciously decides to sit down and creatively attack a problem using one or more techniques to clarify the problem and generate creative ideas for it.

Intuitive vs. Forced Creativity

Teaching
Creativity with
a Computer

Attitudes,
Understanding,
Techniques

Seem Effective

Imagination
Express:
Attitudes,
Techniques

Creative Thinking and Problem Solving (Davis, 1985) is a creativity program on computer disk, currently available for Apple II computers, that teaches the same content and strategies covered in adult and professional creativity courses: sound creative *attitudes,* an *understanding* of creativity—and some effective creativity *techniques,* including several from this chapter and Chapter 6. The disk was prepared for upper elementary and middle school grades, although second and third grade children also like it and learn a lot (Davis & Rudmanis, 1986). Preliminary research indicated that kids enjoy the program, understand creativity better, and feel more inclined to do creative things as a result of working with the disk. A workbook, *Imagination Express* (Davis & DiPego, 1973), written for upper elementary and junior high grades, similarly emphasizes creative attitudes and idea-finding techniques, including all of those in this chapter plus the metaphor-based *synectics* methods in Chapter 6.

Regarding creative attitudes—which are invaluable at all age levels—both the computer disk and the workbook stress:

Creative
Attitudes

1. An awareness of creativity and its importance.
2. A receptiveness to creative ideas of others.
3. Thinking creatively instead of habitually doing things the old ways.
4. The belief that everyone can be more creative than he or she is, with a little effort.

The workbooks *Hippogriff Feathers* and *The Hearthstone Traveler,* both by Bob Stanish (1981, 1988), also teach most of the standard techniques reviewed in this chapter.

BRAINSTORMING

Should We Call
It "BSing"?

Corporate Uses
Are Unlimited

Anyone interested in creative processes or creative problem solving should try group brainstorming. Newcomers to brainstorming always are impressed by the surprising ideas and perceptions of others—ideas that in the group process stimulate further ideas and viewpoints

Classroom:
Creativity
Exercise, or
Solving Real
Problems

("idea hitch-hikes"). Undoubtedly the most popular form of forced creativity, brainstorming is used regularly to prod flights of professional imagination. Corporate and business uses of brainstorming are without limit: finding ideas for new or improved products and processes, solving marketing, advertising, or personnel problems, and others. In the classroom a flexible teacher will schedule brainstorming sessions either for practice in creative thinking or for solving real problems, such as high absenteeism, messy school grounds, traffic safety, bicycle thefts, drug use, raising money, or selling play tickets.

Reasons for the popularity of brainstorming are not particularly mysterious:

Reasons,
Reasons

> It's intuitively appealing.
> It's simple.
> It's fun.
> It's therapeutic.
> It works.

Deferred
Judgment: High
Intuitive Appeal

Creative
Atmosphere

The high *intuitive* appeal stems from the single hard-and-fast rule, the principle of *deferred judgment*—the seemingly self-evident notion that criticism and at least harsh evaluation will interfere with flexible idea production. The originator of brainstorming, Alex Osborn (1963), simply noted that one cannot be critical and creative at the same time. Makes sense. Deferred judgment produces the essential *creative atmosphere* (creative attitudes, psychological safety) that is the single most essential ingredient for innovative thinking.

Simple Enough
For You Kids

Brainstorming is *simple* because, again, the only strict rule is no criticism or evaluation. No training is needed beyond a few minutes' clarification of the groundrules (below). Even young children can brainstorm real or imaginary problem, thereby exercising their creative abilities, learning attitudes and principles of effective thinking, and learning a creativity technique.

Fun

Regarding *fun*, professionals sometimes feel guilty about being paid for having such a swell time. New idea combinations are often humorous. Note that jokes, like other creative ideas, also are made of surprising idea combinations.

Therapeutic

The *therapy* comes from the enjoyable session itself, from being asked for ideas (which is rare in many organizations), from the chance to speak up, kick around ideas and solve problems, and from satisfying basic and often stifled needs to create and construct.

Effective

And it *works,* whether the goal is to stimulate imagination, flexibility and creative attitudes as a training exercise—for children or professionals—or to solve some elusive corporate problem. Osborn (1963) and others have

Post Office:
Saving Person
Hours?

described numerous instances of successful brainstorming outcomes. For example, a Denver postmaster and eleven staff brainstormed the problem "What can be done to reduce man-hour usage?" Some of the 121 ideas led to a saving of 12,666 man hours (okay, person hours) in the following nine weeks. A Pittsburgh department store, stuck with some chair-covering material, brain-

Unusual Uses
Problem

stormed "other uses" for the fabric, leading to advertising that sold the entire stock in a week. A brainstorming

Heinz: 57
Varieties of
Increased Sales

group at Heinz Foods spent just one hour on the problem "How can we help increase the sale of products made at this factory?" They generated more and better ideas than a special committee had produced in ten ordinary conferences. Reynolds Metals brainstormed some "new and

Corny Solution
Wins Award!

more convenient ways to package a client's cornmeal mix." Some of the ideas were included in a prize-winning

Flash!

and sales-winning package. Sylvania Electric's highly successful Flash Cube also was born in a brainstorming session. Finally, the success of the New York advertising

And Don't
Forget BBD & O

agency Batten, Barton, Durstine, and Osborn—the late Alex Osborn's own organization—is good evidence for the effectiveness of brainstorming.

The four groundrules of brainstorming are uncomplicated:

Defer Criticism
and Evaluation

1. *Criticism is ruled out.* This is deferred judgment, which means, as delicately stated in *Imagination Express,* "You don't want some crab knocking down people's ideas before they have a chance." Deferred judgment produces the receptive, encouraging creative atmosphere. The difference is reinforcement, not punishment, for innovative, perhaps even far-fetched ideas.

Wild and Crazy
Can Suggest
Practical and
Useful

2. *Freewheeling is welcomed.* Said Osborn, the wilder the idea the better. Apparently preposterous ideas can suggest imaginative yet workable solutions. And you are more likely to find a creative idea by being wild first and "taming down" the idea second, rather

than criticising, evaluating, and editing as you go. This rule obviously supplements Rule #1 and prepares the thinker to try to be imaginative, to look for different and unusual solutions, to view the problem from novel perspectives, to constructively accept the off-the-wall ideas of others, and to use wild ideas as springboards for workable ideas. In one of the your author's classroom brainstorming sessions, it was suggested that a movie theater could be quickly emptied by collapsible seats that slide patrons out the front of the room. This free-wheeler was followed immediately by the more practical idea of seats that fold down so that in an emergency patrons could rapidly exit by walking over them.

It's That Five Percent!

Are wild ideas wasted? Well, yes. It is assumed that about 95 percent of the ideas will not merit further exploration. The other 5 percent solves the problem creatively.

With More Ideas, More Good Ideas

3. *Quantity it wanted.* This principle reflects the purpose of the brainstorming session, which is to produce a long list of ideas. The mathematically sensible rationale is that with a larger number of ideas there is a better chance of finding good ideas. Further, research has shown that ideas produced later in the session—after the easy and common ones are out—tend to be more imaginative (Manske & Davis, 1968; Parnes, 1961).

Hitch-Hiking Is Legal

4. *Combination and improvement* are sought. This lengthens the idea list. Actually, during the session thinkers will spontaneously hitch-hike on each other's ideas, one idea inspiring the next.

Leadership Simple

Use Chalkboard

It is comparatively simple to run a brainstorming session. The leader reviews the four groundrules, along with procedural details. For example, some groups keep a small bell in the center of the table to ding anyone who criticizes or even asks for justification for an idea ("Why did you suggest that?"). Some leaders prefer to go around the table, letting each participant speak in turn, but allowing someone with a pressing idea to interrupt. It is best to write ideas on a chalkboard where they will be available for combination, modification, and non-duplication. Stenographers and tape recorders also have been used.

Leader
Organizes,
Explains Rules,
Is Focal Point

The leader's role is straight-forward. In addition to organizing the session, explaining the groundrules, and reviewing the problem, he or she occasionally asks "Does anyone else have an idea?" Sometimes the leader serves mainly as place for participants to stare and to address their ideas.

Ask for Facts,
Alternative
Definitions

A more sophisticated leader may take suggestions from the CPS model (Chapter 5) and ask "Well folks, what do we know about the problem?" (fact-finding) or "How else can we define, view, approach, or broaden the problem?" (problem-finding). Helping the group broaden the problem can be especially valuable. For example, instead of redesigning heating elements on an electric range the group can look for innovative ways to "heat food"; instead of building a better mouse trap the group can think of ways to "get rid of mice." We noted in Chapter 5 that asking "Why" after each problem definition produces increasingly more general problem statements.

Group
Composition

In addition to the four main groundrules, Osborn (1963) suggested a few more procedures for effective brainstorming. Group size should be about 10 or 12. An idea panel consists of a leader, an associate leader, about five regular members, and about five guests. Note, however, that one can brainstorm problems alone or with a 500-person audience.

Different
Training,
Same Rank

To increase the source and variety of ideas, members should be heterogeneous in training, experience, and gender. In most circumstances, rank should be roughly equal. Imagine the intimidating and stiffling effect of Chrysler President Lee Iacocca sitting in on managerial-level brainstorming session.

48 Hours
Before, 48
Hours After

With serious problems (not "What can a clever chipmunk do while blindfolded?"), the problem should be circulated 48 hours in advance so that members can come in with ideas. A follow-up request for ideas may be circulated 48 hours after the session in order to catch the ideas participants wish they would have thought of at the time.

For Silent
Periods

During silent periods, if any, the leader may ask the quieter members for ideas, pull out some shirt-pocket ideas of his or her own that were prepared in advance for such an occasion, or else suggest a new way to look at

Idea-Spurring
Questions

the problem. The leader also can roll out Osborn's *idea-spurring questions* (below), which Osborn frequently used in brainstorming sessions.

Do You Really Need a Barnstorming Group?

Oh yes, a critical presession consideration is whether or not to use a group to solve the problem in the first place. Even Osborn recognized that "Despite the many virtues of group brainstorming, individual ideation is usually more usable and can be just as productive" (Osborn, 1963).

Some Ideas Will Look Good

Evaluation Criteria, Evaluation Matrix

Assuming the group has produced a list of ideas, some wild and crazy and some serious, what then? The group, or another group, can evaluate ideas in any of a number of ways. Realistically, sometimes an idea or two will simply look darn good, and they probably are. This makes idea evaluation rather easy. However, it also is possible to brainstorm evaluation criteria and create a formal evaluation matrix as explained in Chapter 5. Some criteria are:

Criteria

> Will it work? Will it do the job? Does it improve present methods?
>
> Does it reduce costs? Eliminate unnecessary work? Increase production? Improve quality? Improve safety? Improve the use of manpower? Improve working conditions? Improve morale?
>
> Does the idea really "grab" people? Do people ask "Why didn't I think of that?"
>
> It is timely?
>
> It is a temporary or permanent solution?
>
> Will it cost too much?
>
> It is too complicated? Is it simple and direct?
>
> Is it suitable? Will others accept it (higher management, the public, the union, parents, the secretary, your mother)?
>
> Are the materials available?
>
> Is it legal?
>
> Are we trying to swat a fly with dynamite?
>
> Are there patent infringements?

Reasons for
Evaluation

In the classroom or corporation using objective criteria for the evaluation process serves several purposes: (1) Of course, using criteria helps evaluate ideas. (2) It also helps children and adults learn to evaluate as part of the overall creative process. (3) It requires people to consider many components of the problem. (4) In some cases an objective evaluation can help the group explore its own value system relative to the problem at hand. Finally, (5) it can prove that thinking of "silly" and "far-fetched" ideas truly can result in good and practical solutions to problems.

Stop-and-Go
Brainstorming

Phillips 66
Is a Gas

Variations. Variations of brainstorming may be helpful in particular circumstances. The first is *Stop-and-go* brainstorming in which short, about 10-minute periods of unrestrained free-wheeling are interrupted by periods of evaluation. The latter serve mainly to keep the group on target by selecting the apparently most profitable directions. The second is the *Phillips 66* technique for use with large audiences. After the problem is explained, small groups of six will brainstorm for six minutes, after which each group reports either all or the best ideas to the larger group.

Reverse
Brainstorming

The third variation is an extremely potent one. With *reverse brainstorming* new viewpoints and perceptions are found by turning around the basic problem: How can we increase costs? Increase waste? Run up the light bill? How can we stimulate absenteeism? How can we promote drug use? Increase traffic or factory accidents? Reduce sales? Increase complaints? Suppress creative thinking? With reverse brainstorming the participants usually list what in reality is actually happening.

Brainwriting

Brainwriting is a quieter version of brainstorming that capitalizes on idea hitch-hiking. Members of each small group are instructed to write down an idea or problem solution, then pass the paper to person on the right. The next person may:

1. Use the idea to stimulate another idea, and write the new idea on the paper.
2. Modify the idea and write down the modification.
3. Write down a completely new idea.

The process is continued until the sheets circulate back to the original owner. Ideas are discussed and informally or formally evaluated.

Sorry, No
Guarantees

No Miracles
Either

Disappointed?
Complain to the
Late Alex
Osborn

Herrmann Is No
Half-Wit

Cautions. Osborn himself did not guarantee brainstorming as a cure-all for every idea-needing person or organization. In reality, some brainstorming programs fail to provide the creative breakthroughs that were anticipated. Osborn (1963) suggested two main reasons for some of the disappointments. First, the organizers and members may not be following the recommended procedures. Second, they may have unrealistically expected miracles in the first place. Further, some individuals can be more creative when alone than in groups. Again, forced creative thinking techniques should supplement, not replace, original individual thinking.

Whole brain approach. Osborn recommended that an effective brainstorming group be composed of persons with different training and experience. William E. Herrmann's "whole brain" approach, brought to you by his Whole Brain Corporation, is a variation on this theme. His underlying theory is that different people are strong in different thought processes. Specifically, a person might be outstanding in *analytical, verbal, intuitive,* or *emotional* abilities, each of which is assumed to be controlled by a different part of the brain. Herrmann devised a questionnaire that identifies the thinking ability that is dominant in each person. He then organizes creative thinking groups that have each type of thought represented. In essence, the group has a "whole brain" that is strong in all of his identified thought processes (Smith, 1985).

Herrmann's exact strategy might be difficult to implement without hiring Mr. Herrmann himself. However, the apparently successful approach underscores the significance of heterogeneity in brainstorming group composition—in training, experience, gender, and particular thinking gifts.

ATTRIBUTE LISTING

Robert
Crawford: a
Theory and a
Technique

Brainstorming is a general thinking strategy that mainly requires creative attitudes and a creative atmosphere. Attribute listing is a more specific technique for generating new ideas that, in fact, can be used within a

Attribute
Modifying,
Attribute
Transferring

brainstorming session. Robert Crawford (1978), the designer of attribute listing, and who in 1931 at the University of Nebraska taught probably the very first creativity course, argued that "Each time we take a (creative) step we do it by changing an attribute or quality of something, or else by applying that same quality or attribute to some other thing." Attribute listing is therefore both a *theory* of the creative process and a practical creative thinking *technique.* Following Crawford's definition, there are two forms of attribute listing: (1) *attribute modifying* and (2) *attribute transferring.* Either strategy may be used individually or in a group.

List Ideas for
Each Attribute

Attribute modifying. With attribute modifying the thinker lists main attributes (characteristics, dimensions, parts) of the problem object or process and then thinks of ideas for improving each attribute. For example, a group might invent new types of candy bars or breakfast cereals by first identifying important attributes (e.g., size, shape, flavor, ingredients, color, texture, packaging, nutritional value, audience, product name) on the blackboard, and then listing specific ideas under each main attribute. Particularly good combinations may be picked out of the lists of ideas. Inset 7.1 includes three exercises from *Imagination Express* (Davis & DiPego, 1973) intended to teach attribute listing to upper elementary and junior high school children. Attribute listing is taught in design engineering courses under the name *substitution method;* you "substitute" different sizes, shapes, colors, materials, etc.

In Engineering,
Substitution
Method

Hi Ho Silver!

Do creative people really use this technique? Fran Striker (1964; Shallcross, 1981) used it for a couple of decades to generate radio and TV episodes for his *Lone Ranger* series. Striker used the attributes of *characters, goals, obstacles,* and *outcomes* in a diagram similar to the first exercise (breakfast cereals) in Inset 7.1. In the first column were listed specific ideas for characters, broadly defined to include objects and animals; goals included things the character(s) wanted to become, to achieve, or to happen; obstacles could be literally a brick wall or wild river, but also person characteristics such as timidity or aggressiveness; and outcomes could include

Characteristics,
Goals,
Obstacles,
Outcomes

Creative
Combinations in
Three Seconds

reaching the goal, changing goals, changing personalities, or getting shot or caught. Striker reportedly would shut his eyes, pick an idea from each column, and think about whether or not it would make a good episode. If not, the combination either could be modified, or it would take about 3 seconds to create another possibility. A modification of Striker's strategy was used in the computer disk *Creative Thinking and Problem Solving* to teach children (1) the attribute listing method, (2) what components go into a short story, and (3) how to create ideas for those components. The technique is simple and it works.

Use with Corporate Problems

Marketing

Attribute modifying may be used with any sort of problem in which the attributes, dimensions, or parts are identifiable. For example, the problem of reducing absenteeism in the corporation could be reduced to dimensions of "sources of unpleasantness" in the company, "type of employees who frequently stay home," "type of inducements, rewards or punishments, that might reduce absenteeism," and perhaps others. Marketing strategists often convert their problem into attributes of "ways to attract new customers," "ways to maintain old customers," and "ways to increase sales to old customers."

New Product Development

Of course, any type of product improvement or new product development problem is a natural for attribute listing. New lines of refrigerators are created by substituting, for example, new colors, new sizes, new shapes, new door arrangements, new materials, new features, or new uses.

Attribute Transferring Is Analogical Thinking

Attribute transferring. Attribute transferring is another name for analogical thinking, which we covered in Chapter 6. To stimulate attribute transferring—or analogical thinking—as described in Chapter 6 one can ask: What else is like this? What have others done? Where could we find an idea? What could we copy? What has worked before? What would professionals do? And so on.

Borrow a Theme

For example, in the classroom or the exhibition hall some truly creative and memorable displays could be created by borrowing attributes (ideas) from a carnival, a circus, Disneyland, MacDonald's, a funeral parlor, a Frankenstein or Star Wars movie, an old west hoedown, and so on.

Inset 7.1
The Attribute Listing Method*

Some breakfast cereals are shaped like tiny little letter O's. Let's invent some new breakfast cereals by thinking of some different *shapes, flavors, colors,* and *sizes.* These are four *qualities* of breakfast cereals, right? Be imaginative.

SHAPES	FLAVORS	COLORS	SIZES
_____	_____	_____	_____
_____	_____	_____	_____
_____	_____	_____	_____
_____	_____	_____	_____
_____	_____	_____	_____
_____	_____	_____	_____
_____	_____	_____	_____
_____	_____	_____	_____

Barron (1988, p. 83) made a strong statement about the creative process that seems to justify Crawford's enthusiasm for attribute listing as a core creative process:

Barron
Emphasizes
Significance of
Attribute Listing

. . . the ability to change things . . . is central to the creative process. New forms do not come from nothing, not for us humans at any rate; they come from prior forms, through mutations, whether unsought or invited. In a fundamental sense, there are no theories

Suppose you were a toy manufacturer with a warehouse full of unsold skateboards. The problem is to change one (or more) parts or qualities of the skateboards to make them really different so they'll once again sell like crazy and make you another million $$$. List some parts or qualities of the skateboards, and then think of ideas for changing these parts. Be creative.

Part or quality   #1_____ #2_____ #3_____ #4_____

Changes: _____ _____ _____ _____

                   _____ _____ _____ _____

                   _____ _____ _____ _____

                   _____ _____ _____ _____

                   _____ _____ _____ _____

What are some *qualities* of

a. a doorbell? _____
b. a bicycle basket? _____
c. a Band-Aid? _____
d. a piece of sandpaper? _____
e. a paperweight? _____
f. a rose? _____
g. an umbrella? _____
h. a potholder? _____
i. a cocker spaniel? _____

*From *Imagination Express,* © 1973 DOK Publishers. Reprinted by permission.

of creation; there are only accounts of the development of new forms from earlier forms.

Understand Sources of Ideas, Valuable Technique

At any age level or with any learners, the attribute listing strategies themselves provide material for a good lesson in "where ideas come from" and in using an effective creative thinking technique, one used by many—Crawford and Barron would say *all*—creatively productive people.

MORPHOLOGICAL SYNTHESIS

A Matrix
Method

Many
Combinations
Quickly

Morphological Synthesis basically is an extension of the attribute modifying procedure (Allen, 1962, 1968; Davis, 1973). Here, specific ideas for one attribute or dimension of a problem are listed along one axis of a matrix. Ideas for a second attribute are listed along the other axis. Lots of new idea combinations are in the cells of the matrix. One sixth-grade Milwaukee class used the technique to invent new sandwich ideas (Figure 7.1). The kids had a swell time designing the new sandwich spreads, many of which are not too revolting. They also learned that they are capable of thinking of clever new ideas and that, if needed, this "checkerboard method" (Davis & DiPego, 1973) can help them find ideas. Note that with a third dimension, for example, 10 types of bread, we would have a three-dimensional cube containing 1,210 (11 $\times$ 11 $\times$ 10) idea combinations.

Morphological
Moral Mentation

Your author (Davis, 1990) used the morphological synthesis method to generate nearly 900 ideas for teaching values and moral thinking. Creativity strategies (e.g., brainstorming, analogical thinking, "What would happen if . . . ?") were listed on the vertical axis, and dozens of specific values on the horizontal axis. Combinations included, for example:

How many ways can we think of to conserve electricity at home? (*Brainstorming/Energy-environment*).

How can we be very rude and discourteous at school? (*Reverse brainstorming/Manners*)

How is an honest person like a comfortable old pair of jeans? (*Analogical thinking/Stealing*)

What would happen if the school were vandalized every night? ("*What would happen if . . .?*"/Vandalism)

Can Use 2, 3, 6
Dimensions

The morphological synthesis method may be used with a half-dozen or so dimensions by listing ideas in columns and, if you wish, cutting the columns into vertical strips. Each strip would slide up or down and new idea combinations would be created by reading horizontally (Fabun, 1968). With the strategy used by Fran Striker to generate *Lone Ranger* episode combinations, four dimensions were used. If Striker systematically examined each and every one of his hundreds of possible combinations, we would

Roof inspector Gilbert Gluefinger used the morphological synthesis technique to find ideas for getting to the building top. "The combination of 'climb' and 'wall' produced this solution," observes the regretful inspector. "Maybe I should have tried 'ride' and 'elevator.'" (The Museum of Modern Art/Film Stills Archive.)

Figure 7.1
A Morphological Sandwich

A sixth-grade Milwaukee class used the morphological synthesis method to generate 121 zany ideas for creative sandwiches. Can you find a tasty combination? A revolting one?

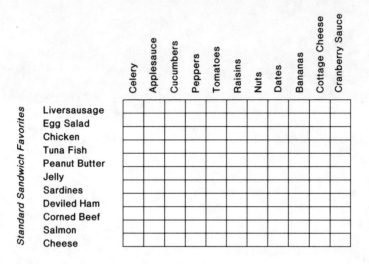

New Companions to Add Zest

Standard Sandwich Favorites

	Celery	Applesauce	Cucumbers	Peppers	Tomatoes	Raisins	Nuts	Dates	Bananas	Cottage Cheese	Cranberry Sauce
Liversausage											
Egg Salad											
Chicken											
Tuna Fish											
Peanut Butter											
Jelly											
Sardines											
Deviled Ham											
Corned Beef											
Salmon											
Cheese											

Ratings of Various Spreads

			Choices		
Flavor	1st	2nd	3rd	4th	5th
Super Goober (Peanut Butter/Cranberry)	17	2	1	0	4
Charlie's Aunt (Tuna and Applesauce)	3	16	2	2	1
Irish Eyes are Smiling (Corned Beef and Cottage Cheese)	0	0	16	2	6
Cackleberry Whiz (Hard-Boiled Eggs/Cheese Whiz)	1	3	2	14	4
Hawaiian Eye (Cream Cheese and Pineapple)	3	3	3	6	9

(Six girls had squeamish stomachs and did not participate.)

call his method *morphological synthesis,* as Shallcross (1981) did, rather than *attribute listing.* The methods are similar.

Can You Create a Novel Sandwich?

How about a little practice with the morphological synthesis method. Look at the sandwich makings in Figure 7.1. Can you substitute a few more exotic entries into the vertical and horizontal axes, add a "bread" dimension, and create some spit-inducing (or is it "mouth-watering") combinations? You might try using two ideas from the vertical axis with one from the horizontal axis. How about pastrami with green peppers on rye? Sliced turkey with a little deviled ham and celery on cracked wheat? Liversausage with tomatoes and walnuts on pumpernickel? Peanut butter with sardines and ginger root on white? Well, three out of four isn't bad.

IDEA CHECKLISTS

May Directly Suggest Ideas, or Indirectly Stimulate Creativity

Yellow Pages

Catalogs, Advertisements

Walk Through the Store

Sometimes, one can find an idea checklist that suggests solutions for your problem. A checklist may directly suggest ideas and solutions, or else items on the list may indirectly stimulate combinations far beyond what actually appears on the list. As some examples, the Yellow Pages of a phone book may be used as a checklist for problems like "Who can fix the TV?" or "Where can I get a haircut?" A high school counselor might use the Yellow Pages for ideas on career counseling—"Look over these 10,000 occupations Chris, maybe you can find a few interesting career possibilities." A Sears or cheese store catalog or a jewelry store advertisement can be an idea checklist for a gift-giving problem. Wandering through a grocery store, department store, gift shop, or florist shop also amounts to reviewing "idea checklists" for creative meals, gifts, clothes, or centerpieces. A trip through the Yellow Pages or a Sears catalog also might suggest product markets or applications for a new process or material.

Table 7.1

Osborn's (1963) 73 Idea-Spurring Questions

Put to other uses? New ways to use as is? Other uses if modified?

Adapt? What else is like this? What other idea does this suggest? Does past offer parallel? What could I copy? Whom could I emulate?

Modify? New twist? Change meaning, color, motion, sound, odor, form, shape? Other changes?

Magnify? What to add? More time? Greater frequency? Stronger? Higher? Longer? Thicker? Extra value? Plus ingredient? Duplicate? Multiply? Exaggerate?

Minify? What to subtract? Smaller? Condensed? Miniature? Lower? Shorter? Lighter? Omit? Streamline? Split up? Understate?

Substitute? Who else instead? What else instead? Other ingredient? Other material? Other process? Other power? Other place? Other approach? Other tone of voice?

Rearrange? Interchange components? Other pattern? Other layout? Other sequence? Transpose cause and effect? Change pace? Change schedule?

Reverse? Transpose positive and negative? How about opposites? Turn it backward? Turn it upside down? Reverse roles? Change shoes? Turn tables? Turn other cheek?

Combine? How about a blend, an alloy, an assortment, an ensemble? Combine units? Combine purposes? Combine appeals? Combine ideas?

Osborn: 73 Idea-Spurring Questions

Arnold's Checklist

Small: Big Ideas from Checklist

Some idea checklists have been designed especially for creative problem solving. These lists indirectly push the imagination into new idea combinations and new analogical problem solutions. The best known of these is Osborn's (1963) *73 idea-spurring questions* (Table 7.1). Slightly simplified versions of Osborn's checklist have appeared in creativity workbooks for children, for example, *Hippogriff Feathers* (Stanish, 1981) and *The Hearthstone Traveler* (Stanish, 1988). As you wander through Osborn's list, ask yourself how a hamburger, TV, suitcase, soda pop product, or other object or process could be improved. The ideas will appear almost involuntarily.

In a creative engineering class at MIT John Arnold (Mason, 1960) developed a short list of self-questions aimed at improving critical engineering features of commercial products (Table 7.2). Think about a bicycle or a proper upright vacuum cleaner as you look through his

While Osborn's checklist did not say *Look stupid*, it did say *Reverse, Turn it backward*, and *Put to other uses*. "I just invented the horse-hair beard!" exclaimed Max Harp. (Wisconsin Center for Film and Theater Research.)

Table 7.2
Arnold's Checklist for Improving
Engineering Features

Can we increase the function? Can we make the product do more things?

Can we get a higher performance level? Make the product longer lived? More reliable? More accurate? Safer? More convenient to use? Easier to repair and maintain?

Can we lower the cost? Eliminate excess parts? Substitute cheaper materials? Design to reduce hand labor or for complete automation?

Can increase the salability? Improve the appearance of the product? Improve the package? Improve its point of sale?

list. Finally, Marvin Small, in a volume modestly titled *How to Make More Money,* created a product-development checklist similar to Osborn's 73 idea-spurring questions (Table 7.3). Pick anything from Band-Aids to children's books to wheel bearings as you peruse Small's idea stimulators.

As with other techniques, using idea checklists can stimulate nonobvious and nonhabitual idea-combinations.

Dictionary Technique: Free Associating

Dictionary technique. The *dictionary technique* works much like an idea checklist. You flip through the pages, find an interesting word, and start making associations that are at least remotely related to your product or problem. For example, artists and writers at Current, Inc., a Colorado greeting card company, free associated to the word *shrink,* leading to their *Wee Greetings,* a line of greeting cards the size of business cards. Associating to *enlarge* led to cards that contain balloons and confetti (Smith, 1985).

SUMMARY

Using a creative thinking technique is a creative process.

Personal techniques are individual idea-finding strategies that all creative people use. Most personal creative thinking techniques involve analogical thinking.

Table 7.3
Small's Checklist for New Product Ideas

Can the dimensions be changed? Larger? Smaller? Longer? Stratify? Converge?

Can the quantity be changed? More? Less? Fractionate? Combine with something else?

Can the order be changed? At the beginning? Assembly or disassembly processes?

Can the time element be changed? Faster? Slower? Longer? Shorter? Chronologized? Renewed?

Can the cause or effect be changed? Energized? Altered? Destroyed? Counteracted?

Can there be a change in character? Stronger? Weaker? Interchanged? Resilient? Uniformity? More expensive?

Can the form be changed? Animated? Speeded? Slowed? Deviated? Repelled? Admitted? Rotated? Agitated?

Can the state or condition be changed? Harden? Soften? Preformed? Disposable? Parted? Vaporized? Pulverized? Lubricated? Drier? Effervesced? Coagulated? Elasticized? Lighter?

Can the use be adapted to a new market? Men? Children? Foreign?

Einstein used "mental experiments" to stimulate new perceptions and ideas.

Artists develop pet topics and styles that lead to their creative products. Ideas for art have been derived from the Bible, mythology, and historical events.

Comedians also use unique sources for their humor, for example, insults, self-criticism, and malapropisms.

To develop personal idea-finding techniques, understand techniques that others use. In addition to looking for analogically related problems and ideas, some problem-solving techniques involve working backward from the goal or speculating on how the problem will be solved in the future. If they work for you, standard techniques can become personal techniques.

Other recommendations are to become involved in creative activities, and to invite creative professionals and consultants to discuss creativity techniques. Creative persons model creative personalities and creative thinking.

Standard creative thinking techniques are taught in university and professional creativity courses. They also can be learned by elementary and secondary students.

Techniques involve "forced" creativity, which contrasts with "intuitive" creativity.

Creative thinking techniques are taught in several creativity workbooks for children, and one Apple II computer program.

Brainstorming, based mainly on the principle of deferred judgment, can be used for any sort of corporate or business problem. Classroom uses include fanciful creativity exercises and solving real problems.

Brainstorming is intuitively appealing, simple, fun, therapeutic, and it works, usually. Osborn's four groundrules included no criticism (deferred judgment), wild freewheeling, quantity is wanted, and combination and improvement are desired.

The leader organizes the session, reviews the groundrules and procedural details, and explains the problem. He or she may ask for problem facts or alternative problem definitions. Group members should vary in backgrounds and training to stimulate different viewpoints; they should be equal in status to reduce inhibitions.

An important decision is whether or not to use a brainstorming group in the first place.

Some ideas simply may stand out, or evaluation criteria and an evaluation matrix may be used. Evaluation teaches people to evaluate as part of the creative process and to look at many problem components. Evaluation may help clarify the group's values, and can prove that silly ideas may suggest productive ones.

Variations include stop-and-go brainstorming, the Phillips 66 technique, and reverse brainstorming.

Brainwriting, used with small groups, involves circulating sheets of paper from person to person, with each person adding modifications or new ideas.

Brainstorming does not always work; even Osborn did not guarantee success.

Herrmann's whole brain approach amounted to building a creativity group composed of people each of whom is strong in a particular ability—which agrees with Osborn's emphasis on heterogeneity of brainstorming group membership.

Crawford's attribute listing included attribute modifying and attribute transferring (analogical thinking). Crawford and Barron have argued that modifying existing ideas is a core creative process.

Morphological synthesis amounts to attribute listing in a matrix form. One normally would use two or three dimensions, but six or more are possible. Many idea combinations are quickly produced.

The Yellow Pages or catalogs can serve as idea checklists. Osborn's 73 idea-spurring questions was deliberately designed to stimulate creative thinking. Arnold's idea checklist was oriented toward improving engineering features; Small's list toward generating new product ideas.

With the dictionary technique one free associates to relevant words, much like using an idea checklist.

8

creativity tests: evaluating creative potential

[*Scene: Laboratory of Dr. Frankenstein. The Frankenstein monster is strapped to his table as Kool-Aid bubbles mysteriously over bunsen burners. Dr. Frankenstein is discussing the future of his creation with his assistant, Igor.*]

Dr. Frankenstein: Well Igor, he looks great! Those insightful eyes and that creative intellect! He's ready for Paramount Pictures anytime!

Igor: I don't now, boss, He's got eyes, but I think I'd worry about his intelligence and creativity.

Dr. Frankenstein: What's this? Do I detect a hint of doubt? Very well, we'll give him a test of creativity!

Igor: What kind of creativity test? There's two kinds, divergent thinking tests and personality-biographical inventories.

Dr. Frankenstein: Both, of course! He'll pass with flying colors! Now, Monster, give my doubting friend here some unusual uses for a brick!

Monster: (Violently) GRRAWL!! GRRAWL!!

Dr. Frankenstein: Excellent, Monster! Did you hear that Igor? He said "gravel." You chop up the brick and use it for gravel! Another idea Monster?

Monster: (Less violently) GRRAWL!! GRRAWL!!

Dr. Frankenstein: Another creative insight! "Gavel"—for bringing the court to order, obviously. Excellent! Excellent! Well Igor, what do you say to that?

Igor: But boss, I don't think he. . . .

Monster: (Beginning to grin) GRRAWL! GRRAWL!!

Dr. Frankenstein: A "girl doll"! Of course! An inspired answer! Slip some doll clothes on the brick and there you have it! The score is Monster 3, Igor zip!

Igor: But boss, he. . . .

Dr. Frankenstein: Now Monster, what unusual or creative hobbies have you had?

Monster: (Grinning from electrode to electrode) ARGHUNH!! ARGHUNH!!

Dr. Frankenstein: Art, huh? VERY good. Anything else?

Monster: ARGHUNH!! ARGHUNH!!

Dr. Frankenstein: Aardvark? You had a pet aardvark? Brilliant! That's a very
   creative trait indeed!

Igor: But boss, he's just. . . .

Dr. Frankenstein: I'm surprised at you Igor. A better man would admit he's wrong!
   I'm calling the studio right away. He can shuffle and growl with the best
   of them!

Igor: If you say so boss.

Creativity Tests Measure Abilities, Personality Dispositions

Countless tests of human traits and abilities have been constructed in part to confirm that (1) a particular trait exists, (2) people that are strong in the trait can be identified, and (3) the trait is related in meaningful ways to other characteristics and behaviors. It is no surprise that many, many tests have been devised to measure creative *abilities* or to evaluate *personality dispositions* for creative thinking. At present, corresponding to the above three points, there is little doubt that creativity exists, that creative people can be identified, and that creative characteristics are systematically related to other characteristics and behaviors.

Due to Complexity, Reliability and Validity Problematic

However, evaluating creative potential is more complicated than evaluating the mastery of a spelling list. Indeed, every purported test of creativity is doomed at the outset to lackluster validity, and perhaps substandard reliability as well. (*Validity* is the degree to which a test measures what it is supposed to measure; *reliability* is the accuracy or time-to-time consistency of a test.) Said one authoritative person recently, "The problem with developing a highly reliable and highly valid creativity test is that creativity is such a complicated construct" (Davis 1989b, p. 257). Torrance (1988, p. 43) noted that "Creativity . . . involves every sense—sight, smell, hearing, feeling, taste, and even perhaps the extrasensory. Much of it is unseen, nonverbal, and unconscious."

Infinite Variety

Regarding this complexity, when we hear the word "creativity" we quickly think of innovation in the arts and sciences. In fact, creative thinking and innovation is found in every facet of human activity. Further, individuals can be creative in any part of their personal, educational, or professional lives. Torrance (1979) emphasized that people can be creative in an infinite number of ways. It also is true that a person may be highly creative in just one area, but quite clunky in others; another person may be creative in many areas.

To note a few more complications, we noted in Chapter 1 Maslow's valuable distinction between *self-actualized* creativity and *special talent* creativity. Can one test measure both?

And
Confusion

Freud emphasized that neurotic conflicts between the libido and superego motivate creativity; equally suspect claims are that paranormal abilities and experiences are important for creativity (Honorton, 1967). Jung's (1933, 1976) unique position that creative persons are (uncontrollably) inspired by the unconscious animation of archetypal images adds still more confusion; but his theory also underscores the complexity and mystery of human creativity.

Testing
Conditions
Influence
Reliability

Callahan (1991) recently itemized a number of test conditions that can influence creativity test scores, that is, decrease their reliability: changing the time limits, removing the time limits, interrupting children from an interesting vs. an uninteresting classroom activity for the testing, administering creativity tests in the same room where intelligence tests had been previously administered, administering the tests in an enriched or barren environment, preceding the testing with a brief warm-up activity, and making seemingly innocuous changes in the test-taking instructions.

Optimism

Is it a challenge to design a test that accurately evaluates "creativeness"? The conclusion of one optimistic reviewer is that "At present, there seem little question that tests measuring creative abilities, creative personality, and biographical traits, or else evaluating the creativeness of products, work reasonably well" (Davis, 1989b, p. 15). However, a pessimistic reviewer, comparing the simplicity of some creativity test items with the riddle of complex human creativity, concluded

And Pessimism

". . . that the measures of creativity currently available to us measure creativity in a less meaningful (some might say trivial) way than would correspond to people's implicit theories of creativity. Thinking of unusual uses for a paper clip, for example, and similar tasks, would seem to draw relatively little upon the . . . unconventionality, integration and intellectuality, aesthetic taste and imagination, decision skills and flexibility, perspicacity, and drive for accomplishment and recognition that are seen as essential aspects of creativity" (Sternberg, 1986, p. 189).

Test Builders
Make
Assumptions

Finally, another given in creativity testing is that "Each instrument mirrors the particular set of beliefs and preconceptions of its developer concerning the nature of creativity" (Treffinger, 1987; also Treffinger, Renzulli, & Feldhusen, 1971). As you review the creativity tests in this chapter, keep in mind the test developer's assumptions about creativity and the abilities or traits contributing to creativity that are the basis for each test.

USES OF CREATIVITY TESTS

There appear to be three main uses of creativity tests, for identifying creatively gifted children for G/T programs, for research, and for counseling.

Identifying Creatively Gifted Children

Selecting Kids
for G/T
Programs

Currently, the most common use of creativity tests is for selecting creatively gifted students for participation in programs for the gifted and talented. State directors, district G/T teacher-coordinators, and other program planners (e.g., school board members, parents) are becoming more and more aware that high intelligence is just one type of giftedness. Students who are creatively gifted also deserve the frog-kissing, prince-becoming benefits of G/T programs. In Chapter 9 we will review the U.S.O.E definition of giftedness (Marland, 1972) and Renzulli's three-ring definition of giftedness (Renzulli & Reis, 1990), both of which stress creativity as an important gift or talent. Probably the majority of current G/T programs have formally adopted the U.S.O.E. definition, the Renzulli definition, or both (which is tricky, because they are slightly inconsistent). Most G/T programs, especially those that formally endorse the U.S.O.E and/or Renzulli definitions, accept as foundation principles that (1) creative students should be identified, and (2) creativity should be taught.

Use Two
Criteria of
Creativeness

Single Criterion
Too Shaky!

Obviously, selecting children who are creative requires some index of creativeness, which frequently means creativity test scores, hopefully supplemented with teacher, parent, or peer ratings, or perhaps ratings of creative products, usually by an art, English, or science teacher. If you wish to have high confidence in your selection of creative children, it is wise to use two criteria of creativity. For example, if a given child scores high on a creativity test *and* a teacher rates the child as high in creativity, you can be 99 percent certain you have a genuine creative kid. Two different creativity tests, perhaps a personality inventory and a divergent thinking test, also could be used. No creativity test nor any teacher's rating is so reliable and valid that just one measure, by itself, will produce a highly accurate and dependable estimate of creative potential.

Research

A second use of creativity tests is in research. Research helps us understand the nature of creativity and creative people, helps us understand the development of creativity, and, as Treffinger (1987, p. 104) noted, "Helps to remove the concept of creativity from the realm of mystery and superstition."

In Research,
Tests Used to
Identify
Creative People

Relate Test
Scores to Other
Traits

In research, creativity tests typically are used in either of two ways. First, a researcher may need to identify creative children or adults in order to compare them in some way with "regular" children or adults. For example, a researcher might wish to determine if creativeness is related to personality or biographical characteristics such as the ones described in Chapter 4, or to other personality traits, behavior patterns, intellectual abilities, preferred learning styles, academic or career choices, and so on. After all, if one wishes to test the propositions that creative people are more likely to believe in flying saucers, own a cat, have an imaginary playmate, become involved in theatre, or be self-accepting, low in anxiety, or left-handed one must first identify a group of creative people.

Also Used to
Evaluate Effects
of Creativity
Training

The second research use of creativity tests is to evaluate any beneficial effects of some educational or creativity training experience upon the creativeness of the participants. For example, in a primary or secondary school a researcher may wish to evaluate the effects upon students' creativity of a creative dramatics class, a three-week unit on creativity, or a year-long gifted and talented program. Creativity tests, inventories, and questionnaires can help assess these training effects.

Counterbalance
Test Forms

As a research suggestion, if the research design includes both a *before* and an *after* measure using two different test forms, such as Form A and Form B of the *Torrance Tests of Creative Thinking*, it is best to give half of the subjects Form A and half Form B as a pretest. Each subject would take the other form as the post-test. This strategy controls for the possibility that the test forms may not be equivalent. That is, average scores on Form A (or Form B) might tend to be higher regardless of any intervening training. It would not do to provide objective test evidence that (1) the gifted and talented program depressed creativity (because the group happened to take the difficult form as a post-test), or (2) that the program was wildly successful in teaching creativity (because the group happened to take the easy form as a post-test).

Use Control
Group—Please!

Confounded
Research
Results

An another research suggestion, kindly include a *control group* of comparable subjects who do not receive the training, or who receive different training, so that a logical person can conclude that the improvement from pretest to post-test is truly attributable to the creativity training, and not due to having taken the creativity test once before nor to other educational experiences. One recently published study made several mistakes: Following a creativity training experience, post-test creativity scores on one test form were higher than pretest scores on a different form, which led the researcher to conclude that his training methods were effective. Perhaps they were, but we will never know for sure. The higher post-test scores might have been due to practice with the pretest, to a post-test that was easier than the pretest, or to other educational activities that also intervened between the pretest and the post-test.

Original
Questionnaire
May Be Better
Than Published
Creativity Test

Incidentally, sometimes the most effective way to evaluate creativity training effects is not with a published creativity test, but with an original questionnaire that asks: Did you enjoy the experience? Was it worthwhile? Do you feel more creative as a result of the experience? Are you more likely to engage in creative activities as a result of the experience? Very often, such a direct approach will show benefits of creativity training when a popular published creativity test will not.

Counseling

Helpful
Information for
Counselor

Aversion to
Rigidity,
Routine

The third use of creativity testing is in counseling and guidance. A counselor or school psychologist in the elementary or secondary school may want more information about a student who is referred because of apathy, underachievement, uncooperativeness, disruptiveness, or other personal or educational problem. For example, a creative child who is independent, curious, artistic, risk-taking, and who has high energy and a good sense of humor may not be well-rounded and may have few friends (Torrance, 1981a). Further, he or she may well acquire an aversion to routine, rigid, authoritarian classrooms—resulting in a refusal to complete work, becoming aggressive or a class clown, feigning illness to stay home, or other maladaptive behavior (Davis & Rimm, 1989). Information regarding creativeness will help the counselor diagnose the problems.

Creativity
Scores: Unique
and Valuable
Data

Actually, a student need not have "problems" at all to benefit from creativity testing in the counseling setting. Creativity testing can be used to help counselors, teachers, parents, and the students themselves recognize, understand, and develop a student's perhaps untapped creative talent. Treffinger (1987) stressed that creativity scores are unique and valuable data that should be included in the profile of a learner's characteristics. Such information enables teachers to better define instructional activities that will be appropriate and challenging. Especially, and obviously, a highly creative student should be engaged in projects (art, science, literature, etc.) that challenge and strengthen his or her creative abilities.

TYPES OF CREATIVITY TESTS

Present Review:
Published Tests
Only

Lots and Lots of
Creativity Tests

A thorough review of all living creativity tests, their rationale, format, administration and scoring directions, and the research evidence for reliability and validity would fill a good-sized encyclopedia with reasonably dull reading. However, only a handful of tests have been commercially published, and the present overview will be restricted to those. The reader interested in collecting a sizeable file of published and unpublished creativity tests should see the lists available in the *Journal of Creative Behavior* (Davis, 1971; Kaltsoonis, 1971, 1972; Kaltsoonis & Honeywell, 1980), Davis (1989b), Callahan (1991), and in the appendix of Davis (1973).[1] The reader will discover tests of creativity in music, math, chemistry, physics, creative writing, motor behavior, and play; there are tests of curiosity, humor, risk-taking, regression, and empathy with story characters; there are surveys of creative activities and background (family, education) characteristics; there also are open-ended tests that ask you to list unusual uses, improvements for products, questions, meanings, answers to "What would happen if?", and instances of things that are round or purple. A computerized information retrieval search of "creativity testing" will provide an updated list of tests of general creativeness, tests that evaluate creativity in particular artistic or academic areas, and research related somehow to creativity testing. Overall, the variety is astonishing.

Two Main
Categories:
Divergent
Thinking Tests

Inventories That
Assess
Personality,
Biographical
Information

In measuring a general tendency toward or potential for creative thinking, however, there are two main categories of instruments. First, we have *divergent thinking* tests in which the examinee freely lists all of the ideas he or she can think of in response to an open-ended question (e.g., listing unusual uses for a brick is the classic divergent thinking test). Second, there are inventories that evaluate *personality and biographical characteristics* (e.g., attitudes, awarenesses, motivations, values, interests, and histories of creative activities and hobbies).

1. As of April, 1979, Davis himself no longer has an appendix; and if he did, he hardly would fill it with lists of tests. The appendix referred to is in *Psychology of Problem Solving*, by Davis (1973).

These inventories are based upon studies of the personality and biographical backgrounds of creative people (see Chapter 4).

Good Construct Validity

Good Criterion-Related Validity

Both types of tests have a solid theoretical base and good supporting validation research, and both work reasonably well at age levels between preschool and adult. For both types of tests there is strong evidence for *construct validity*—persons who possess those divergent thinking abilities or those personality traits tend to show other characteristics of creative people, including a tendency to do creative things. There also is good *criterion-related* validity. Criterion-related validity usually is concurrent in the sense of establishing significant correlations between test scores and some other current criteria of creativity, for example, ratings of a creative product, ratings of creativeness by a teacher or supervisor, or scores on another creativity test.

The Criterion Problem

There is a *criterion problem* (Taylor, 1988). How do you decide *who* is creative or *what products* are creative in order to validate creativity tests? If the criterion is shaky—for example, scores on another creativity test or ratings of "creativeness" by someone who believes that creativity means neatness, high grades, and pleasing the teacher—the correlations between test and criterion cannot be high. It is no surprise that many creativity test developers rely heavily on establishing construct validity. Two well-known creativity test batteries, the Wallach and Kogan (1965) and the Getzels and Jackson (1962) tests (described later) were developed based entirely on construct validity, with no criterion-related validity research at all.

Critics Do Not Study Validation Research

Incidentally, writers who disparage the validity of creativity tests normally do not closely examine the details of the validation research (nor do they acknowledge that high IQ scores do not always assure intelligent behavior).

Inventories Are More Efficiently Administered, Scored

While both divergent thinking tests and personality-biographical inventories work reasonably well, as we noted, the administration and scoring of the personality-biographical inventories are considerably more efficient.

DIVERGENT THINKING TESTS

Torrance Tests of Creative Thinking

Most Widely
Used Creativity
Tests

The *Torrance Tests of Creative Thinking* (Torrance, 1966) are by far the best known, most widely used, most extensively validated, and, because of their popularity and importance, the most soundly criticized of all creativity tests. Said Torrance (1984a, p. 3), "The basic battery of the *Torrance Tests of Creative Thinking* has been used in over 1,000 published research studies. These tests have been translated into over 30 different languages and have been published and standardized in France, Italy, Czechoslovakia, and Taiwan . . . According to the best estimates available, about 150,000 children and adults are being tested with these instruments each year." Because the Torrance Tests are so well known and widely used, we will describe this battery in more detail than others.

10 Years in
Development

Test Booklets,
Administration
and Scoring
manuals, Norms
and Technical
Manual

The Torrance Tests were derived in the 1950s and 1960s from Torrance's *Minnesota Tests of Creative Thinking,* which themselves were based upon Guilford's Structure of Intellect creativity tests (described next). The Torrance Tests survived ten years of development, during which Torrance firmed up administration and scoring procedures, assembled normative data, gathered reliability and validity data, and put it all into four test booklets, four administration and scoring manuals for the *Verbal* Forms A and B and *Figural* Forms A and B, and a norms and technical manual, now in its second edition. All of the subtests are timed, with either a 5- or 10-minute limit.

Verbal Test:
7 "Activities"

1. List
Questions

2. List Causes

3. List
Consequences

The verbal test (*Thinking Creatively With Words*) is built of seven subtests or "activities." The first three subtests evolve around a curious picture (imagine an elf with pointed ears and pointed shoes looking at his or her reflection in a stream). Torrance feels that the ability to ask questions (sense problems, detect gaps in information) is an important creative ability. In fact, it is part of his definition of creativity (Torrance, 1977, 1988; see Chapter 3). Therefore, the first activity, *Asking,* requires the test taker to list all of the questions he or she can think of about the events in the picture, questions that cannot be answered by simply looking at the picture (e.g., are the ears pointed?). The second subtest, *Guessing Causes,* asks the test taker to list possible causes of the events shown in the picture. The third activity, *Guessing Consequences,* asks for a list of consequences of the events taking place in the drawing.

4. List Product Improvements

5. Unusual Uses

6. Unusual Questions

The fourth verbal subtest, *Product Improvement,* includes a sketch of a stuffed monkey (or elephant). The examinee lists all of the improvements he or she can which would make the stuffed animal more fun to play with. A fifth subtest, *Unusual Uses,* asks the taker to list uses for cardboard boxes (or tin cans). The related sixth subtest, *Unusual Questions,* again focuses upon question asking: List all of the questions you can about cardboard boxes (or tin cans).

7. What Would Happen If?

The final, seventh verbal subtest, *Just Suppose,* is an old creativity favorite—the "what would happen if . . ." question. In this case, the unlikely event is clouds with strings attached to them, or in the other test form, clouds so low you could only see people's feet. What would happen? Would you wear anything but shoes?

Figural Test: 3 "Activities"

All: Complete A Drawing

1. Picture Construction

2. Picture Completion

3. Circles

There are just three nonverbal or figural subtests in the *Thinking Creatively With Pictures.* In all three cases, an incomplete or abstract sketch is presented and the examinee is asked to complete the drawing—making the picture into something meaningful and imaginative. The first subtest, *Picture Construction,* presents a sausage-shaped (or egg-shaped) form which is used as the basis for an imaginative drawing. The second subtest, *Picture Completion,* presents the test taker with ten simple, abstract shapes similar to those in Figure 8.1 which he or she completes and labels. Finally, the third figural activity, *Circles,* includes two pages of circles (or parallel lines) which again are incorporated into complete, meaningful, and perhaps clever drawings.

Scores of Fluency, Flexibility, Originality, Elaboration: Creative Abilities

The subtests of the Torrance Tests, verbal and figural, are scored for *fluency, flexibility, originality,* and *elaboration.* These are considered basic creative abilities, as well as dimensions of the scoring. A newer, streamlined scoring scheme for the Figural Forms A and B, which produces 18 creativity scores (and which seems to be a well-kept secret, shhhh!) will be described later.

Figure 8.1
Torrance Tests of Creative Thinking

The *Torrance Tests of Creative Thinking* (Torrance, 1966) measure creative abilities of *fluency* (number of ideas), *flexibility* (number of different types or categories of ideas), *originality* (uniqueness) and *elaboration* (number of embellishments). Exercises similar to Torrance's subtests are presented below. Spend a few minutes on each one. Are you fluent? Flexible? Original? Are you elaborate?

Directions: Make a meaningful picture out of each of the nonsense forms below. Try to be original. Give each one a name.

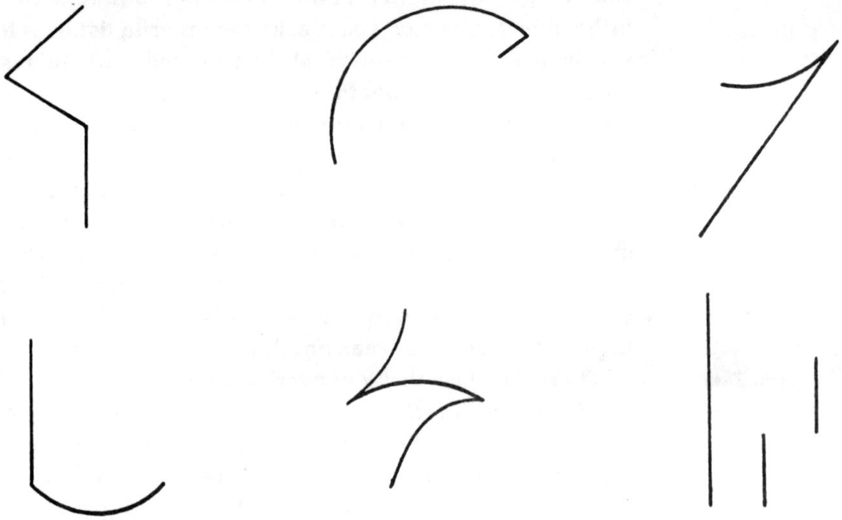

Directions: List as many unusual uses as you can for discarded rubber tires.

_____   _____
_____   _____
_____   _____
_____   _____
_____   _____
_____   _____
_____   _____
_____   _____

(For additional space use inside back cover of book.)

Test of originality: How many explanations can you think of for the action, or lack of it, in this photo? (The Museum of Modern Art / Film Stills Archive.)

The fluency score is simply a count of ideas listed or drawings completed, after duplications and irrelevant entries (e.g., recopying instructions, writing one's name 20 times, or reciting Mary Had a Little Lamb) are excluded. Originality scores are based upon *statistical infrequency* norms. That is, each idea is listed in a table in the scoring guide where it is awarded 0, 1, or 2 points depending upon how infrequently (rarely) that idea was listed by subjects on whom the test was normed. Scoring for originality is not as simple as scoring for fluency. Because some ideas will be ambiguous or not in the scoring guide, the test scorer must make a judgment as to the degree of "creative strength" shown by the ambiguous idea, and therefore the number of points to award. For example, using a cardboard box for a dog house is not original, but what about using it for a house for a pet anteater, pet Martian, or politician?

Flexibility refers to the number of different categories of ideas or the number of different approaches one takes to a problem. For example, if Roberta Rutt's list of tin can uses includes put buttons in it, put pennies in it, put bottle caps in it, put nails in it, put washers in it, put feathers in it, etc., Roberta would have a very low flexibility score. In scoring the Torrance Tests, as the scorer looks up the originality weight he or she also will find a number indicating the flexibility category. The number of different flexibility category numbers is the flexibility score for that subtest. Read that sentence fast.

The figural tests may be scored for elaboration by counting the number of details beyond the basic picture. These are details that are added to the figure itself, its boundaries, and/or to the surrounding space (e.g., additional ideas, decorations, emotional expressions, color, shading). *Title originality,* on a 0 to 3 scale, is an optional *verbal* score that may be derived from figural Activity 1, *Picture Construction,* and Activity 2, *Picture Completion.* Bonus points (2 to 25) are awarded for Activity 3, *Circles* (or *Parallel Lines*), if the clever person combines two or more circles into a single picture. These points are added to the figural originality score. The verbal tests typically are not scored for elaboration, although directions for this optional scoring are available. One would count the number of additional details in each response beyond what is needed to communicate the basic idea. This could be useful if one were specifically interested in a person's or group's elaboration abilities.

High Interscorer Reliability

Good Test Retest Reliability

The norms and technical manual (Torrance, 1974) reports interscorer reliabilities (the correlation between scores produced by two independent scorers) as high as .99 (for fluency) and almost always above .90. Test-retest reliabilities are in the satisfactory .60 to .80 range, with a few lower and many higher. The test-retest reliability figures are undoubtedly depressed by Torrance's peculiar procedure of using Form A for the first administration and Form B for the later administration, which muddles test-retest reliability with alternate forms reliability.

Construct Validity

Wild Reputations, Original Drawings, High Humor, Ink Blot Creativity

Lower Rigidity

Creative Activities, Hobbies, Career Preferences

Validating creativity tests is not an easy chore, for reasons cited earlier. Much of Torrance's validation work, in fact, has been of the construct validity type—demonstrating that high scorers on the Torrance Tests show characteristics commonly associated with creativity. One study indicated that high scorers on the Torrance Tests had reputations for producing wild or silly ideas; their drawings were described as highly original; and they tended to be humorous and playful (Torrance, 1974). Another study showed that high scorers were rated high in humor and gave ink blot responses traditionally associated with imagination and creativity—responses were unconventional, fanciful, and included human movement and color (Weisberg & Springer, 1961). Fleming and Weintraub (1962) found a significant inverse relationship between creativity scores and rigidity scores. Still other studies showed Torrance Test scores to be significantly correlated with the originality of imaginative stories (Yamamoto, 1963); involvement in creative activities and hobbies (art, drama, literature, music; Cropley, 1971, 1972); preferences for creative and unconventional careers (Torrance & Dauw, 1965); and teacher nominations of, for example, "Who thinks of the most unusual, wild or fantastic ideas?" (Torrance, 1974).

Torrance's Landmark Longitudinal Studies

Research which provides the best evidence of a relationship between Torrance Test scores and real-life creative achievement comes form two longitudinal studies, one involving high school students tested in 1959 and followed up 7 and 12 years later (i.e., in 1966 and 1971); and another involving elementary school students tested in

High Scorers:
Greater
Quantity and
Quality of
Creative
Achievements
and Higher
Creative
Aspirations

1958 (and 5 subsequent years) and followed up 22 years later (i.e., in 1980; Torrance, 1988). The results of these landmark research projects should increase the confidence of Torrance Test users. Compared with low Torrance Test scorers, high scorers reported a larger *quantity* of creative achievements, higher *quality* of their creative achievements, and a higher level of *creative motivation* (career aspirations). For example, the "quantity of publicly recognized and acknowledged creative achievements" included such items as patents and inventions, plays or music compositions that were performed publicly, art work awards, founding a business, journal, or professional organization, or developing an innovative technique in medicine, science, business, teaching, etc. The quality criterion was ratings of the "three most creative achievements" of each person. Creativeness of aspirations was primarily assessed via answers to two direct questions: (1) "What are your career ambitions? For example, what position, responsibility, or reward do you wish to attain? What do you hope to accomplish? (2) "If you could do or be whatever you choose in the next 10 years, what would it be?" (Torrance, 1988, p. 58).

Torrance (1984a, p. 4) reported that after 22 years, as young adults

Compared
with a High
IQ Group

. . . the creatively gifted group excelled a high IQ group on the quality of their highest creative achievements, their high school creative achievements, the number of creative lifestyle achievements, and the creativity of their future career images. They also tended to excel the IQ gifted group on number of post-high school creative achievements but the difference fell short of statistical significance. The doubly gifted group [high creativity, high IQ] equalled but did not excel the creatively gifted group on all five of the criteria of young adult creative achievement.

Over Time, Highs Got Higher, Lows Did Not

Scoring Is Time Consuming; Only Divergent Abilities Measured

Streamlined Scoring: Fluency, Originality, Elaboration, Abstractness of Titles, Resistance to Premature Closure, 13 Creative Strengths

Five Norm-Referenced Scores

13 Criterion-Referenced Scores

Interestingly, the difference in creative achievements and motivations between high and low creatives increased over time—while the highs got higher, the lows did not change.

Streamlined scoring. Torrance confessed that, despite generally satisfactory reliability and validity evidence and proven usefulness in education, "many users have made two major criticisms: The scoring is too time-consuming and the tests assess only the divergent production abilities and do not tap the essence of creativity" (Torrance & Ball, 1984, p. 5).

Torrance's (Torrance & Ball, 1984) *streamlined* scoring system (for the Figural tests only) was designed to (1) streamline the scoring (surprise!), and (2) assess other dimensions of creativity beyond the divergent thinking abilities of fluency, flexibility, originality, and elaboration. The new system, nine years in development, maintains the *fluency* measure essentially "as is" (which was easy to score in the first place), expedites the scoring of *originality* and *elaboration,* and adds two easily-scored dimensions called *abstractness of titles* and *resistance to premature closure.* Also added were no less than 13 "creative strengths."

To be as brief as possible, the five scoring dimensions of fluency, originality, elaboration, abstractness of titles, and resistance to premature closure, are considered *norm-referenced,* which means that the number of points earned are relative to the norm group. (Strictly speaking, fluency is not scored relative to a norm group.) The other 13 creative strengths are *criterion referenced,* which means that the criterion (the creative strength) either appears in the person's test or it does not.

Fluency, as in the original scoring guides, is a count of relevant, nonduplicated ideas. If two or more figures are combined, credit is still given for the number of figures used.

Originality is simply the number of original ideas. That is, non-original ideas, listed in tables, are eliminated.

One *elaboration* point is given for adding: decorations, color, shading, each major variation of design, and each elaboration of the title beyond minimal labeling.

Abstractness of titles is scored from 0 to 3 points according to degree of abstractness, for example, a 3-point idea involves ". . . the ability to capture the essence of the information involved, to know what is important . . . (and) enables the viewer to see the picture more deeply and richly" (Torrance & Ball, 1974, p. 19).

Resistance to premature closure earns 0 to 2 points depending upon the degree to which the test taker (prematurely) closes the incomplete figure, "cutting off chances for more powerful original images" (p.22)

"+" and "++"   Turning to the list of 13 creative strengths, in general, one plus sign ("+") is awarded if 1 or 2 instances of the creative strength occur (in the entire test booklet); two plus signs ("++") are given if 3 or more instances occur.

Emotional expressiveness is the communication of feelings or emotions (sad, happy, angry, scared, lost) in either the drawing or the title.

Storytelling articulateness is including enough detail to put the picture in context and tell a story.

Movement or action is scored if it appears in the title or the picture (e.g., running, flying, dancing, swimming).

Expressiveness of titles is scored if emotion and feeling are shown in the title (e.g., "lonely," "ambitious").

Synthesis of incomplete figures, a rare occurrence, is the combination of two or more figures in the Picture Completion subtest.

Synthesis of lines or circles is the tendency to combine two or more circles or sets of lines, which is " . . . an important indicator of a creative disposition or thinking ability" (Torrance & Ball, 1984, p. 34).

Unusual visualization is the tendency to present ideas or objects in usual visual perspective, for example, from underneath, on top, or a cutaway view.

Internal visualization is the tendency to visualize the internal workings of things, for example, body parts seen through clothing, the internal parts of a machine, or ants in an anthill

Extending or breaking boundaries may occur by lengthening some lines in the Parallel Lines activity (e.g., to make a table), dividing a pair of lines for different aspects of a picture, or by adding depth perception with circles.

Humor—puns, word play, exaggeration, absurdity—may appear in the figures or in the titles.

Richness of imagery is scored if the drawing " . . . shows variety, vividness, liveliness, and intensity . . . has freshness . . . and provides delight for the tired scorer" (p. 44), for example, a pair of cat eyes, an alligator, or a surfer.

Colorfulness of imagery "is defined as exciting in its appeal to the sense of taste, touch, smell, feel, sight, etc." (p. 44), for example, a whale ride, banana store, ghost, or toothache.

Finally, *Fantasy* is reflected in fairy tale episodes or characters from fables, science fiction, or other fantasy literature; also original fantasy, such as talking rain drops or a parachute hat creation.

High Agreement Between Original and Streamlined Scoring

A comparison of the original scoring of fluency, originality, and elaboration with the new streamlined scoring showed very high agreement (correlation coefficients of .92, .94, and .92, respectively; Torrance & Ball, 1984). The streamlined scoring test manual presents extensive validity coefficients (correlations between scores and criteria of creativity) for all 18 measures for students in grades 3 through 12, derived from the longitudinal data mentioned earlier plus other research, that range mostly between .30 and .60.

All 18 Streamlined Measures Validated

Is 18 Scores Really "Streamlining"?

On one hand, changing the scoring system from four to 18 scores somehow loses the flavor of "streamlining." On the other hand, the new scoring system, with practice, is indeed expedient and includes rich information that could be very useful in understanding a person's creative tendencies and talents. The reader interested in further details regarding scoring and validation should see Torrance and Ball (1984).

Rich Information

Creativity and school achievement. Creative traits such as unconventionality and independence, sometimes mixed with a little resistance to domination and indifference to rules and conventions, surely can work against school achievement. However, other traits and abilities of creative students are definite assets in school: flexibility, curiosity and inquisitiveness, perceptiveness and the ability to see relationships, resourcefulness, high energy and enthusiasm, confidence, inner-directedness,

Bad for School Success

Good for School Success

Verbal Creativity Related to School Achievement

"Okay, okay! I'll take a look at the new streamlined scoring system!" (The Museum of Modern Art / Film Stills Archive.)

an experimental attitude, intuitive thinking, open-mindedness—and verbal creativity generally. Torrance (1974)
reported correlations roughly in the range of .35 to .45
between verbal creativity scores and scores on standardized achievement tests (reading, language, arithmetic),
with intelligence held constant. Figural creativity scores
showed lower correlations (.16 to .25) with achievement.
Torrance noted that correlations between creativity
scores and achievement will be lower when children are
"taught by authority," higher when taught in creative
ways such as using ". . . discovery, experimentation and
the like."

Importantly, summarizing the results of many studies,
Torrance reported the median correlation between figural creativity and intelligence as .06 and between verbal
creativity and intelligence as .21. These figures indicate
that creative abilities and abilities measured by intelligence tests are not the same, especially with nonverbal
creativity.

Especially When Children Taught in Creative Ways

Low Correlations With IQ Scores

The Guilford Tests

Guilford's SOI Model

Secret Information

Original Model: 120 Cells

Latest and Final Model: 180 Cells

Some problem-sensitive readers may have wondered
why Guilford's (1967, 1977) *Structure of Intellect* (SOI)
model did not appear in Chapter 3 with other theories of
creativity.[2] Answer: It was saved until now. Guilford created a three-dimensional cube—a theory of intelligence—which was intended to describe anything anyone
could every do with his or her brain. Figure 8.2 presents
the 1988 (and final) edition of the SOI cube, with its three
dimensions of *contents, products,* and *operations.* This
newest version is known only to the readers of his five-
page 1988 article or this chapter. In its original form
(Guilford, 1967), four types of contents combined with six
products and five operations to produce 120 cells (4 × 6
× 5 = 120). Most people who write about Guilford's model
stopped here—with "120 SOI abilities" forever ossified
on their frontal lobes. In fact, Guilford (1977) extended
the model by subdividing the "figural" content into *visual*

2. Have you wondered why Joy Paul Guilford never used his first name?

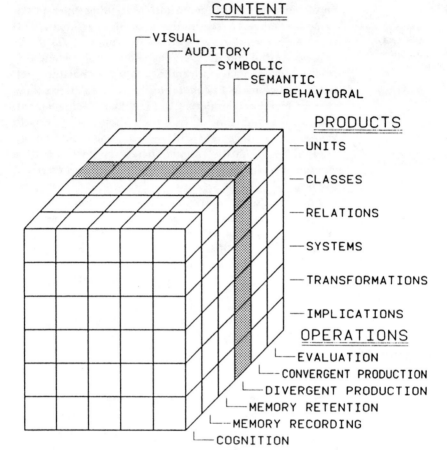

Figure 8.2. The Revised Structure of Intellect Model. X-Ray examination confirmed that Guilford's cerebral cortex looked exactly like this. Reprinted by permission of *Educational and Psychological Measurement*.

content and *auditory content,* creating 150 cells. Shortly before his death he also subdivided the "memory" operation into *memory retention* (long-term memory) and *memory recording* (short-term memory)—producing no fewer than 180 cells (Guilford, 1988).

Each Cell Equals a Cognitive Ability

Our limited space will not permit a complete description of the SOI model (which makes tedious reading anyway). Briefly, each of the 180 cells of the model is interpreted to be a unique cognitive ability. This approach stands in sharp contrast to the two IQ scores of the WISC-R or the four scores of the *Stanford-Binet Intelligence Scale, Fourth Edition.* J. Paul Guilford invested about three decades creating tests that measure each one of those 180 abilities.

Creativity: Divergent Thinking Abilities

The darkened slab of the model in Figure 8.2 includes the operations of *divergent production.* Tests that measure a few of these 30 abilities (6 products $\times$ 5 contents) currently are marketed as tests of creativity. For example, *Word Fluency* is a 4 minute test that requires the examinee to produce a list of words containing a specified letter or letters (e.g., R _____ M). In the SOI cube this is divergent production of symbolic units, or DSU. The *Expressional Fluency* test, divergent production of semantic systems (DMS), allows 8 minutes to verbally express an idea using a given first letter for each word (e.g., E ____ R ____ L ____ P ____). Other fluency tests listed in a 1988 publisher's catalog included *Ideational Fluency* and *Associational Fluency;* there also are *Consequences* ("What would happen if . . .?") and *Alternate Uses* tests.

Published SOI Tests

Transformations: Also Creative Abilities

In addition to the divergent production abilities (the darkened slab), Guilford 91986) explain how *transformations* (a product; can you find the transformation slab in Figure 8.2?) also are important creative abilities. For example, a scientist might be strong in cognition of visual transformations (CVT); a cartoonist strong in cognition of semantic transformations (CMT); and the creativity of scientists, inventors, and decorators will involve the evaluation of visual or semantic transformations (EVT, EMT; Guilford, 1986).

This Puzzle Ignites Thinking

One cell in the SOI model is the divergent production of figural transformations—combining the divergent production operation with the transformation product. One test of DFT may be familiar—matchstick problems. For example, given the six squares in Figure 8.3, one problem is to remove three matchsticks and leave four squares; another problem is to remove four matchsticks and leave three squares. See Guilford (1967, 1977, 1986) for descriptions of the many, many other specific SOI tests.

Supportive Validity Studies

Regarding validity, Guilford's 1967 book reviewed some elderly research showing that, for example, artists scored higher on divergent production of figural systems

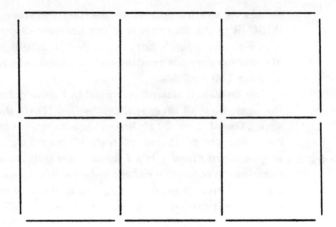

Figure 8.3. Matchstick problem measuring the divergent production of figural transformations (DFT). Try removing three matches to leave four squares; four matches to leave three squares. Do not leave excess, dangling matches.

(DFS) tests than did unselected college students (Welch, 1946); creative writing samples of sixth-grade students correlated .46 and .58 with verbal divergent production composite scores, while their creative drawing samples correlated .50 and .54 with figural test composite scores (Jones, 1960); originality ratings of Air Force captains correlated .30, .36, and .32 with scores on the three divergent production tests Alternate Uses, Consequences, and Plot Titles (creating titles for simple story plots; Barron, 1955); and the ability to design an experiment on transfer of training correlated .41 with a composite divergent thinking score based on Alternate Uses, Consequences, and Plot Titles (Bass, Hatton, McHale, and Stolurow (1962).

Not-So-Supportive Validity Studies

Other studies, equally elderly, have reported less impressive validity coefficients. For example, Brittain and Beitel (1961) found mostly insignificant correlations between scores on a number of semantic divergent production tests and creativity in art students; and Piers, Daniels, and Quackenbush (1960) found that teachers' rating of creativity correlated .23 with a composite divergent production originality score, but −.02 with a composite semantic fluency score. Guilford's 1977 and 1986 books included no validity data.

Meeker:
Diagnostic-
Remediation
Approach With
SOI-LA Test

Incidentally, Meeker (1969, 1981) has used groups of the Guilford tests in a diagnostic-remediation (medical model) approach to teaching reading, math, writing, and creativity. Specific weaknesses are diagnosed with the *SOI-Learning Abilities* test which are then remediated with equally specific exercises (Meeker, 1976; Meeker & Meeker, 1986; Meeker, Meeker, & Roid,1985).

Monitor Test of Creative Potential

Monitor Tests
Measure Some
SOI Abilities

The *Monitor Test of Creative Potential* (TCP; Hoepfner & Hemenway, 1973) is available in Forms A and B and may be used with children as young as age 7 (second grade) and with adolescents and adults. There are three subtests designed to measure some of Guilford's Structure of Intellect creativity factors, with each page of each subtest producing two scores.

Writing Words

The *Writing Words* subtest is a verbal test said to measure Guilford's divergent production of semantic units (DSU) and divergent production of semantic classes (DSC). The person is given two minutes to "Write words that mean about the same as (say, DARK)" and, on the bottom half of the page, "Write words that mean about the same as (say, SOFT)," and then another two minutes to do the same with another two words on the next page. Each page produces an *associational fluency* score and a *spontaneous flexibility* score.

Picture
Decorations

The *Picture Decorations* test is considered a figural test intended to measure divergent production of figural units (DFU) and divergent production of figural implications (DFI). This test involves two copies of each of three simple pictures (e.g., two teepees). The person is given two minutes to decorate both copies of a given picture, for a total of six minutes. It produces a *design element* score, based on shading, symbols and figures that are not "pictorial," and a *pictorial element* score, based on decorative elements that represent real things or objects.

License Plate
Words

The third subtest, *License Plate Words,* is said to measure symbolic abilities—Guilford's divergent production of symbolic units (DSU) and divergent production of symbolic transformations (DST). The examinee is given three minutes to create words from three sets of three letters (like PST, LOS, and FRD, with the letters kept in order), and then another three minutes to create words from another three license plates. the license plate words are scored for *word fluency* and *originality,* the latter defined as words with letters inserted between the given three letters and words containing 8 or more letters.

Total Fruit Salad Score

And Subtest Scores

Like the Torrance Tests, the administration of the Monitor TCP is standardized and scoring guides permit objective and reliable scoring. The treatment of TCP scores is creative and not at all strange, if you do not mind adding oranges, apples, and bananas for a total fruit salad score. Each of the seven pages (two *Writing Words,* three *Picture Decoration,* two *License Plates*) earns two qualitatively different scores, for example, associational fluency and spontaneous flexibility for the *Writing Words* test. For each page the two scores are added together for a page score; the two or three page scores add together for a subtest score; and the three subtest scores add together for a total creativity score. This unique method provides the efficiency-minded user with one total score with which to easily rank students, yet research could be conducted with various subtest scores.

Interscorer reliability estimates reported in the manual were a satisfactory .94 to .99. A type of combined test-retest/alternate forms reliability was produced by having 7–9 year olds take the test using one form, then retake the test three months later using the other form. (We explained this incorrect procedure earlier.) The two reported reliability figures (correlations) were .62 and .67, which are reasonable.

Reliability Information Okay, but No Validity Data

Generally then, the reported reliability (accuracy, consistency) information is satisfactory. However, validity data is not sketchy; it is absent. The manual only presents correlations between Monitor TCP scores and IQ scores from the *Lorge Thorndike Intelligence Tests,* which range from .52 to .59. These are much higher than those noted above for the Torrance Tests (Torrance, 1974). The authors interpret these correlations to mean that ". . . scores on the TCP are not determined by IQ status." A reasonable person could reach exactly the opposite conclusion—that the TCP scores are, in fact, much more highly correlated with intelligence test scores that they should be. It is conceivable that the time pressure enabled more intelligent students to do better than less intelligent students. The 1973 manual promised that "Additional empirical external validity information will be provided . . . in later editions of this manual." However, this writer's copy was obtained in 1984, still with no validity data.

Exercise in Divergent Thinking

CAP: Assesses Divergent Thinking and Personality Traits

Frank Williams (1980) did not have the decency to consider the neat organization of this chapter nor your author's feelings when he devised his *Creativity Assessment Packet* (CAP). What he did consider was that a sensible evaluation of children's creative potential could reasonably involve both a divergent thinking test and inventories for assessing creative personality traits. His CAP therefore must awkwardly be described in two places.

Picture Completion: Figural and Verbal Scores

Fluency, Flexibility, Originality, Elaboration

One Total Creativity Score

Williams' *Exercise in Divergent Thinking* is almost identical to Torrance's figural subtest *Picture Completion,* although Williams considers it both a figural and a verbal test because the title of each artistic creation is assigned a verbal creativity score. The test includes 12 incomplete drawings, similar to those in Figure 8.1, which students have a generous 25 minutes (grades 3–5) or 20 minutes (grades 6–12) to complete, producing fluency, flexibility, originality, and elaboration scores. With young children, the required title for each drawing may be written in by teachers or aides. Instructions encourage students to "Try to draw a creative picture that no one else would think of . . . think of a clever title for your picture . . . (and) Draw as many pictures as you can in the time given." Each title is awarded 0 to 3 points, based largely on length, complexity, creativeness, and humor. Williams adds the five scores together for a total creativity score.

Unclear Validity Criteria

Ten-month test-retest reliabilities for the three CAP instruments for 256 students in grades 3 through 12 were said to be " . . . in the sixties." Williams claimed validity coefficients (correlations) for CAP between .59 and .76, which in creativity testing would be considered extremely high. However, the specifics of which CAP test scores were correlated with what validity criteria were not clear. Fekken (1985), another perceptive test reviewer, soundly criticized the CAP tests for poor norming samples and unclear and inadequate reliability and validity data.

Wallach and Kogan Tests

Freebies

The Wallach and Kogan (1965) creativity tests are not published in the sense that you could buy a box of 25 for eight or ten dollars. The deal is much better. The tests appear in their entirety in *Modes of Thinking in Young Children,* complete with administration and scoring directions. It would appear that educators or researchers can use the tests without charge.

Gamelike
Atmosphere

No Time Limits

Removes
Influence of IQ

The Wallach and Kogan test administration procedure is unique and well known on two counts. First, a relaxed, gamelike atmosphere is established. Second, the tests are untimed. The purpose of these two manipulations is to remove the pressured, test-like atmosphere that characterizes intelligence testing. According to Wallach and Kogan, these gamelike and untimed conditions reduce the influence of intelligence upon the creativity scores to about zero.

Fluency,
Uniqueness

There are five tests. Each test is scored for *fluency,* the total number of ideas listed, and *uniqueness,* the number of ideas that are not given by any other person in the testing group. Obviously, the uniqueness score will depend upon the group size—with only 5 or 10 test takers, uniqueness scores will be much higher than with 100 or 500 students. The Wallach and Kogan sample consisted of 151 fifth-grade children.

Valid For
College
Students

This is not to say it is a children's test battery. In your author's personal experience the tests worked very well with a group of 37 college students (Bartlett & Davis,

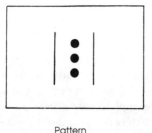

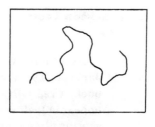

Pattern   Line

Figure 8.4. Items similar to those in the Wallach and Kogan (1965) Pattern Meanings and Line Meanings tests.

1974). Fluency and uniqueness scores were correlated .33 and .35 with overall ratings of the creativeness of actual art and writing products and ideas for inventions and creative teaching methods.

Instances

With the *Instances Test* the students list instances or examples of each of four class concepts. For example, "Name all of the *round* things you can think of." Ditto for "things . . . that will make a noise," "square things," and "things . . . that move on wheels."

Alternate Uses

Similarities

Alternate uses is, of course, our old friend the unusual uses test. In eight questions subjects were to "Tell me the different ways you could use a newspaper (knife, automobile tire, cork, shoe, button, key, and chair)." The *Similarities* test asks the person to "Tell me all the ways in which a potato and a carrot (cat and mouse, train and tractor, milk and meat, grocery store and a restaurant, violin and piano, radio and telephone) are alike."

Pattern Meanings

Line Meanings

Two similar tests use visual materials. With *Pattern Meanings* subjects list possible meanings or interpretations of eight abstract visual designs: "Tell me all of the things you think this could be." With *Line Meanings,* instead of neat symmetrical patterns subjects list interpretations of line drawings, some squiggly and abstract, others simple. One, in fact, is a straight line. "Here is another line. You can turn it any way you want to. Tell me all the things you can about it. What does it make you think of?" Drawings similar to those in *Pattern Meanings* and *Line Meanings* appear in Figure 8.4

Getzels and Jackson Tests

As with the Wallach and Kogan tests, the Getzels and Jackson (1962) tests are published only in the authors' book, *Creativity and Intelligence*. Four of the subtests appear in their entirety, complete with administration and scoring directions. The fifth is copyrighted by others. The four tests again appear to be available for general use without charge.

Word Association: List Meanings

Scoring: Number of Different Meanings

The *Word Association Test* presents the person with a list of 25 words, each of which has multiple meanings (e.g., *arm, duck, bolt, punch,* and *tender*). Fifteen minutes are allowed to list as many meanings as possible. The creativity score is the total number of *different* meanings listed (e.g., *arm of chair* and *arm of sofa* would receive just 1 point, not 2).

Uses Test

Scoring: Different Uses, Unique Uses

Different + Unique = Total

The *Uses Test* asks the person to—what else—list as many different uses as he or she can for five objects (bricks, pencils, paper clips, toothpicks, a sheet of paper). Again, 15 minutes are allowed. The test is scored for the number of *different* uses for an object and for the relative *uniqueness* of the uses. The test taker receives a unique-ness point for each idea listed by less than one-fifth of the group of responders. The number of different uses is added to the number of unique uses to produce a total *Uses Test* score.

Hidden Shapes

Scoring: Number Correct

Hidden Shapes, the copyrighted test, consists of 18 simple geometric figures, each of which is accompanied by four complex figures. For each test item, the problem is to identify which complex figure contains the simple figure. The test is supposed to measure "critical exact-ness" or "critical practicality," "predictive of individual and creative work thoroughly done" (Cattell, 1955). A full 3½ minutes are allowed. See Cattell (1956) for a look at the test.

Analytic vs. Global Thinking?

Analytic Thinker: Less Social

We should note that some versions of this type of test are called *hidden figures* or *embedded figures* tests, and are interpreted to reflect a cognitive style of *analytic* (or *field independent*) vs. *global* (or *field dependent*) thinking (see Witkin, Moore, Goodenough, & Cox, 1977). The an-alytic (but not the global) thinker can separate the figure from the complex ground in which it is embedded. The

A Convergent
Test

analytic thinker also is less social, less dependent upon others, less well liked, and probably has a college major or career in an analytic nonsocial area—math, engineering, architecture, or biology, but not social work, clinical psychology, elementary education, sales, or personnel management. Getzels and Jackson's *Hidden Shapes* probably is not the best measure of creativeness. Certainly it requires convergent, not divergent thinking processes.

Fables Test:
Moralistic,
Humorous, Sad
Endings

The *Fables Test* consists of four fables whose last lines are missing. The test taker is allowed 30 minutes to supply (a) a moralistic, (b) a humorous, and (c) a sad ending for each fable. For example:

Starving
Grasshopper

A grasshopper, that had merrily sung all summer, was almost perishing with hunger in the winter, so she went to see some ants that lived near, and asked them to lend her a little of the food they had put by.

"You shall certainly be paid before this time of year comes again," she said.

"What did you do all the summer?" asked they.

"Why, all day long, and all night long too, I sang, if you please," answered the grasshopper.

"Oh, you sang, did you?" said the ants
. . . .

Scoring:
Appropriateness,
Relatedness

The answers are scored for *appropriateness* (is it really moralistic, humorous, or sad?) and *relatedness* (does the ending logically follow from the given material?). Appropriateness and relatedness scores are added together for a total *Fables* score.

Make-Up
Problems

Scoring:
Elements,
Operations

Finally, with the *Make-up Problems* test students are given four paragraphs, each of which contains a number of numerical statements about the activities of (1) building a swimming pool, (2) doing a science experiment, (3) earning money at odd jobs, and (4) conducting a survey of apartment rental rates. Students are allowed approximately 30 minutes to make up as many mathematical problems as they can with the given information. Each problem is scored for the number of *elements* (pieces of numerical information) and number of *operations* (addition, subtraction, multiplication, division). Again, the two scores are added together for a total *Make-Up Problems* score.

Mathematical Creativity

Incidentally, Getzel's and Jackson's *Make-Up Problems* test has been used as a test of mathematical creativity.

Thinking Creatively in Action and Movement

TCAM: Preschool Creativity Test

Developmentally Appropriate

Torrance's (1981b) *Thinking Creatively in Action and Movement* (TCAM) is a preschool measure of creative potential. The tests grew out of Torrance's observations of the ways in which preschool children in day-care centers expressed their creativeness. Said Torrance, these tests of creativity in movement are developmentally appropriate to preschoolers and ". . . sample the kinds of creativity that are important in the lives of such children . . . (and the tests) . . . make sense to them." Torrance conceded that his *Torrance Tests of Creative Thinking* ". . . proved to be only marginally successful with five-year olds and were unsuitable with three and four-year olds . . . (because) . . . children at these ages . . . have only marginal skills for expressing their ideas in words and drawings."

How Many Ways?

The first subtest, *How Many Ways?*, asks children to ". . . think up as many ways as you can to walk or run" between tape markers on each side of the room. The experimenter records the ideas, which are later scored for *fluency* (number of ideas) and *originality* (according to a scoring guide and influenced by judgments of creative strength, with 0 to 3 points per idea). The second activity is *Can You Move Like?*, for example, a tree in the wind and assorted animals, totaling six situations. It is scored in one category, *imagination,* which is rated as the student performs each of the six movements. Activity 3, *What Other Ways?*, requires a large supply of paper cups and one waste basket. The test administrator asks the child how many ways he or she can put a paper cup in the wastebasket. A little known fact is that Wilt Chamberlain got his start by taking this test. The fourth and final subtest

Can You Move Like?

What Other Ways?

A Stilted Fact

What Can You Do with a Paper Cup?

Creative
Flourishes

is *What Can You Do With A Paper Cup?*, a children's form of the unusual uses test. Both Activities 3 and 4 are scored for fluency and originality, as with Activity 1. Extra credit (up to 4 points) is given for ". . . unusual flourishes and choreographing executed by some children." The student winds up with a total fluency, total originality, and an imagination score.

Untimed, No
Bias

The tests are basically untimed, although the tester is urged to record the time required for each subtest. Students usually need between 10 and 30 minutes. Scores on the tests appear to have no racial, gender, or socioeconomic bias and are relatively unrelated to previous preschool attendance and measure of intelligence. They can be used with handicapped groups such as emotionally disturbed students and deaf students (Torrance, 1981b).

High Interscorer
Reliability

Torrance (1981b) reported interscorer reliabilities of .99 for fluency and around .96 for originality. Similarly, Tegano, Moran, and Godwin (1986) reported an interscorer reliability of .95, and Cropley (1986) reported interscorer reliabilities between .93 and .99 for various TCAM subscores. The test manual also reported a high test-retest reliability coefficient of .84 for the overall test, with subtest test-retest reliabilities from .58 to .79.

Construct
Validity

Who's There

Regarding validity, Torrance again notes the difficulty of finding a suitable criterion against which to validate the tests. Several studies were cited that produced significant correlations between TCAM scores and criteria associated with creativeness. For example, TCAM fluency and originality scores were correlated .44 and .42, respectively, with children's Knock-Knock joke humor. Knock Knock. (Who's There?) Ithsmus. (Ithsmus who?) Ithsmus be about the best data Torrance could find, under the circumstances. Another study showed that 5-year old children trained in problem-solving sociodrama scored higher on the TCAM test than control children without the training, which is exactly what one would expect if the TCAM truly measures the construct of creativity.

No Support
Here

However, on the negative and eyebrow-raising side, Tegano *et al.* (1986) found significant correlations between TCAM fluency scores and IQ scores, suggesting that TCAM performance is not independent of intelligence. Evans (1986) felt that more construct and predictive validity evidence is needed before TCAM scores could be used for making important educational decisions, such as admission to G/T programs.

Helps Creativity Consciousness

Incidentally, some users' comments reported in the TCAM Manual suggest that the test helps improve teachers' creativity consciousness, and helps them recognize specific creative children: "What a splendid tool this is . . . . The staff . . . were so awakened, saying such things as 'Why I never saw that in (name) before!' or 'Why I never paid attention to that before!' or 'Oh! Look what I have missed!' or 'I'm going to have a whole new way of teaching now!' "

Sounds and Images, Onomatopoeia and Images

2 LP Records

Different Than Other Divergent Thinking Tests

Thinking Creatively With Sounds and Words (Torrance, Khatena, & Cunnington, 1973) takes the form of two long-playing records that include the two tests *Sounds and Images* and *Onomatopoeia and Images*. They are not "divergent thinking tests" in the strict sense that a test taker will brashly list every idea he or she can think of. However, the test taker does think up and write down ideas that are scored for originality. The tests are clearly performance tests rather than self-estimates of one's creative personality, and they fit best in this divergent thinking category.

Abstract Sounds Stimulate Creative Images

Sounds Repeated: More Originality

Statistical Infrequency Scoring

The *Sounds and Images* test presents four abstract sounds. After each sound the test taker is given a few seconds to describe on the score sheet the mental images stimulated by that sound. The set of four sounds is presented three times, under the assumption that the associations will become more and more original with the repetitions. They usually do. Each of the 12 responses receives between 0 and 4 originality points, based upon the norms in the scoring guide. We saw this *statistical infrequency* scoring procedure in the discussion of the Torrance Tests, above.

Onomatopoeia and Images: Same Procedures

The *Onomatopoeia and Images* test is similar, except that 10 image-stimulating onomatopoeic words (e.g., *zoom, boom, fizzy* and *moan*) are used instead of four sounds. Again, the 10 words are presented three times, and 0 to 4 points are awarded for each answer according to tabled norms.

Two Forms

As with the *Torrance Tests of Creative Thinking,* there are two forms of *Sounds and Images* and two forms of *Onomatopoeia and Images.* The forms differ only in the specific abstract sounds or onomatopoeic words used. Also, the tests are available in an adult form and a children's form. The introductory narratives of the children's forms are simpler.

Adult, Children's Versions

The authors present extensive reliability and validity information for the two tests. Considering both tests, interscorer reliabilities ranged form .88 to .99. Alternate forms reliability, the correlation between scores on Form A with scores on Form B, ranged from a disturbingly low .36, reflecting poor consistency and low accuracy, to .92. Validity criteria were highly varied and so were the validity coefficients, usually between .13 and .45. To its credit, correlations between *Onomatopoeia and Images* and measures of intelligence were close to zero.

Useful as Exercises, Too

Apart from its use as a test, *Sounds and Images* makes a very good imagination stimulating creativity exercise, which is what it was created for in the first place (Torrance, Khatena, & Cunnington, 1973)

PERSONALITY AND BIOGRAPHICAL INVENTORIES

As noted earlier, creativity inventories are designed to measure the kinds of recurrent personality and biographical characteristics that appear in Chapter 4. Of course, as we have underscored in this chapter, there are many forms of creativity, creative thinking, and creative people, which makes the task of designing a super-valid creativity inventory (or divergent thinking test) rather challenging. Perhaps "next to impossible" would be more accurate.

Not All Traits Apply to All Creative People

Not every creative person is confident, curious, energetic, humorous, artistic, etc., and shows a plump history of creative activities and hobbies. However, these kinds of traits are sufficiently common among creative people

Characteristics
Approach
Words at All
Age Levels

that the "characteristics" approach to identifying creative persons works effectively, efficiently, and with high reliability and good validity with persons from preschool age to professional adults.

How Do You Think?

HDYT

The *How Do You Think?* (HDYT) test (Davis, 1975, 1991a; Davis & Subkoviak, 1978) is a high-school and adult-level test that includes 100 items in a five-point rating scale, "No," "To a small extent," "Average," "More than average," and "Definitely." The items measure self-evaluations of creativeness; self-ratings of independence, self-confidence, risk-taking, energy, adventurousness, curiosity, reflectiveness, humor and playfulness, liking for complexity, and artistic interests; belief in ESP, mental telepathy, flying saucers, and other psychic and extraordinary phenomena; and one's background of creative activities, interests, and hobbies.

High Internal
Reliability

Good
Concurrent
Validity

Construct
Validity

Internal consistency reliability coefficients have been high, about .91–.95 (Davis, 1975, 1991a; Shields, 1988), which means all items measure components of the same trait. Regarding concurrent validity, in its original development HDYT test scores correlated .41 with an overall creativity rating of four college student projects (creative writing, art or handicraft, ideas for inventions, and ideas for creative teaching). Davis and Bull (1978) demonstrated that HDYT scores increased as a result of taking a college creativity course, which is evidence of construct validity; that is, you would expect HDYT scores to increase if (a) the test measures creativity and (b) the training trained creativity.

Perceptual
Aberration Plus
Magical
Ideation:
Creative
Characteristics

Impulsive
Nonconformity

Further evidence of construct validity comes from Schuldberg, French, Stone, & Heberle, 1988). These researchers found that normal (?) male and female college students who were high in a combined measure of schizotypal tendencies, *perceptual aberration* (e.g., "My hearing is sometimes so sensitive that ordinary sounds become uncomfortable") and *magical ideation* (i.e., having superstitious and supernatural beliefs)—yes, these are traits of creative people—scored significantly higher on

HDYT than did a control group. Further, college students who were high in a measure of *impulsive nonconformity* produced significantly higher HDYT scores than a group who scored low (Schuldberg *et al.,* 1988). Interestingly Shields (1988) found that items in HDYT that measure belief in paranormal phenomena formed the strongest subscale. Moss (1991) found a correlation of .51 between HDYT scores and *intuition* scores on the *Myers-Briggs Type Indicator.*

Still More Construct Validity

Runco, Okuda, and Akau (1988) used HDYT scores as a criterion against which to validate a nine divergent thinking scores. Correlations (.14 to .45) between the divergent thinking measures the HDYT scores also provide construct validity for HDYT.

Useful in Predicting Success of Math/Science G/T Students

Runco, Okuda, and Hwang (1987) compared the ability of HDYT to predict success in a math and science program for gifted and talented high school students. HDYT scores were significantly related to a composite performance score (three exams plus two reports). Further, HDYT scores were related to combined exam scores and combined report scores when ability (PSAT-Math) scores were controlled. Runco recommended that "The use of the HDYT test was strongly supported," along with PSAT-Math, for selecting students for participation in such programs.

The *How Do You Think?* test does seem to measure the tendency to think and act in creative ways.

Group Inventory for Finding Interests II

GIFFI II

The *Group Inventory for Finding Interests II* (GIFFI II; Davis & Rimm, 1980, 1982; Rimm & Davis, 1983) is built of 60 items from the *How Do You Think?* test. A sample of GIFFI II items appears in Table 8.1.

Subscales Available

One advantage of GIFFI II is the subscale scoring. In addition to a total creativity score, test users receive scores on *confidence, challenge-inventiveness, imagination, creative arts and writing,* and *many interests.* These can have useful diagnostic value, for example, in identifying and understanding the timid creative student

Table 8.1

Sample Items from GIFFI II

Item	Trait
I have a very good sense of humor.	Humor
I have done a lot of creative writing.	Creative Activity
I enjoy thinking of new and better ways of doing things.	Originality
I tend to become childishly involved with simple things.	Playfulness, Curiosity
I am quite original and imaginative.	Self-rating of Creativity
I am very curious.	Curiosity
I have had many hobbies.	Wide Interests, Many Hobbies
I have been active in photography or film making.	Creative Activity
I am able to work intensely on a project for many hours.	Energy, Commitment
I would like to learn mountain climbing.	Adventurousness, Risk-Taking
I have a great many interests.	Wide Interests
I have participated in theatrical productions.	Creative Activity
I am artistic.	Artistic
I am a risk-taker.	Risk-Taking

who is high in everything except self-confidence, and who therefore avoids creative activities out of fear of rejection.

Works with Many Groups

The test appears to work very well. Internal consistency reliabilities have ranged from .91 to .96. The test has been validated with urban, suburban and rural students of many ethnic groups and all socio-economic levels. Table 8.2 summarizes validity coefficients using a validity criterion of teacher ratings of student creativeness (on a 5–point scale) combined with ratings of the creativeness of students' short stories (also on a 5–point scale). The median (central) correlation is .45, which is quite reasonable.

Table 8.2
Validity Coefficients for GIFFI II, Combined Criterion

School	N	Validity Coefficient	Mean Score
Rural Texas			
Grade 9	39	.62	175.8
10	63	.41	175.5
11	32	.20	175.5
12	26	.60	177.9
Overall	160	.45	
Milwaukee, Wisconsin			
Grades 9, 10, 11	28	.68	
Rural Wisconsin			
Grade 9	24	.40	157.8
10	21	.48	170.8
11	17	.59	174.8
12	22	.69	175.4
Overall	84	.53	
Suburban Wisconsin			
Grade 10	16	.28	208.9
11	20	.31	178.2
12	11	.28	179.5
Overall	47	.29	

Note: Combined criterion is teacher ratings plus story ratings.

Average Scores Not Related to Grade

Note in Table 8.2 that mean GIFFI II scores do not systematically increase over grades as would achievement or ability scores, which is evidence of the relative (not total) independence of creativity and intelligence.

Group Inventory for Finding Interests I

GIFFI I

The *Group Inventory for Finding Interests I* (GIFFI I; Davis & Rimm, 1982; Rimm & Davis, 1979, 1983) was designed for middle school students, grades 6 through 9. The test is very similar to the secondary level GIFFI II, although the wording and concepts naturally are more simple. As with GIFFI II the test includes 60 items in a 5-point rating-scale format from "No" to "Definitely." It produces a total creativity score and scores on the same subscales as GIFFI II. GIFFI I also shows internal consistency reliability coefficients above .90, indicating that all items are measuring the same trait, and validity coefficients comparable to those of GIFFI II (see Davis & Rimm, 1982).

Group Inventory for Finding Talent

GIFT

Creative Traits Appear in Elementary School

The *Group Inventory For Finding Talent* (GIFT; Rimm, 1976; Rimm & Davis, 1980) includes three forms, *Primary* for grades 1 and 2, *Elementary* for grades 3 and 4, and *Upper Elementary* for grades 5 and 6. The inventories are relatively brief, just 32, 34 and 33 yes-no items in length, with 25 items common to all three levels. The main difference between the forms is the size of the print.

The GIFT inventories primarily assess traits of independence, flexibility, curiosity, perseverance (energy), breadth of interests, and past creative activities and hobbies. Some items and the traits they measure appear in Table 8.3. Along with a total score, three subscale scores are available, *imagination, independence,* and *many interests.*

Valid With Many Groups, Many Nationalities

The GIFT tests have been used with children who are white, black, Spanish surnamed, high SES, low SES, urban, suburban, rural, immigrant, learning disabled, gifted, Israeli, French, Australian, and Chinese (Rimm & Davis, 1976, 1980). Internal reliability figures, using data from several studies, for the primary, elementary and upper elementary forms were .80, .86, and .88, respectively. Frequently, the validation research conducted by others was more favorable than our own, which testifies not only to the value and virtues of GIFT but to our unquestionable honesty as well. Validity coefficients usually range from about .25 to .45, sometimes lower and sometimes higher.

Preschool and Kindergarten Interest Descriptor

PRIDE

Preschool? Yes indeed, the creative traits are there and can be evaluated (by parents) with high reliability and good validity. PRIDE is the *Preschool and Kindergarten*

Table 8.3
Sample Items from GIFT
(Elementary School)

Item	Trait
I like to make up my own songs.	Creative activity
I like to paint pictures.	Interest in art
*I would rather play old games than new.	Flexibility
I have some really good ideas.	Independence
I like to take things apart to see how they work.	Curiosity
*Making up stories is a waste of time.	Interest in writing.
*A picture of the sun should always be colored yellow.	Independence
*I'd rather color or paint in a coloring book than make my own pictures.	Independence
*Easy puzzles are the most fun.	Perseverance
I ask a lot of questions.	Curiosity
It's all right to sometimes change the rules of the game.	Flexibility
I like things that are hard to do.	Perseverance
*I wish other children wouldn't ask so many questions.	Curiosity

*Negatively related to creativeness

Interest Descriptor. (The acronym PRIDE does not fit its title too well, but it sounds better than PKID.) PRIDE may be used with children age 3–6. It consists of 50 five-point rating scale items ("Not" to "Definitely"), and it measures the same kinds of traits assessed by GIFT, the two GIFFI tests, HDYT, and other creativity inventories— ". . . many interests, curiosity, independence, perseverance, imagination, playfulness, humor, and originality" (Rimm, 1983).

Filled out by Parents

Unlike the others, parents fill out the questionnaire, requiring about 20–35 minutes. Rimm (1983) noted that "Since a student self-report inventory tends to be unreliable for children who are ages 3–5, PRIDE was developed for use by parents based on their observation of their children."

Subscales

An internal consistency reliability of .92 was reported. Like GIFT, validity was established by correlating PRIDE scores with scores derived by combining teacher ratings of creativeness with experimenter ratings of the creativeness of children's pictures and short stories. With three samples of children, three validity coefficients were .38, .50 and .32. As with GIFT and the GIFFI tests, there are subscale scores (*many interests, independence-perseverance, imagination-playfulness, originality*) that may prove useful.

Exercise in Divergent Feeling

Another
CAP Test

Subscale Scores

We mentioned in the divergent thinking section that Frank Williams' *Creativity Assessment Packet* (CAP; Williams, 1980) included a divergent test and inventories for evaluating creative personality traits. One inventory is entitled *Exercise in Divergent Feeling,* which includes 50 items in a four-point rating-scale format. It asks students (grades 3 through 12) ". . . how curious, imaginative, complex and risky they believe they are" and produces four subscale scores (*curiosity, imagination, complexity, risk taking*) and a total creativity score. Reliability and validity data for the three CAP tests were mentioned earlier in conjunction with Williams' *Exercise in Divergent Thinking.*

The Williams Scale

Filled Out by
Parents,
Teachers

The *Williams Scale* is not a skin disorder, but the third of the three CAP tests. It consists of 48 three-point ("Often," "Sometimes," "Seldom") rating-scale items used by a parent or teacher to evaluate student creativeness. Eight sections assess factors of fluency, flexibility, originality, elaboration (which normally are considered divergent thinking abilities), curiosity, imagination, complexity, and risk-taking, with six questions per section. However, only a total creativity score is used.

Yeasayers
Score High

Open-Ended
Questions a Plus

One problem with this inventory is that all 48 items are positively related to creativity, which means that a busy "yeasayer" parent or teacher could quickly check the "Often" column with only a sketchy reading of the actual questions, thus inflating the scores. A unique and positive feature of the *Williams Scale* is the set of four open-ended qualitative questions on the back page. These ask parents to explain *why* they believe their child is intelligent or creative, and what they expect of a school program for creative students.

Creativity Attitude Survey

Elementary
Level

Similar to Other
Inventories

Schaefer (1971) created an elementary level creativity inventory designed for grades 4–6 entitled *Creativity Attitude Survey* (CAS). The CAS is 32 yes-no items in length and seems to measure many of the same traits evaluated by GIFT and the GIFFI's: confidence in one's own ideas and imagination, appreciation of fantasy and wild ideas, humor, an interest in art and writing, a desire for novelty, and an attraction to the abstract and magical. The manual reported internal consistency reliabilities of .75 and .81 and a five-week test-retest reliability coefficient of .61. Adequate.

Creativity
Training
Worked (and
Validated the
Test)

Evidence for validity was provided by research with 31 fifth-grade children who participated in a creativity training program for one hour per week for 14 weeks. Their CAS scores significantly improved from pretest to post-test while the scores of students in two control groups did not. Interestingly, 20 months later the children who received the creativity training still scored higher on the CAS than the others. Said Schaefer (1970), ". . . favorable changes in attitudes toward creativity seem to be a primary effect of creativity training programs, and these attitudinal changes seem to be relatively resistent to extinction over time."

Creativity
Training Helped
Minority
Students

A second validity study in primarily black and Puerto Rican schools with 321 experimental and 366 control children essentially replicated the earlier project: Post-test CAS scores for the children who received creativity training were significantly higher than for the control children. Finally, 17 students who were nominated by a fifth-grade language arts teacher as having shown "concrete evidence of creativity" scored higher on the CAS than 18 other students who were judged "equally bright." One review (McKee, 1985) concluded that, although the CAS has not been widely adopted, it could be used for evaluating the success of programs designed to teach creative thinking in elementary age children.

Renzulli-Hartman Rating Scale

It's the SRBCSS

Used By Teachers

As part of his series of rating scales entitled *Scales for Rating the Behavioral Characteristics of Superior Students* (Renzulli, 1983), gifted education leader Joseph Renzulli designed a scale that may be used by teachers to evaluate creativity in students. A teacher who knows the student well would rate him or her on each of 10 characteristics; the sum of the points for the 10 scales produces a total score. Because the scale is brief, and Joe has generously given permission, the scale is reproduced in its entirety in Table 8.4

Adjective Check List

From Absent-Minded to Zany

Creative Chimpanzee?

Convert to Standard Scores

The *Adjective Check List* (ACL; Gough, 1952) contains 300 adjectives, from *absent-minded* to *zany*. The test taker takes the test by marking those adjectives which apply to him or her. The ACL test manual does not include a scoring key for creativity. However, Domino (1970) devised a creativity key which includes 59 of the 300 adjectives. In scoring the ACL for creativity it is necessary to control for the number of adjectives checked, since an enthusiastic chimpanzee could endorse all 300 items and thereby earn a perfect creativity score. Domino's scoring system includes a table in which the raw score (number of the 59 creativity items checked) is converted to a standard score; a given standard score will depend upon the total number of adjectives checked.

Table 8.4
Renzulli-Hartman Scale for Rating Characteristics of Creative Students

	1	2	3	4
1. Displays a great deal of curiosity about many things; is constantly asking questions about anything and everything.	___	___	___	___
2. Generates a large number of ideas or solutions to problems and questions; often offers unusual ("way out"), unique, clever responses.	___	___	___	___
3. Is uninhibited in expressions of opinion; is sometimes radical and spirited in disagreement; is tenacious.	___	___	___	___
4. Is a high risk taker; is adventurous and speculative.	___	___	___	___
5. Displays a good deal of intellectual playfulness; fantasizes; imagines ("I wonder what would happen if. . . ."); manipulates ideas (i.e., changes, elaborates upon them); is often concerned with adapting, improving and modifying institutions, objects, and systems.	___	___	___	___
6. Displays a keen sense of humor and sees humor in situations that may not appear to be humorous to others.	___	___	___	___
7. Is usually aware of his impulses and more open to the irrational in himself (freer expression of feminine interest for boys, greater than usual amount of independence for girls); shows emotional sensitivity.	___	___	___	___
8. Is sensitive to beauty; attends to aesthetic characteristics of things.	___	___	___	___
9. Is nonconforming; accepts disorder; is not interested in details; is individualistic; does not fear being different.	___	___	___	___
10. Criticizes constructively; is unwilling to accept authoritarian pronouncements without critical examination.	___	___	___	___

Reproduced by permission of the author.

"Between you and me, it's the Torrance Tests or GIFT and GIFFI." (The Museum of Modern Art / Film Stills Archive.)

Sensitive to
Creativity
Training

The ACL, with the Domino scoring system, appears to be a very good adult creativity test. In one study with college students (Davis & Bull, 1978) the ACL showed very high internal consistency reliability and good validity (in predicting the rated creativeness of students' creative art and writing projects). Furthermore, the ACL was sensitive to creativity training effects: Students who had taken your author's creativity course scored higher than students who had not yet taken the course. Not all creativity tests will show changes in personality and self-concept as a result of creativity training experiences.

Scoring Key
and Conversion
Table

Since the ACL has proven valuable, the 59 adjectives in the scoring key (Table A) and the table for converting the raw scores to standard scores (Table B) are reproduced at the end of this chapter, both courtesy of Professor George Domino.

Barron-Welsh Art Scale

Preference for
Complexity

Many lists of characteristics of creative people will include "preference for complexity and asymmetry," a finding attributable to the research of Welsh and Barron (1963) with their *Barron-Welsh Art Scale.* This test is a set of 80 drawings, some simple and balanced and others complex and asymmetrical. Artists tend to like the complex and asymmetrical and to not like the simple and balanced, Interestingly, so do more creative people. Some patterns similar to those in the Art Scale have been created in Figure 8.5.

There is a "correct" answer for each of the items ("like" or "don't like"). The creativity score is the total number of correct answers. The test has not been widely used in the schools (translation: your author doesn't know of *any* studies with elementary or secondary students). The test may or may not be useful below the college level.

Comment

As a final word, we must repeat the opening cautions. Creative thinking, creative processes, creative behavior, and creative people are indisputably complex, involving a mix of experience, abilities, drives, personality dispositions, and thinking processes. The apparent simplicity

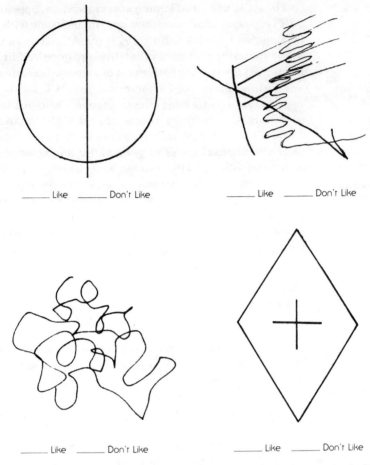

_____ Like _____ Don't Like   _____ Like _____ Don't Like

_____ Like _____ Don't Like   _____ Like _____ Don't Like

Figure 8.5. Patterns similar to those in the *Barron-Welsh Art Scale*. Are you simple and balanced? Or complex and smudgy?

of the tests described in this chapter stands in stark contrast with the complexity of "creativity." Nonetheless, many of these tests are remarkably successful in producing reasonable correlations with sound criteria of creativeness. They are useful. To repeat another point, to be truly confident of creativity test results, two criteria should be used. If a student scores high on both a personality/biographical inventory and a divergent thinking test, or on one of these along and is rated as "highly creative" by a teacher or parent, one can be quite confident that the student has strong creative tendencies.

SUMMARY

Creativity is exceedingly complex. For example, creativity is found in every area of human endeavor; it may appear in our personal, educational, or professional lives; there is self-actualized and special-talent creativity; it can be forced or intuitive; and it happens in children and the elderly. Freud blamed unconscious neurotic conflicts, while Jung cited his mysterious archetypal images.

We also noted that creativity test scores may be influenced by such factors as having time limits, removing children from interesting activities, giving the tests in a barren environment or a room where intelligence tests were given, having a warm-up activity, or making small changes in instructions.

Some critics complain that simplistic creativity test items do not correspond to peoples' implicit conception of creative thinking. Also, each creativity test reflects the beliefs and preconceptions of the test developer.

Nonetheless, creativity tests have confirmed that creativity exists, that creative people can be identified, and that creativity is systematically related to other characteristics and behaviors.

Creativity tests are most widely used to help select creatively gifted children for programs for the gifted. The U.S.O.E. and the Renzulli definitions of giftedness include high creativity. For confidence in selecting creatively gifted children, two criteria of creativeness should be used.

Creativity tests are used in research. The tests also are used to evaluate the effectiveness of creativity training.

Creativity tests can provide helpful information to guidance counselors, particularly regarding troubled or underachieving students who may be highly creative; the tests also permit the prescription of more suitable (creative) learning activities.

Two main categories of published tests are divergent thinking tests and personality/biographical inventories, both of which usually show good evidence of construct validity and criterion-related validity.

Among divergent thinking tests, the Torrance Tests of Creative Thinking are by far the most widely used. There are seven verbal tests and three figural tests, both in Form

A and B. The tests virtually always are scored for fluency, flexibility, originality, and, for the figural tests, elaboration.

The streamlined (?) scoring system, designed to expedite scoring and provide conceptually rich additional information, includes 5 norm-referenced scores plus 13 criterion-referenced "creative strengths."

The 1988 version of Guilford's Structure of Intellect includes 180 cells. His creativity tests stem from the divergent thinking (operation) part of the model. Meeker uses the SOI model and her SOI-Learning Abilities tests in a diagnostic-remediation fashion.

The Monitor Test of Creative Potential includes three subtests (Writing Words, Picture Decorations, License Plates) that measure SOI factors.

Williams' Exercise in Divergent Thinking is part of his Creativity Assessment Packet (CAP). It is similar to Torrance's Picture Completion subtest, and produces both figural scores (fluency, flexibility, originality, elaboration) and a verbal score based upon title originality.

Wallach and Kogan administered their tests in an untimed and gamelike atmosphere. The battery includes verbal and non-verbal subtests which are scored for fluency and uniqueness.

The Getzels and Jackson tests also include verbal and non-verbal subtests. Their unique Fables Test requires a moralistic, humorous, and sad ending for each of four fables. Their Make-Up Problems test has been used to measure mathematical creativity.

Torrance's Thinking Creatively in Action and Movement is a preschool measure of creativity. Three subtests ask for different kinds of movements, actions or pantomimes; a fourth asks for unusual uses for paper cups.

Thinking Creatively With Sounds and Words includes the two tests Sounds and Images and Onomatopoeia and Images, which are a different sort of "divergent thinking" test. With Sounds and Images, test-takers write down mental images stimulated by four abstract sounds. Onomatopoeia and Images is similar, except that the stimuli are words.

Regarding personality/biographical inventories, not all traits apply to all creative people, of course.

How Do You Think? is a high-school and adult-level inventory that has shown high internal consistency reliability, good concurrent validity, and good construct validity.

GIFFI II, based on How Do You Think?, is a high school inventory; GIFFI I is a middle school inventory. Both produce subscale scores and a total creativity score.

GIFT measures some of the traits assessed by GIFFI I and II, for example, independence, curiosity, motivation, humor, wide interests, and past creative activities. GIFT also has subscales and has been validated in many countries.

PRIDE is a preschool inventory filled out by parents; it measures many of the same traits as GIFT and GIFFI I and II.

Exercise in Divergent Feeling is part of Williams' CAP. Like the above inventories, it measures traits commonly associated with creativity and produces subscale scores.

The Williams Scale, the third CAP test, is used by a parent or teacher to evaluate a child's creativeness.

Schaefer's Creativity Attitude Survey is an elementary level inventory that also measures creativity traits.

The Renzulli-Hartman Rating Scale, used by teachers to evaluate student creativeness, includes just 10 items that measure important traits of creative people.

Domino's scoring key for Gough's Adjective Check List includes 59 of the 300 adjectives.

The Barron-Welsh Art Scale is a different type of personality inventory. Eighty abstract drawings measure a preference for complexity and asymmetry.

As a final comment, despite their apparent simplicity, many of the tests show high reliability and good validity.

Table A
Creativity Scale for the Adjective Check List
Developed by George Domino

absentminded	disorderly	logical
active	dissatisfied	moody
adaptable	distractible	original
adventurous	egotistical	outspoken
alert	energetic	quick
aloof	enthusiastic	rational
ambitious	humorous	rebellious
argumentative	hurried	reflective
artistic	idealistic	reserved
assertive	imaginative	resourceful
autocratic	impulsive	restless
capable	independent	sarcastic
careless	individualistic	self-centered
clear-thinking	industrious	sensitive
clever	ingenious	serious
complicated	insightful	sharp-witted
confident	intelligent	spontaneous
curious	interests wide	tactless
cynical	intolerant	unconventional
demanding	inventive	

The 300 item *Adjective Check List* is available from Consulting Psychologists Press, 577 College Avenue, Palo Alto, California. It is an adult personality test which can be scored for creativity by counting (a) the number of the above 59 adjectives checked and (b) the total number of adjectives checked. These numbers are used in Table B to find the standard (T) scores for creativity. It is a good creativity test.

Conversion of ACL Raw Scores to T Scores

Total # of Adjectives Checked	MALES				FEMALES			
	1–75	76–95	96–121	122–300	1–78	79–98	99–119	120–300
Raw Score								
59	116	108	102	87	126	116	105	83
58	115	106	100	86	124	115	103	82
57	113	105	99	84	123	113	101	80
56	111	103	97	82	121	111	99	79
55	110	101	95	81	119	109	98	77
54	108	100	93	79	117	107	96	76
53	107	98	91	77	115	105	94	74
52	105	96	89	76	113	103	92	73
51	103	94	88	74	112	101	90	71
50	102	93	86	72	110	99	89	70
49	100	91	84	71	108	98	87	68
48	99	89	82	69	106	96	85	67
47	97	87	80	67	104	94	83	65
46	95	86	79	66	102	92	82	64
45	94	84	77	64	101	90	80	62
44	92	82	75	62	99	88	78	61
43	91	80	73	60	97	86	76	59
42	89	79	71	59	95	84	75	58
41	87	77	69	57	93	82	73	56
40	86	75	68	55	91	80	71	55
39	84	73	66	54	90	79	69	53
38	83	72	64	52	88	77	68	52
37	81	70	62	50	86	75	66	50
36	79	68	60	49	84	73	64	49
35	78	66	59	47	82	71	62	47
34	76	65	57	45	80	69	60	46
33	75	63	55	44	78	67	59	44
32	73	61	53	42	77	65	57	43
31	72	60	51	40	75	63	55	41
30	70	58	50	39	73	62	53	40

Conversion of ACL Raw Scores to T Scores

Total # of Adjectives Checked	MALES				FEMALES			
	1–75	76–95	96–121	122–300	1–78	79–98	99–119	120–300
Raw Score								
29	68	56	48	37	71	60	52	38
28	67	54	46	35	69	58	50	37
27	65	53	44	34	67	56	48	35
26	64	51	42	32	66	54	46	34
25	62	49	40	30	64	52	45	32
24	60	47	39	29	62	50	43	31
23	59	46	37	27	60	48	41	29
22	57	44	35	25	58	46	39	28
21	56	42	33	24	56	44	38	26
20	54	40	31	22	55	43	36	25
19	52	39	30	20	53	41	34	23
18	51	37	28	19	51	39	32	22
17	49	35	26	17	49	37	30	20
16	48	33	24	15	47	35	29	19
15	46	32	22	14	45	33	27	17
14	44	30	20	12	44	31	25	16
13	43	28	19	10	42	29	23	14
12	41	26	17	9	40	27	22	13
11	40	25	15	7	38	25	20	11
10	38	23	13	5	36	24	18	10
9	36	21	11	3	34	22	16	8
8	35	20	10	2	33	20	15	7
7	33	18	8	1	31	18	13	5
6	32	16	6		29	16	11	4
5	30	14	4		27	14	9	2
4	28	13	2		25	12	8	1
3	27	11	1		23	10	6	
2	25	9			21	8	4	
1	24	7			20	7	2	

9

creativity in gifted education

[*Scene: Hell. Devil with short horns, pointed tail, and dressed in red long johns sits behind desk in office cluttered with fat record books and an old typewriter. A flickering Hellish fire illuminates the room. A sign on the desk reads "GIFTED DEMON PROGRAM." A portly applicant is just entering.*]

Devil: (Impatiently) Well, c'mon sonny, we haven't got all eternity you know! What's your problem?

King Henry VIII: Sonny? Sonny? My good sir, I'm Henry the Eighth, former King of all England! I'm interested in your Gifted Demon Program. I assure you I've had plenty of experience in heinous torture and corrupt leadership. Besides, I've been boiling in fish oil for 450 years and I'm becoming an extraordinarily smelly prune! A change, good sir, would be most welcome.

Devil: Hmmmm. Look Hank, we've got too many kings, kaisers, caliphs, commissars, and you-name-it in the program now. How about a transfer to Flogging and Eye Gouging?

Henry: Not really.

Devil: Well Hank, what we really need are creative troublemakers—how did you do on the *Evil and Skulduggery Test?*

Henry: 87 out of 100.

Devil: Not bad, not bad! Any special accomplishments? Evidence of sinister gifts? Villainous talents? Awards for diabolical evil-doing? How are you on debauchery and depravity? Can you make college students come up one credit short for graduation?

Henry: Well, I've had six wives, beheaded two of them, and I tossed the Catholic Church right out of England.

Devil: (Smiling). Not bad at all! Actually Hank, I like your style. Beheading's okay, but what you did to the Pope just tickles my tail! You're in! On your way out, would you send in the next applicant?

Henry: My pleasure, sir, and thank you so much. You'll never regret this.

(Henry VIII leaves; Cinderella's stepmother Rubella enters)

Devil: Well, hello Rubella! How are things down on Brimstone IV?

Rubella: (Noticeably upset) Oh, it just couldn't be worse, your Rogueful Royalty! All the time burn, burn, burn! My mascara is a mess and look at my hands!

Devil: Glad to hear things are so infernal! Now, you're interested in our Gifted Demon Program. Wicked Stepmothers' Division I assume?

Rubella: Oh yes, your Sinful Sovereignty! I'm good at beating step-children, dressing them in rags, and making them stay home to sweep up cinders. And I can be very cruel to Walt Disney's mice!

Devil: Not much imagination, I'm afraid. What about glitching computers? Causing accidents and fires? Starting wars? Promoting social diseases?

Rubella: Sir! I have my morals!

Devil: That's what I was afraid of, Rubella—it's back to Brimstone IV. Nobody ever said I was a nice guy!

Rubella: (Sobbing) But my eye shadow is streaking, your Heinous Highness, and
. . .

Devil: Now would you send in Rasputin and tell the Wicked Witch of the West it'll be just a few minutes.

Gifted Kids Have Special Needs, Require Differentiated Services

G/T Education Growing Worldwide

The education of the gifted and talented has become a highly visible educational reform movement. At present, every state in the USA has enacted legislation which (a) recognizes that gifted students exist, (b) acknowledges that they have special needs which usually are not met in regular educational programs, and (c) recommends or requires differentiated educational services for them. Gifted programs also are being created across Canada and in such exotic spots as mainland China, People's Republic of China, Hong Kong, Manila, South Africa, Egypt, Saudi Arabia, India, Australia, Mexico, Dominican Republic, Guam, Brazil, and Russia.

Creativity Plays Core Role

As We will see in this chapter, creativity plays a key role in all aspects of gifted education—defining "giftedness," formulating goals and objectives of a program, identifying gifted and talented students, and planning acceleration and enrichment activities that enhance students' creative potential.

Two Aims of Gifted Education

The two fundamental aims of G/T programs are: ". . . to help individual gifted and talented students develop their high potential, and to provide society with educated professionals who are creative leaders and problem solvers" (Davis & Rimm, 1989).

DEFINITIONS OF GIFTEDNESS

Definition of
"Gifted"
Determines Who
Gets Services

Defining *gifted and talented* is extremely important because the particular definition adopted by a school district will determine who is selected for the special services and training of a gifted program. Also, there is continual danger that one's definition, and consequent identification methods, will discriminate against such special populations as poor, minority, handicapped, underachieving, and even female gifted students.

Terms
Sometimes Used
Interchangeably

Or on a
Continuum

There is no great consensus on the distinction between "gifted" and "talented," even among experts. For example, it is common and acceptable to use the terms interchangeably—we can speak of a "gifted artist" or a "talented artist." In contrast, based on our common use of the terms, the general public and some scholars see *talent* and *giftedness* on a continuum, as when we speak of "talented" musicians, writers, and scientists, only a few of whom are truly "gifted." But we never reverse this usage.

No Term for
Extremely
Gifted

As another definitional consideration, every G/T program includes students who barely meet admission criteria, along with one or two others who are extraordinarily gifted. We have no special term to designate extremely gifted students, although "extremely gifted" and "low-incidence gifted" are used, as are "child prodigies" and the tongue-in-cheek terms "severely gifted" and "profoundly gifted."

Five Categories of Definitions

As an introduction to the definition problem, Stankowski (1978) outlined five categories of definitions of "gifts" and "talents." All but the first currently are used in various programs to guide the identification process.

Outstanding
Achievements

First, *after-the-fact* definitions emphasize established prominence in one of the professions. The "gifted" are those who have shown consistently outstanding achievements, usually creative ones.

IQ Cutoff

Second, *IQ* definitions set a cutoff point on the IQ scale. "Gifted" students are those scoring at or above the cutoff, for example, an IQ score of 120 or 130.

Percentage
Cutoff

Third, *percentage* definitions set a fixed proportion of the school (or district) as "gifted," based on IQ scores, overall grades, or sometimes grades in particular areas, such as math, and science. The percentage may be a restrictive 3 to 5 percent or a more generous 15 to 20 percent, as in Renzulli's Schoolwide Enrichment Model (described later).

Talent Area
Focus

Fourth, *talent* definitions focus on students who are outstanding in art, music, math, science, or other specific aesthetic or academic area.

Creativity
(Right on!)

Finally, *creativity* definitions emphasize creative abilities and talents, as reflected in creativity test scores, teachers nominations, or ratings of creative products.

General Innate Gifts vs. Specific Talents (Performances)

Cohn: Domains
of Giftedness
with Specific
Talents within a
Domain

Some educators use the word *gifted* to describe highly intelligent "intellectually gifted" persons and the word *talented* to refer to persons who demonstrate superior skills and abilities—"talents"—in one or a few specific areas (e.g., art, math, science, language, or social areas). In one version of the general gifts vs. specific talents approach, Cohn (1981) identified three central domains of giftedness, each of which subdivided into specific talents. *Intellectual* giftedness was subdivided into quantitative, verbal, spatial, and "other specific talent dimensions." The *artistic* domain split into the fine arts, performing arts, and "other specific talent dimensions." *Social* giftedness separated into leadership talent, empathic/altruistic talent, and (you guessed it) "other specific talent dimensions."

Gagne': Innate
Abilities (Gifts)
vs.
Performances
(Talents)

Under-Achiever
Has Gifts, Not
Talents: Gagne'

In another variation, Gagne (1985, 1991) stressed the distinction between innately determined *abilities* (or aptitudes) and *performances.* He identified four domains of aptitudes: *intellectual, creative, socio-emotional,* and *sensorimotor,* each of which subdivided into specific types of gifts. Said Gagne (1991), "*Giftedness* corresponds to competence which is distinctly above average in one or more domains . . . *Talent* corresponds to performance

Gifts Activated
by Catalysts

which is distinctly above average in one or more fields of human activity." One thus would speak of math talent, music talent, or sculpting talent to describe the activities of persons who *perform* well in these areas. With Gagne's distinction, an underachiever is one who possesses the gifts (aptitudes), but not the talents (performances). The gifts are assumed to be activated into performances by such catalysts as motivation, personality, and a supportive environment (Gagne', 1985, 1991).

U.S. Office of Education Definition

The sun rises and sets with the 1978 U.S. Office of Education definition of "gifts and talents," which was modified from an earlier statement (Marland, 1972). The definition reads:

U.S.O.E
Definition: Five
Categories

(The gifted and talented are) ". . . children and, whenever applicable, youth who are identified at the pre-school, elementary, or secondary level as possessing demonstrated or potential abilities that give evidence of high performance capability in areas such as *intellectual, creative, specific academic* or *leadership* ability or in the *performing and visual arts,* and who by reason thereof require services or activities not ordinarily provided by the school" (U.S. Congress, Educational Amendment of 1978 [P.L. 95–561, IX (A)]).

A Multiple
Talent
Definition

Note that the definition recognizes not only high general intelligence, but gifts in specific academic areas, creativity, leadership, and the arts. It is considered a "multiple-talent" definition. Note also that by including "demonstrated or *potential* abilities" the definition includes underachievers, whose abilities may not be demonstrated in actual high-quality performances.

Curious
Inconsistency

As an ironic fact, most states and individual school districts accept the U.S.O.E definition in their formal legislation and in written program plans. But then blithely

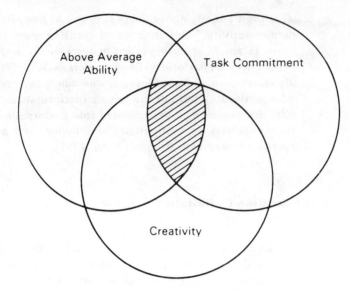

Figure 9.1. Renzulli's three-ring model. Reprinted by permission of J. S. Renzulli.

base actual identification upon intellectual criteria—
ability scores, grades, teacher nominations for academic
excellence—and ignore the other categories. This is called
"paying lip service" (can you say "paying lip service"?).

Renzulli's Three-Ring Definition

High Creativity,
High
Motivation,
Above-Average
Ability

Joseph Renzulli's *three-ring definition* of giftedness
also is well-known and widely accepted. Renzulli (1977;
Renzulli & Reis, 1991; Renzulli, Reis, & Smith, 1981) has
argued that people who truly make creative contributions
to society—that is, truly gifted and talented persons—
possess three characteristics: They have high *creativity,*
high *task commitment* (motivation), and at least above
average (though not necessarily outstanding) *ability* (intelligence; Figure 9.1). It has been a common mistake
among people who endorse Renzulli's three-ring definition to select for gifted and talented programs only those

"I'm above average in ability and high in creativity," said Sleazy Sam, "but motivation was always a problem!" (The Museum of Modern Art/Film Stills Archive.)

children who appear to be strong in all three character-istics—creativity, motivation, and intelligence. In fact, says Renzulli and Reis (1991), schools should use var-ious—and flexible—criteria to select students, including both objective test scores and subjective non-test cri-teria. Students should

Creativity and Motivation: "Developmental Objectives"

". . . display or have the potential to display above average ability in one or more academic areas, or in special aptitudes such as music, art, drama, leadership, or interpersonal skills. The other two rings [motivation, cre-ativity] are considered *developmental objectives* that we attempt to promote in the target population . . ."

That is, as we will see in the discussion of Renzulli's Schoolwide Enrichment Model later, students who show or develop the creativity and motivation will volunteer to work on individual projects with a resource room G/T teachers.

Taylor's Multiple-Talent Totem Poles

Most or All Students Are Above Average (or Gifted) in Something

Thinking Talents

Talents for Getting Ideas Implemented

Calvin Taylor's (1986, 1988) *multiple-talent totem pole* concept does not define "gifts and talents." Rather, it raises our awareness that virtually all students possess special skills and talents of some variety. A recent ver-sion of Taylor's totem poles appears in Figure 9.2. The second through sixth talents (productive thinking, com-municating, forecasting, decision-making, planning) were called "thinking talents," and were described as ones that contribute to creative thinking and problem solving. The final three (implementing, human relations, discerning opportunities) are essential for getting ideas into action.

The multiple-talent totem pole concept complicates the question: Who should be selected to participate in the G/T program? Different children would be chosen de-pending upon which talent is emphasized. Said Taylor (1986, p. 317), "Everyone has both strengths and weak-nesses all the way across the totem poles . . ." Further,

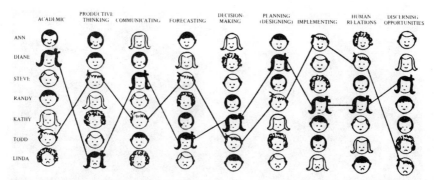

Figure 9.2. Taylor's multiple-talent totem poles, 1984 extended version. Copyright © 1984, Calvin W. Taylor. Reprinted by permission.

"The more talents that students have activated in schooling, the more chance that the students will find one or more talents in which they are above average or even highly talented" (p. 320).

CHARACTERISTICS OF GIFTED STUDENTS

Developmental Advancement

Motivation, Confidence, High Moral Thinking, Humor

While high creativity is one characteristic that is important in selecting students for G/T programs, intellectual giftedness usually is valued even more. Apart from its appearance in high IQ scores and high grades, intellectual giftedness can be seen more informally in precocious language skills, including an advanced vocabulary, superior comprehension, and very logical thinking processes. Also common among the intellectually gifted are early reading, writing, math, music, and art skills, along with advanced interests and very wide interests. There also are many common affective traits, such as high motivation and persistence; confidence, low anxiety, better self-concepts, and an internal locus of evaluation; plus higher levels of moral thinking, due to a strong empathy ability and good sense. Superior humor also is common.

Prefer Independent Study, Projects

Due to their ability, creativity, independence, and motivation, gifted students prefer to learn in less-structured, more flexible ways—independent study and projects, for example (Griggs & Dunn, 1984).

"I don't know about academic talent, productive thinking, or communicating, but she has terrific sleeping talent," said Captain Calvin Taylor. (The Museum of Modern Art/Film Stills Archive.)

**Terman's
Termites**
We should mention the Terman studies, since so many lists of characteristics of gifted and talented students are based on his and his colleagues long-term research (e.g., Terman & Oden, 1947). In the 1920s Lewis Terman (1925) and others used the *Stanford-Binet Intelligence Scale,* which Terman developed, to identify 1,500 boys and girls with IQ scores of 140 and above—the top 1 percent. The personal and professional activities of these people were studied and followed-up in a series of interviews and mailings for the next 60 years. (Many are now happily in their graves—the only escape from Terman's project.)

Recall test: In Chapter 4 we saw the 1895 claim of Cesare Lombroso that "men of (creative) genius" were:

a. sickly and generally emaciated.
b. hunched-back, lame, or club-footed, due to rickets.
c. short, bald, and forgetful.
d. sterile and stuttering.
e. any or all of the above.

Terman:
Lombroso
Wrong:

Yes, "e" is correct. In fact, Terman actually found that "the average member of our group is a slightly better physical specimen than the average child . . ." As reflected in the traits listed above, they also were superior in all academic areas. They were more trustworthy, and they were better adjusted and more emotionally stable in their youth and adulthood, as evidenced by lower rates of mental illness and suicide.

IDENTIFICATION OF GIFTED STUDENTS

Identification:
Related to
Definitions,
Characteristics

Space will not permit a detailed discussion of the tests, inventories, rating forms, and the matrix systems that combine data, nor the problems and delicate issues of deciding who is and who is not "gifted and talented" (see Davis & Rimm, 1989). The identification methods are, or should be, related to both the definitions and the characteristics of giftedness described in the previous sections. Selection should include both objective scores and subjective nominations and ratings.

Use Two
Creativity
Criteria

Results of Using
Criteria Rigidly

Torrance: Using
Only IQ Scores
Misses 70% of
the Most
Creative

Creative talent is one criteria for selection, based on teacher ratings of "creativeness" or creativity test scores. For accurate identification of creative students, as noted in Chapter 8 teachers should use *two* criteria of creativity. A student scoring high on both is extremely likely to be identified correctly as "creative." Unfortunately, many state governments and school districts ignore creativity altogether in favor of teacher recommendations, grades, or ability (IQ) scores. As a sample of not uncommon happenings: An unimaginative and unmotivated student with an IQ score of 130 (the cutoff score) may be stamped "gifted" and admitted to a G/T program, while an energetic creative person with an IQ of only 129 is excluded. Said Paul Torrance (1983), "The use of intelligence tests to identify gifted students misses about 70 percent of those who are equally gifted on creativity criteria." Bureaucracies are not particularly famous for fairness, flexibility, or agreeing with your author's totally sensible concern for creative talent.

The following is an unelaborated list of identification methods, which are used singly or in various combinations.

Methods

Intelligence test scores
Achievement test scores
Teacher nominations (informal or using rating scales)
Creativity test scores
Parent nominations (usually using a structured form)
Peer nominations
Self-nominations
Product evaluations

Talent Pool
Approach More
Reasonable

As we noted in the section on percentage definitions, some programs will select a restrictive 3 to 5 percent; others will use a *talent pool* approach and identify 15 to 20 percent, with a flexible and more reasonable "when in doubt, admit" philosophy.

GOALS AND CURRICULA OF PROGRAMS FOR THE GIFTED

There have been many lists of the needs of gifted and talented students, which translate into the goals and curricula of G/T programs (see Davis & Rimm, 1989, pp. 103–104). An abbreviated overview of curriculum for the gifted would include the following:

G/T Program
Goals

1. Maximum achievement in basic skills, including learning at an appropriate level and pace, and based on needs rather than grade-level appropriateness.
2. Content beyond the prescribed curriculum, related to broad-based issues, abstract ideas, theories, and problems that require reflective, evaluative, critical and creative thinking; using materials and resources beyond the designated grade-level, perhaps to develop products.

Product and performance evaluations are one way to identify creative talent. "It would be easier if you didn't keep time on my nose," said the budding pianist. (The Museum of Modern Art/Film Stills Archive.)

3. Exposure to a variety of fields of study, including new disciplines and new occupations.
4. Student-selected content based on interests and needs, including in-depth studies of self-selected topics.
5. Experience in creative thinking and problem solving; futuristic thinking.
6. Development of thinking skills, such as independent and self-directed study skills, library skills, and research/scientific skills; critical thinking in the sense of evaluating biases, credibility, logic, and consistency; decision-making, planning, organizing, analyzing, synthesizing, and evaluating.
7. Development self-awareness and self-understanding regarding one's capabilities, interests, needs; appreciating individual differences; relating to other gifted students.

8. Development of motivation, including independent and self-directed thinking and work, and increased achievement motivation that includes high-level educational ·and career aspirations.

Avoid "Fun and
Games,"
Busywork

All acceleration and enrichment activities should be planned with these types of objectives in mind. Although it is essential that the learning experiences be enjoyable, they should not just be "fun and games" or busywork designed to keep students occupied.

ACCELERATION AND ENRICHMENT ALTERNATIVES

Acceleration

Acceleration:
Results in
Advanced
Placement

Enrichment: All
Else

A handy way to differentiate *acceleration* from *enrichment* in gifted education programs is to define *acceleration* as any strategy that results in advanced placement or credit. *Enrichment* includes strategies that supplement or go beyond standard grade-level work, but do not result in advanced placement or credit (that is, anything else).

Some popular acceleration strategies are:

Acceleration
Strategies

1. Early admission to kindergarten or first grade
2. Grade skipping ("full acceleration")
3. Subject skipping ("partial acceleration")
4. Early admission to junior or senior high school
5. Credit by examination
6. College courses while in high school
7. College correspondence courses in high school
8. Early admission to college (early high school graduation)
9. Telescoping, for example, four years of high school into three

Julian Stanley's
SMPY

The best-known example of accelerating bright secondary students into college level mathematics courses is the Study of Mathematically Precocious Youth (SMPY)

Top SAT-M
Seventh
Graders

Do SMPY
Students Get
No Sleep?

Smorgasbord of
Opportunities

Many Benefits

program. SMPY was born at Johns Hopkins University in 1971, brainchild of Julian Stanley. Over a 12-year period more than 10,000 predominantly seventh-grade boys and girls were identified as mathematically precocious (top 1 percent) based on their *Scholastic Aptitude Test-Mathematics* scores (Benbow, 1991). The students participated in fast-paced summer math programs at Johns Hopkins, usually covering one to two years of high school algebra and geometry in three weeks, because, said Stanley, they are working, not sleeping. In addition, they are counseled regarding the suitability of a smorgasbord of acceleration options: They may attend college part-time, earn college credit by examination by taking Advanced Placement tests, skip a grade, collapse two or more years of math into one, or enter college early, perhaps by skipping high school graduation. The results, said Stanley and Benbow (1986), are an increased zest for learning, enhanced feelings of self-worth, reduced egotism due to the humbling effects of working with intellectual peers, far better preparation for college, better fellowship opportunities, and the opportunity to enter a professional career at an earlier age.

Talent Search:
Based on High
SAT-M or
SAT-V

In recent years the SMPY model has evolved into the *talent search* concept, which uses both the SAT-Math and the SAT-Verbal to identify and provide advanced (summer) course work for both mathematically and verbally talented students. See Benbow (1991) and Cohn (1991) for details.

Acceleration
Indirectly
Fosters Creative
Productivity

Most acceleration strategies do not "teach creativity" directly in the same sense that this book teaches creative attitudes, techniques, and an understanding of the topic of creativity. However, by advancing students' knowledge in a subject matter field we indirectly enable them to think creatively in that area, and prepare them to make creative discoveries and innovations. They have advanced information with which to be creative.

Enrichment: Grouping Plans

The Old Pull-
Out Plan

Many school districts offer enrichment activities within some type of *grouping* structure. For example, the most common grouping plan is the *pull-out* program. Elementary students are "pulled out" of their regular classes two or three hours per week to participate in enrichment activities guided by a G/T teacher-coordinator. If the students must be transported to a resource room elsewhere in the district to work with a "resource teacher," the plan is called a *resource room plan*, which is extremely similar in operation to a pull-out plan. The recurrent criticism of pull-out programs is that they are a part-time solution to a full-time problem.

Cluster Grouping

With *cluster grouping*, usually five to ten gifted, say, fourth-graders are "clustered" together in one class, along with other students. They work on independent research projects or advanced academic subjects individually or in small groups.

Special Classes

Some schools will create *special classes* for gifted students within a particular grade level or age range. In addition to covering prescribed grade-level objectives, a variety of enrichment, personal development, and skill development experiences—including creative skills—are planned.

Mainstreaming

Many schools *mainstream* their gifted students, allowing each teacher to provide appropriate activities for the one or more G/T students in his or her class. In some cases mainstreaming is a default plan—the school has made no other provisions to meet the special needs of its gifted and talented children. In other cases, such as in the Pyramid Model described later, mainstreaming the majority of G/T students is a carefully considered and effective plan.

Special Elementary Schools

Magnet Schools Are Attractive

Some large cities have *special elementary schools* for the gifted, to which students from throughout the school district are bused daily. A similar large-city option is *magnet high schools,* in which an entire high school attracts students interested or gifted in, for example, math and science, the performing arts, business, or technical and trade skills.

School-within-a-School

With the *school-within-a-school* plan, gifted students from around the district attend with regular students for part of the day (e.g., physical education, study hall, manual arts, home economics), but also attend special classes taught by special teachers.

Enrichment: Activities

The following are enrichment activities that may be planned within most or all of the grouping options described above.

Library Research Projects

With *library research projects* students pursue answers to a specific problem, such as "Why and how was the Great Wall of China built?" The final product need not be a neatly written report. It could be a more creative demonstration of some activity or skill, a student-made movie or slide show, a TV news report, a mini-play, or a newspaper column.

Art Projects, Science Projects

Many Abilities Strengthened

There are virtually limitless types of art, theatre, and scientific research projects, all of which will require creative thinking and problem solving. Many abilities that underlie and contribute to creative productivity will be stretched, such as problem defining, analytic thinking, and critical thinking; Taylor's totem pole talents of communicating, forecasting, decision making (evaluation), and planning; affective traits such as confidence, risk-taking; and others.

Learning Centers

Some teachers effectively use *learning centers,* either teacher-made or commercial, to engage gifted students in art, math, science, social studies, creative writing, music, or language-learning projects.

Field Trips

Field trips can acquaint students with cultural or scientific topics or with career possibilities. Field trips are valuable for all students; gifted students should have specific problems to solve or questions to be answered.

Saturday and Summer Programs: Mini-Courses

A few colleges and universities sponsor *Saturday programs* and *summer programs.* These typically take the form of mini-courses in art, theatre, biology, TV production, limnology, and so forth, and are taught by college undergraduates, graduate students, or faculty. There is much creative involvement within subject areas.

Mentorships

A *mentorship* traditionally involves an extended relationship between a student and a community professional. The student learns the activities, responsibilities, problems, attitudes, and life style associated with the career. While normally a high school plan, mentorships are becoming a popular elementary level enrichment alternative for gifted students.

Gifted and regular students benefit from mentorships. This student is learning the skill of boat chimney repair from Captain Sally Sailorsuit. "Just don't forget your lantern," reminded the captain. (The Museum of Modern Art / Film Stills Archive.)

Future Problem
Solving

Many schools use the *Future Problem Solving* program as an enrichment activity. A team of five students (in an upper elementary, middle school, or high school division) is registered with the National Future Problem Solving Program at St. Andrews College in Laurinburg, North Carolina.[1] The team is sent three future-oriented practice problems. For 1989–90 the problems dealt with shrinking tropical forests, the arms race, and poverty. Past problems have concerned UFO's, ocean communities, robotics, nuclear war, prisons, lasers, nuclear waste, genetic engineering, the greenhouse effect, drunk driving, education, and the militarization and industrialization of space (Crabbe, 1985). Each problem is solved with the following model. Note that the model follows almost exactly the CPS model described in Chapter 5.

[1] A non-competitive Primary Division for children in grades K–3, designed to instruct children in the problem-solving process, began in the Fall of 1984. An Advanced Division, consisting of the most competent problem-solving teams, began in 1982. They work on real business and government problems.

Follows CPS
Steps

1. They research information related to the general future-oriented topic. Specific articles are provided; students search out books, magazines, or other sources, and perhaps visit agencies and interview experts (Crabbe, 1985).
2. They brainstorm 20 possible problems related to the situation, and then select one underlying problem they feel is central to the situation.
3. They brainstorm solutions for this problem.
4. They brainstorm evaluation criteria and then, using their five best criteria, they evaluate ideas using an evaluation matrix of the type described in Chapter 5. Their ten most promising solutions are rank-ordered.
5. Finally, their best solution is described carefully in a few paragraphs.

State, National
FPS Bowls

Their work for steps 2–5 is sent to the state Future Problem Solving office for evaluation and feedback. Based on the quality of the third problem, the top 10 percent of the teams are invited to participate in a state FPS bowl; the winner of which is sent to the National FPS competition. For 1989–1990, students in the state bowls dealt with the problems related to medical advances; at the national FPS bowl they grappled with crime.

Good Skill
Development

Overall, the FPS experience develops creativity, analytical and critical thinking, research skills, speaking and writing skills, and teamwork and interpersonal skills.

OM

Long-Term
Problems

Like Future Problem Solving, *Odyssey of the Mind* (OM; formerly Olympics of the Mind) is a national problem designed to foster creative development. A team of seven (five players, two alternates) registers with the state OM committee in an elementary, middle school, or high school division. The OM Association provides each team with detailed directions for preparing *long-term problems* that they will work on usually in weekly meetings throughout the school year. For example, for the 1988 competitions the *Atlantis* problem required students to construct the illusion of a deep-sea expedition to explore the lost city of Atlantis. The team constructs and operates a submersible vessel that maneuvers two remote arms that are operated from inside the vessel. The *Straddle Structure* problem required students to build a balsa wood and glue structure that will straddle an octagon 1½ inches high

Odyssey of the Mind always includes an excellent creativity-stimulating theatre activity. "Just watch your hands," said Cleopatra, "This ain't 'The Best Little Pyramid in Egypt'." (Wisconsin Center for Film and Theater Research.)

and 7 inches wide, and support as much weight as possible. With *It's Show Time,* students develop a musical scene based on a play (for example, *The Emperor's New Clothes, Much Ado About Nothing*); they also prepare a Playbill and an oral summary of the play.

Short-Term Problems   In addition to long-term problems, students also solve on-the-spot *short-term* problems, both in practice and in competition (e.g., "List all of the giants you can think of").

Creative, sometimes off-the-wall answers receive three points (e.g., "Eddie Murphy is a giant of comedy," "Cheerios are giant wheels to an ant"), common answers receive one point. Within each state there are regional competitions, the winners of which participate in annual state competitions. State winners compete in an annual world OM competition.

Many Other Creativity-Stimulating Competitions

In addition to the Future Problem Solving and Odyssey of the Minds programs, there are other national programs and competitions that stimulate creative thinking, academic excellence, or both, for example, the Junior Great Books program, Academic Decathlon, Mock Court, and National Forensics League. See Davis and Rimm (1989) for suggestions.

PROGRAM MODELS

Program models provide the theoretical structure within which specific enrichment activities, including creativity training, may be planned.

Enrichment Triad Model

Triad Model: Renzulli

Type I: General Exploratory Activities

Probably the best known curriculum guide is the *Enrichment Triad Model* (Renzulli, 1977). It may be implemented with students of any age and in any grouping arrangement. There are three more-or-less sequential but interactive stages (Figure 9.3). With Type I enrichment, General Exploratory Activities, students are exposed to topics that are not a normal part of the school curriculum. While Type I (and Type II) enrichment are recommmended for all students, one purpose of Type I exploratory activities is to help motivated gifted students to find and pursue a later independent project (Type III enrichment). Type I enrichment may involve a well-stocked resource center (books, magazines, other media) and field trips to meet dynamic, creative and productive professionals.

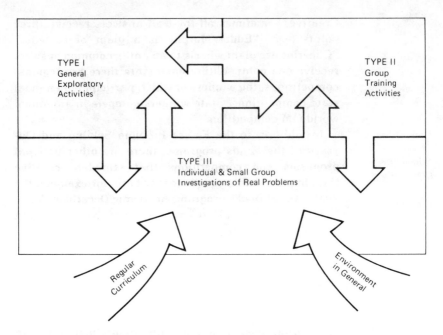

Figure 9.3 Renzulli's Enrichment Triad Model. From J. S. Renzulli, *The Enrichment Triad Model: A Guide for Developing Defensible Programs for the Gifted and Talented.* Mansfield Center, Conn.: Creative Learning Press, 1977. Reprinted by permission.

Type II: Thinking and Feeling Processes

Four Categories of Type II Enrichment

The purpose of Type II enrichment, Group Training Activities, is to ". . . promote the development of a broad range of thinking and feeling processes" (Renzulli & Reis, 1985). Renzulli and Reis (1991) recommend developing general and specific skills in the four categories of:

(1) *Cognitive and affective thinking,* including creative thinking, problem solving, decision making, critical and logical thinking, and affective processes such as appreciating and valuing.

(2) *How-to-learn skills,* such as listening, observing, perceiving, reading, note-taking, outlining, interviewing and surveying, and analyzing and organizing data.

(3) *Advanced research skills and reference materials* that prepare the students for Type III investigations, including using the library, information retrieval systems, and community resources.

(4) *Written, oral, and visual communication skills* that will be directed toward maximizing the impact of students' products.

Type III:	Type III enrichment, Individual and Small Group In-
Investigations of	vestigations of Real Problems, is exactly that. The young
Real Problems	person becomes an actual researcher or artist dealing

with a real problem in an artistic, scientific, literary, business, or other area. Students should be producers of knowledge, not merely consumers or reproducers.

| Product, | It is important for students to (a) produce a product, |
| Audience | and (2) have an audience for their products. The teacher |

may need a lively imagination to help locate or create audiences for students' Type III products.

Schoolwide Enrichment Model

SEM	The Enrichment Triad Model is incorporated into Ren-
	zulli's more recent and broader Schoolwide Enrichment
I Counted Them	Model (SEM; formerly known as the Revolving Door Iden-
Talent Pool	tification Model; Renzulli, Reis, & Smith, 1981). Briefly,
Concept	there are two main characteristics of the SEM, and an

even one billion minor details (see Renzulli & Reis, 1985, 1991). First, unlike traditional G/T plans, which identify about 5 percent of the students for participation, the SEM identities 15 to 20 percent of the school population for a *talent pool.* Identification is flexible, designed to include students, not exclude them. This strategy not only is more fair, it minimizes criticisms of elitism.

With High	Second, talent pool students (and occasionally non-
Creativity,	talent pool students) who show or develop high creativity
Motivation:	and motivation and wish to work on an independent pro-
Revolve into	ject are "revolved" into a resource room to carry out the
Resource Room	project with the resource teacher. When the project is
Details, Details	completed, the student revolves back out. See Renzulli

and Reis (1985, 1991) for the other 999,999,999 details pertaining to the history of SEM, underlying theory, issues, supportive research, identification forms and strategies, curriculum compacting (to "buy time"), parent communications, forms for everything (some of which insure that staff work gets done), learning style assessments, implementing Types I, II, and III enrichment, lists of specific art, science, language, etc. topics, lists of specific thinking skills to be fostered, project evaluation, and much more.

Feldhusen's Three-Stage Enrichment Model

Emphasizes
Creative
Thinking

Feldhusen's *three-stage enrichment model* (Feldhusen & Kolloff, 1986; Kolloff & Feldhusen, 1984) centers on three types or stages of instructional activities that are largely intended to foster creative development.

Creativity (and
Other) Exercises

Stage 1 focus upon *basic divergent and convergent thinking abilities.* Corresponding instructional activities include relatively short-term, teacher-led exercises mainly in creative thinking, but also in logical and critical thinking. Some creativity exercises include unusual uses, product improvement, and "What would happen if . . . ?" problems.

Techniques,
CPS, FPS

Stage 2 requires *more complex creative and problem-solving activities* that (1) may extend over a longer period of time and, importantly, (2) require less teacher direction and more student initiative. Learning and practicing creative thinking techniques such as brainstorming and the synectics methods; working through systematic problem-solving models such as the CPS and FPS models; or solving detective mysteries in the *Productive Thinking Program* (Covington, Crutchfield, Olton, & Davies, 1972).

Projects

Stage 3 activities aim at strengthening *independent learning abilities.* Said Feldhusen and Kolloff (1981), "Stage 3 projects should involve gifted youngsters in challenging efforts to define and clarify a problem, ambitious data gathering from books and other resources, interpretations of findings, and the development of creative ways of communicating results."

Other Curriculum Models

Pyramid Project

Your Mummy
Will Like It

The models summarized above focus on creative development as main program goals. There are many more models that guide G/T program and curriculum planning. All of these include creative development either directly, as in group creativity exercises, or indirectly, as when students work on independent projects. For example, the *Pyramid Project* (Figure 9.4) is an organizational plan that prescribes different services for different

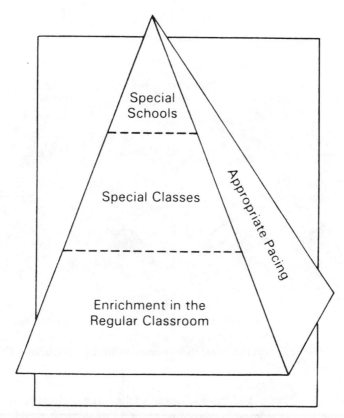

Figure 9.4. The pyramid model. Reprinted from *Educating Able Learners: Programs and Promising Practices,* by June Cox, Neil Daniel, and Bruce O. Boston, copyright © 1985. Reprinted by permission of J. Cox, Gifted Students Institute, and the University of Texas Press.

levels of giftedness. The largest number of "able learners" (the base of the pyramid) receive advanced material in the regular classroom, for example, using learning centers, cluster grouping, and resource room projects. A smaller number of more superior students are placed in full-time special classes for advanced material and skill development. The few at the top of the pyramid attend special schools for the gifted.

ALM: 5 Steps   The *Autonomous Learner Model* (ALM; Betts, 1985, 1991), like Renzulli's Schoolwide Enrichment Model, is an overall program plan. The ALM includes five steps of (1) orienting students and parents to giftedness and program opportunities, (2) individual development of learning

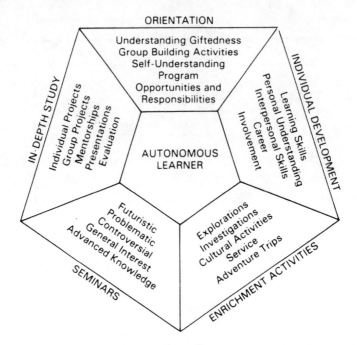

Figure 9.5. Autonomous Learner Model (Betts, 1985). Reprinted by permission of the author and Autonomous Learning Publications.

skills and interpersonal skills, (3) enrichment activities, including investigations of high-interest problems and "adventure trips" (e.g., studying geology in the Grand Canyon), (4) seminars in which students research and present topics, and (5) in-depth long-term research projects. These five steps are slightly elaborated in Figure 9.5.

Taylor's Totem
Poles Guides
Curriculum
Planning

(Popular in the
Northwest)

Taylor's *multiple-talent totem pole* model (Figure 9.2) also may be used as the basis for curriculum planning. That is, activities may be planned in the areas of *academic, productive thinking, communicating, forecasting, decision-making, planning, implementing, human relations,* and *discerning opportunities.* Slichter's (1986) *Talents Unlimited* in-service training model acquaints teachers with Taylor's model, describes exercises for strengthening the totem pole talents, and allows practice planning and teaching the totem pole talents.

SUMMARY

Creativity is central to all aspects of gifted education—definitions, goals and objectives, identification, and
acceleration and enrichment activities.

One's definition of giftedness determines who gets the
special services. There is no consensus in defining
"gifted" vs. "talented"; some use the terms interchangeably, others do not. There is no special term for the extremely gifted child.

Stankowski suggested five categories of definitions:
after-the-fact, IQ, percentage, talent, and creativity definitions.

Cohn differentiates general domains of gifts from specific talents within each domain. Gagne' defined giftedness as having innate competence, talents as
performances.

The widely-endorsed U.S.O.E. (multiple talent) definition includes the five categories of general intellectual
ability, specific academic talent, creativity, leadership,
and ability in the performing and visual arts.

Renzulli's three-ring definition includes high creativity, high motivation (task commitment), and at least
above-average ability—characteristics of people who
make creative contributions to society.

Taylor's multiple-talent totem pole model raises our
awareness that almost everyone can be above average or
even outstanding, if we look at many types of talents. His
totem pole subdivides into one intellectual talent, five
thinking (creativity) talents, and three talents important
for implementing ideas.

Intellectually gifted students are developmentally advanced in many areas. They also tend to show high motivation, confidence, humor, and higher moral thinking.
These traits appeared in Terman's classic research.

Identification methods should be related to both definitions and characteristics of giftedness. Both objective
and subjective information should be used. The over-use
of IQ scores discriminates against creative students.

There are many identification methods: Ability scores, achievement scores, teacher nominations, creativity test scores, parent nominations, peer nominations, self-nominations, and product evaluations.

Goals of G/T education include: maximum achievement, content beyond the regular curriculum, exposure to a variety of fields, student-selected content, creative thinking and problem solving, thinking skills, self-awareness and self-understanding, and the development of motivation and self-directedness.

Acceleration strategies, as defined here, result in advanced placement or credit.

In Julian Stanley's SMPY, mathematically precocious seventh-grade students participate in fast-paced summer math programs. Talent search programs accommodate both mathematically and verbally precocious students.

Enrichment plans include pull-out (resource room) programs, cluster grouping, special classes, mainstreaming, special elementary schools, magnet high schools, and school-within-a-school plans.

Enrichment activities can include library, art, theatre, or science projects, learning centers, field trips, Saturday and summer programs, mentorships, or participation in Future Problem Solving, Odyssey of the Mind, or other competitive programs.

Program models structure the enrichment activities.

Renzulli's Enrichment Triad Model includes general exploratory activities (Type I enrichment), group training activities (Type II), and individual or small group research projects (Type III).

The Triad model expands into the Schoolwide Enrichment Model, which includes the talent pool concept—identifying a full 15 to 20 percent of the school for participation. When a student shows or develops high motivation and creativity, he or she "revolves" into a resource room to work on an independent project.

Feldhusen's three-stage enrichment essentially outlines three levels of creativity training: basic exercises to strengthen divergent and convergent thinking abilities, more complex creative activities such as learning creativity techniques, and involvement in independent projects.

The Pyramid Project is an organizational plan that prescribes mainstreaming for the largest number of "able learners," full-time special classes for more superior students, and special schools for the few most gifted children.

Betts' Autonomous Learner Model is an overall program plan that includes the five steps of orientation, individual development of learning and interpersonal skills, enrichment activities, seminars, and in-depth long-term research projects.

Taylor's Multiple-Talent Totem Pole model also has guided curriculum planning in each of his totem-pole areas.

10

let's be a cuckoo clock: creative dramatics

[*Scene: Principal's Office of the Wonderland Elementary School. Principal Alice is interviewing a prospective creative dramatics teacher.*]

Principal Alice: Well now, what is your name?

Interviewee: Hearts, Queen of Hearts. You may call me 'Your Majesty.' I wonder, don't I know you from somewhere?

Principal: Oh I don't think so. İ've been the Wonderland principal for some time. Now, Ms. Hearts. . . .

Interviewee: That's 'Your Majesty.'

Principal: Now . . . Your Majesty . . . have you any experience in teaching creative dramatics? Have you done movement exercises? Awareness exercises? Pantomime? Playmaking?

Interviewee: Well . . . in a way. I formerly played a great deal of croquet with flamingos and hedgehogs. That certainly takes movement! Hmmm, you still seem very familiar.

Principal: Any pantomime or playmaking?

Interviewee: Well, I used to help out with tea parties—pretending to pour make-believe tea and that sort of thing. And I always played the part of an irate queen. Would you like to hear my "Off with their heads!"? It's very inspiring.

Principal: Actually, I think I've heard it. Do you, by any chance, remember playing croquet with a little girl who was looking for a White Rabbit wearing a red vest? He was always two days late.

Interviewee: Alice? Is it really you? Imagine, all grown up and running your own school! Do I get the job?

Principal: I can't say for sure yet, although it is nice to see you. At present, the choice has narrowed to you, a Mr. March Hare, and a very strange Hatter fellow.

CD: Unusual
Subject

Compared with most academic topics, creative dramatics is a strange subject. There is no standard course content, no achievement tests, and no behavioral objectives. However, creative dramatics does things that no traditional classwork can accomplish.

Imagination,
Problem
Solving,
Concentration,
Physical Self,
Sensory
Awareness,
Emotions, Pride,
Self-Confidence,
Empathy

In a sense, creative dramatics is the education of the whole person by experience (Way, 1967). Like many of the exercises in this book, especially in Chapter 11, creative dramatics stimulates thinking, imagination, and problem solving. It also uniquely works on increasing awareness and concentration, developing control of the physical self, sharpening the senses, learning to discover and control emotions, developing pride in individuality, strengthening self-confidence in speaking and performing, fostering a sense of humor, and increasing an empathic understanding of others (Davis, Helfert, & Shapiro, 1971; Way, 1967). Yes, creative dramatics makes ambitious claims.

CD is Not
Children's
Theatre

It is important to note that creative dramatics is not children's theatre. With children's theatre a published or original play is obtained, the best actors and actresses are selected and trained (after all, we must impress the principal and the parents), and everyone else paints scenery, turns on the lights and tape player, sells tickets, and hands out programs. Creative dramatics is for everyone, not just the few gifted actors and actresses. An audience is not needed nor desired, since it would only interfere with the imaginative, concentrated, and sensitive involvement necessary for successful creative drama.

The Leader:
Humor and
Energy

The leader of creative dramatics should have two personality qualifications: a sense of humor and lots of energy. He or she will need them to survive swinging through the jungle like a monkey, wading across a field of fly-paper, being anchor man for an imaginary tug-of-war, or turning the crank to wind up a giant people machine.

Adults Need It,
Love It

Your author teaches undergraduate and graduate college courses in creative thinking and problem solving. The highlight is always the creative dramatics session. As a totally new experience, these adults (some in their 30's and older) bend and twist their bodies into dozens of shapes and forms. As a warm-up they shrink into the "smallest thing" they can, then pick themselves up as rag-doll puppets with strings fixed on noses and elbows. They stare at a fellow student, almost a total stranger, mimicking his or her every move in the mirror exercise. They beep, chug, hum, and scrub a fellow student who rolls along on all fours—a Volkswagen in a people-machine car wash. In groups of about eight, each person in turn lifts the lid on an invisible trunk, takes out an invisible thing—a basketball, can of beer, make-up kit, hoola-hoop, saxophone, or inflatable horse—and pantomimes the appropriate action. They listen in silence to sounds that are near and sounds that are far. Then as 1-inch Lilliputians they relax, shut their eyes, and explore the inside of a coffee pot.

It is a time of creative regression, one they do not soon forget.

The remainder of this chapter is divided into five parts: warm-up exercises, movement exercises, sensory and body awareness exercises, pantomime, and play-making.

WARM-UP EXERCISES

It always is best to begin a session with some sort of stretching, loosening-up activity—to get the blood flowing and to clear the cobwebs out of the cortex. Three suggestions for this are:

Warm-Up
Exercises

1. *Holding up the Roof.* All participants strain to hold up the roof; slowly let it down (to one knee), then push it back up. It is quite strenuous, if done properly.
2. *Biggest Thing.* Everyone stretches his or her body into the biggest thing he or she possibly can. Guess what the second part of this exercise is?
3. *Stretching.* Beginning at their heads and working down, students stretch the various parts of their bodies.

MOVEMENT EXERCISES

1. *Circles.* Students stand in large circle. Each person, in turn, thinks of a way to make a circle by using his or her body. All others make the same circle. The circle can be made with part of the body or all of the body; it can be a fixed circle (e.g., a halo) or a moving circle (e.g., a circular motion of the foot or rolling on the floor). Names add to the fun, e.g., "This is a halo circle," "This is an eyeball circle," "This is a chicken circle." "This is a Groucho Marx circle." Squares and triangles may be used, but circles seem to work best.

2. *Tug-of-War.* Pick two five-person teams. The leader narrates, e.g., "This side seems to be winning. Look out! The rope broke!" Students will fall into two heaps without coaching. Be sure they hear the last five words.

3. *Mirrors.* Everyone needs a partner. One person becomes a mirror that mimics the movements of the partner who might be brushing teeth, pulling faces, or putting on clown makeup. Reverse roles in two or three minutes.

4. *Toe Tips.* This might be a good follow-up to the mirrors exercise. The pairs of students face each other with toe tips stuck together. They explore moving sideways, forward (or is it backward), hopping, bowling, skating, and anything else they can think of.

5. *Puppets.* There are several variations. The leader can narrate as rag-doll marionettes are lifted from the floor by strings attached to nose and elbow—then dropped! With children in pairs, one is the marionette and the other is the string-pulling puppeteer. The marionette, not the puppeteer, initiates the action which the puppeteer tries to follow.

6. *People Machines.* This is everyone's favorite. There are two main approaches. Students can form groups of 6–12 people and take 10 minutes or so to design and practice their machine. Alternatively, the "add on" strategy can be used: One student begins creating, e.g., a cat-petting machine, and others add themselves. Beeps, boops, hums, buzzes, and dings are important. You can slow it down, speed it up. One of the best "add ons" is a pinball machine, with as many as 50 people adding themselves to the growing game!

7. *Ice Cubes.* Everyone is an ice cube which melts; different effects if melted by sun or by stove. A variation is to be sand bags which leak.

8. *Statues.* According to "Go" and "Stop" signals, or the beginning and ending of leader's drum beat, students freeze in ugliest positions imaginable. Student observers or the statues themselves describe what they are, as soon as they figure it out.

9. *Ridiculous Poses.* On a signal, students strike the most ridiculous pose they can.

10. *Biggest Thing, Smallest Thing Variations.* The biggest/smallest exercise was described above. This can be extended to the lightest/heaviest, stiffest/most rubbery, angriest/happiest, bravest/most frightened, etc. Transitions from one form to its opposite may be in slow motion.

11. *Circus.* Each child becomes a different circus performer or animal. Variations include the leader directing what everyone should be, e.g., tightrope walkers, trained elephants, lion tamers, jugglers, etc.; or the performers can create a circus parade, each selecting his or her own character.

12. *Obstacles.* With chalk, draw "start" and "finish" lines about eight feet apart on the floor. One at a time, each student makes up an imaginary obstacle which he must climb over, dodge past, wade through, overcome, etc., to get from start to finish. Observers guess the obstacle. Works best with small groups.

13. *Gym Work-Out.* Participants pantomime activities as if they were in an imaginary gym. They run in place, lift weights, roll a medicine ball, climb a rope, etc.

14. *Leader Game.* Students form a large circle. One person goes outside the room until called. Another person is selected to start some motion which the other children follow. The first person is brought back into the center of the circle and tries to guess who the leader is. The leader changes the motion when the observer is not watching. When found, it is the leader's turn to leave the room.

15. *Robot Walk.* Each person is a robot with a sound. Whenever one robot touches another robot, both stop, sit down, and begin again to rise, with a new sound and a new walk.

16. *Balloon Burst.* All students are on the floor as *one* deflated balloon. The leader begins to blow the balloon up and the students work together to expand. Variations of balloon bursting: Let the air out slowly, pop with a pin, or blow it up until it bursts. With the individual variation, each person is a balloon that gets blown up and bursts, or else is released and flies with predictable craziness about the room.

17. *Making Letters.* Have two people at a time make any alphabet letter with their bodies. Others guess the letter. Or have larger groups spell ENVIRONMENT or words of their choice.

18. *Nature's Shapes.* Children shape their bodies to become a tree, stone, leaf, growing flower, rain, sun, etc.

19. *Sticky Floor.* Have students glue a portion of their bodies (e.g., elbow) to the floor. Discover movements they can make while glued.

20. *Creative Locomotion.* Have children walk like a Crooked Man, Jolly Green Giant, Raggedy Ann, Robot; run like a mouse or Miss Muffet frightened by a spider, or like the fattest person in the world running for a bus; jump like a kangaroo, popcorn, or plow horse. Walk on a different planet, with gravity double that of Earth.

SENSORY AND BODY AWARENESS

1. *Body Movement.* Children discover their moving parts when the teacher asks them to move their fingers, then hands, wrists, elbows, shoulders, neck, head, face (chew, make faces, bat eyelashes), back, hips, legs, ankles, feet, and toes. Variations: Ask students for more ideas (e.g., eyeballs, tongue, stomach muscles); ask students to keep *all* parts moving as more are added.

2. *Waking Up the Body.* Have the children lie on the floor in any position with their eyes closed and body relaxed. With slow, quiet music have the children begin waking up the various parts of their bodies one at a time until they are on their feet.

3. *Ordering by Height.* With eyes closed and no talking, a group of 8 or 10 students line themselves up according to height.

4. *Swinging.* Let the group discover all the ways a body can be made to swing—head, arms, legs, waist, etc.

5. *Warm-Up at Different Speeds.* Have children run in place in slow motion, then speed up until children are moving very fast. Variations include jumping, skipping, hopping.

6. *Rag Doll-Tin Soldier.* Have children walk as a limp rag doll, then as a stiffened tin soldier. Ask how their movements changed.

7. *Paper Exploration.* Give each child a piece of paper. Have them balance the paper on different parts of the body (especially the foot); run with the paper on the palms of their hands. Discover what sound effects can be made with the paper.

8. *Exploring an Orange.* Give everyone an orange to examine closely. How does it look, feel, smell, taste? What is unique about *your* orange? Could you pick it out from a crowd of oranges? Have groups of 5–6 students put their oranges in a paper bag; then identify them by touch. Take the orange apart and look at it; taste, touch, and smell the inside. Eat it.

9. *Blind Walk.* An absolute awareness favorite. Divide participants into pairs. The member with eyes shut (or blindfolded) is led under tables and chairs and allowed to identify objects by touch, smell, or sound. Get a drink of water, read names and numbers on doors (such as "boys" or "girls"). Go outside and explore trees, the sun, shade, a flower, etc. Ask students about experiences and discoveries. This exercise can lead to a discussion of blindness and replacement senses.

10. *Empathic Vision.* Ask students to inspect the room through the eyes of an artist, fire inspector, lighting engineer, a termite. Look at today's weather from the point of view of a duck, a skier, a field mouse, smoke jumpers. Who else?

11. *Invisible Balls.* An invisible ball is passed from person to person around a circle or up and down rows. As each person receives the ball, it changes size, shape, weight, smell, etc.

12. *Face Touching.* About 6 to 8 volunteers form a front-facing line with eyes shut. Another set of 6 to 8 volunteers become partners. Each new partner places one or both hands of the "blind" person on his or her face.

The blind partner feels hair, noses, cheekbones, whiskers, earrings, collars, glasses and so forth, gathering information which will allow him or her to identify the partner (who returns his or her previous spot before eyes are opened). Accuracy is very high, and so the game becomes more sporting when the partner tries to fool the blind person by removing earrings or glasses, standing on a chair, or quickly changing hairdos or sweaters.

13. *Listening.* Have students sit (or lie) silently, listening for whatever they can hear. Encourage concentration, letting sounds evoke associated images and memories. Variations: Listen only for close sounds or far sounds. With eyes shut, have students describe the source of the sounds with their hands, communicating without words.

14. *Imaginary Sounds.* Ask students to suggest and imagine sounds found in particular places—a factory, zoo, railroad station, department store, gas station, police station, etc.

15. *Touching.* Have students touch many surfaces, concentrating fully on the feel. Use strange things (e.g., a piece of coral) and familiar things. A paper sack or a box may be used to hide the objects from sight.

16. *Imaginary Touching.* Have children imagine the feel of different objects and surfaces, e.g., warm sand between the toes, a hot sidewalk, a wet paw and a lick on the face, ice cream, a Twinkie, mud, etc.

17. *Body Contacts.* Have participants concentrate on contacts of body places with, e.g., soles of shoes, shirt collars, chair seats, contacts between fingers. Can they feel the shirt or blouse in the middle of the back? Can they feel heart beats, stomach, lungs?

18. *Texture Walk.* Have group walk through imaginary substances, e.g., jello, flypaper, deep sand, chocolate pudding, tacks, swamp, etc., with leader and students calling out new substances and surfaces.

19. *Smelling.* Small bottles are prepared in advance with familiar scents in them—Vicks Vaporub, vanilla extract, peanut butter, used coffee grounds, lilac perfume, cinnamon, cloves, rubbing alcohol, antifreeze, face cream, lipstick, and so on. In small groups the scents are passed around one at a time and students discuss the memories that are stimulated by each smell.

20. *Imaginary Smells.* Have students imagine good smells. What are they? Can everyone imagine them? Have them imagine the smell of, e.g., tulips, his or her mother, a bus, barn, bakery, hamburger, etc. Ask for suggestions.

21. *Tasting.* Encourage students to be aware of and to concentrate upon different tastes of food. Imaginary tastes can be suggested; perhaps some new taste experiences can be shared, with reasonable sanitary precautions.

PANTOMIME ACTIVITIES

Pantomime involves acting out a story, a scene, or other activity or event without speaking. When a child is asked to pantomime an action, full attention is given to the elements that compose the activity. The student creates the proper shape and movements of his or her body and even intently fixes eyes upon objects in the imaginary environment. With encouragement, students will use face, hands, and body to display such emotions as sadness, glee, surprise, love, anger, or fear. If the same persons were allowed to speak, they might ignore bodily and facial expressions and let only words convey the message. With pantomime students are encouraged to "show me, don't tell me."

Note that many of the exercises described above also can serve as pantomime activities. Some candidates are Holding Up the Roof, Tug-of-War, Mirrors, Puppets, People Machines, Circus, Obstacles, Gym Work-Out, Sticky Floor, Creative Locomotion, Rag Doll-Tin Soldier, and Invisible Balls.

Additional pantomime activities include:

1. *Animal Pantomimes.* Have the children imitate the way a particular animal moves. Each child can come into the center of the circle to pantomime his or her animal. The rest of the group can guess the animal, perhaps by moving into the center to feed it. For variety, two or three animals can act out a simple plot, for example: (a) a cat sneaking up on a mouse, (b) a bear looking for honey, but finding bees, (c) a bloodhound tracking down a possum, (d) a bull spotting some picnickers, or (e) a fox stalking a chicken.

This creative dramatics student is pantomiming a cannonball. Will the result knock his socks off? (The Museum of Modern Art / Film Stills Archive.)

2. *Toy Shop.* Each student purchases a toy from a make-believe toy shop clerk, then plays with the toy.

3. *Invisible Trunk.* Students form a circle of 6 to 8 persons. In the center is an invisible trunk (or box). In turn, each person lifts the lid, takes something out, does something with it, then puts it back in the box and shuts the lid.

4. *Hats.* Create a hat shop, real or imagined, in which various kinds of workers come in to select a hat fitting their job, e.g., baseball player, policeperson, fireperson, clown, cowboy, movie star, nurse, miner, railroad engineer, etc. With hat in place, each child pantomimes the behavior matching the hat.

5. *Inside Out.* Many pantomimic activities can be explored from the inside out. Children become fish in a tank and others look in. Zoo animals in cages are good possibilities for this activity.

6. *Creating an Environment.* This exercise is much like an add-on people machine. The students think of and create an environment. For example, with a bowling alley environment one child begins rolling a bowling ball down a lane. Others become the ball, pins, the scorecard, a drinking fountain, and whatever else they can think of until the picture is complete. If available, sound effects records are helpful. Other worthwhile subjects or environments are fishing, croquet, baseball, a playground, hanging clothes on the line, a circus, an orchestra, marine fish and animals (octopi, star fish, crabs, lobsters), zoo animals, farm animals, an assembly line processing fish, and so on. Your people will think of more.

7. *Miscellaneous Pantomime.* Many brief sketches may teach characterization, for example, a jolly ice cream shop person making an ice cream soda, a fussy lady trying on hats, a scared mountain climber scaling a cliff, a tired pirate digging for treasure, giggly kids watching a funny movie, a grouchy cab driver fighting five o'clock traffic, a nervous, sneaky thief entering a candy store, an awkward cook flipping pancakes, a burglar surprised by the homeowners. Again, you and your students can think of additional possibilities.

PLAYMAKING

Give Scene,
Characterization

Playmaking as a type of creative drama can take many forms. With one straightforward strategy, students are given a simple scene or plot, characterization, and then are turned loose to improvise the action and dialogue. In some examples from Way (1967), one group of three students could be the three stooges robbing a bank. They are so half-witted they do everything wrong, backwards, or both. Other groups of the same idiots can act as a surgery team performing a heart transplant ("Gimme a knife and a blood bucket!"); perform as a musical quartet for trombone, drum, nose harp, and garbage can; erect a tent on a windy, rocky hill; or paint and wallpaper a kitchen.

This Is No
Chair, This Is
My Wife

The *Chair Smuggling* exercise requires problem solving and on-the-spot improvising. Chairs are illegal in this imaginary country. Each of about 10 students will try to smuggle a chair past a border guard—whose job it is to keep chairs out of the country. The border guard normally is played by the creative dramatics leader who, after some improvised suspicion, allows each student and his or her non-chair to enter. Each student must improvise a story about, and demonstrate, what it is that he or she is trying to bring across the border—certainly not a chair! Real or imaginary chairs may be used.

Reduces Self-
Consciousness,
Strengthens
Confidence,
Risk-Taking,
Humor

Note that by giving students a perfectly logical reason for being silly, they are helped in overcoming feelings of self-consciousness. Fear of failure is reduced and such creative traits as confidence, risk-taking, and humor are strengthened.

Serious
Playmaking

Mini-plays need not always be silly. Way (1967) suggested that groups can be miners working against time to reinforce a mine about to cave in; slow-moving astronauts assembling something on the moon; toyshop toys (or museum displays) coming alive at the stroke of midnight; or witches cooking up a magic brew. Historical events also present possibilities: Columbus discovering America, the Boston Tea Party, Pilgrims landing at Plymouth Rock, and so forth.

Making a Play

A more involved playmaking strategy runs as follows. After a few warm-up exercises, the leader tells a story.

Events
Characterization

Scene by Scene

Without and
with Dialogue

Use Fairy Tales,
Myths, History,
Stories

Then the leader and students review the sequence of events—what happened first? Second? The group then discusses characterization, considering physical, emotional, and intellectual qualities (nervous, calm, slow-witted, happy, angry, excited, scientific-minded, beautiful, quick-stepping, limping, stuck-up, etc.). The play typically is broken into scenes and worked out scene by scene. The group may first act out a scene without dialogue to explore the physical possibilities, believability of the characters, and the overall effect. After the group thinks of ways to make the scene better, it is replayed with improvised dialogue. A given scene may be played many times with different students experiencing various roles. This general strategy may be adapted for use with such familiar tales as Goldilocks or Peter Cottontail for small children, Cinderella for third graders, and Pandora's Box for the sixth grade. Generally, fairy tales, nursery rhymes, myths, folklore, historical material, and animal stories provide good sources for ideas.

Ask Questions:
Affective,
Empathic
Understanding

Direct questioning may add to the educational experience. For example "Was Goldilocks a burglar?" "Did Cinderella's stepmother hate her?" "Could you hate your mother?" "Why were Cinderella's ugly sisters so mean?" Questions such as "How would you feel if. . . ?" and "What would happen if. . . ?" also will stretch creative, empathic imaginations.

SUMMARY

Creative dramatics is a unique educational experience aimed at strengthening problem solving, imagination, physical control, sensory awareness, self-confidence, humor, and empathic awareness and understanding of others.

Creative dramatics is not children's theatre; creative dramatics involves everyone.

The leader should have energy and a sense of humor.

Sessions begin with a stretching, warm-up activity or two.

The next activities may include movement exercises, for example, mirrors and people machines; sensory and body awareness exercises, such as the blind walk and exploring an orange; pantomiming, as in animal pantomimes or creating an environment; and playmaking.

Playmaking can be simple, as when students are merely given a scene and characterization before jumping in. Playmaking also can be extensively and carefully developed, including a discussion of events and characterization, exploration of different possibilities, rehearsing first without dialogue, continual modification and improvement, and rotating parts.

Discussion of roles, characters, dilemmas, etc., adds to the experience by increasing human empathy and understanding.

11

teaching for creative growth

[*Scene: Cottage of Cinderella, her stepmother, and her two ugly stepsisters Drisella and Esmerelda. Stepmother and stepsisters are about to begin brainstorming ideas for harassing Cinderella.*]

Stepmother: Come now girls, we've got to find new ways to make you-know-who as miserable as we can!

Esmerelda: Yes mama. I'm so tired of her pretty hair, gorgeous face and sweet disposition—why can't she be like the rest of us?

Drisella: OH SHUT UP, ESMERELDA! WE'RE JUST AS DAMN CHARMING AS SHE IS!

Stepmother: Girls! Girls! Don't let the little twit upset you like that! Now, you both know the brainstorming rules.

Esmerelda: Yes mama. We don't criticize or evaluate, we. . . .

Drisella: You nitwit! Everybody knows that! Well, go on . . . let's hear the rest!

Esmerelda: We suggest whatever wild ideas occur to us, we list lots of ideas, and we modify and combine ideas in order to produce even more ideas. Let's hide her socks.

Drisella: That's a dumb idea. If we're going to hide something, let's be more creative. Let's hide her broom—and then demand that she sweep up the whole house and the front walk!

Stepmother: That's the WORST idea I ever heard, you nincompoop! She'd just find another broom and have everything spiffy in a few minutes! What about strangling her cat?

Esmerelda: That's really a stupid one, mama! The cat would put up a big fuss and Cinderella would hear us. Let's put cracker crumbs in her bed, milk in her shoes, vinegar in her yogurt, break the teeth of her comb, cut the strings on her vest, burn her sewing basket, send her to the next kingdom for some salt, and make her clean the chimney—from the inside.

Drisella: You ignorant big-nosed toad, we did all those last week! Look, let's have her take some hot soup over to Tom Tom, the piper's son. Tom Tom has the plague!

Stepmother: She'd just bring it home, you fool! I've got it! Let's stop her from going to the Prince's ball!

Esmerelda: Oh mother, that's a super idea! Isn't it wonderful how a warm, receptive, and encouraging atmosphere can stimulate creative thinking!

1. Issues

This chapter will consist of three main parts. First, we will look at some issues and considerations that relate to strengthening skills, abilities, and predispositions for creative thinking—beginning with the core question, "Can creativity be taught?" Teaching creative thinking is not a simple issue. Second, we will review concepts, ideas, and assumptions related to teaching for creative growth that appeared in every earlier chapter. Finally, we will describe five core goals of creativity training and strategies for achieving them.

2. Earlier Chapters

3. Five Core Goals

ISSUES IN CREATIVITY TRAINING

Issues

This section will look at these issues:

Can creativity be taught?
Individual differences in responsiveness to creativity training
Individual differences in motivation to create
The importance of a creative climate
Must creativity be taught within a content area?

Can Creativity Be Taught?

The most frequent question your author is asked is, "Can creativity be taught? Or are you born with it?" Sometimes the issue is raised in a more negative form— "I don't think you can teach creativity," followed by the inevitable rationale, "You either have it or you don't!"

Individual Differences

Of course, there are tremendous individual differences in innate creative abilities and in affective dispositions toward creativity, just as there are wide variations in every other mental and physical characteristic. Realistically, no amount of the most carefully orchestrated creativity training can mold an average person into a Leonardo DaVinci, Marie Curie, Thomas Edison, William Shakespeare, Booker T. Washington, or Orson Welles.

Creative thinking and your creative development are important in any career. "I'm sure glad my dental school taught me to use my imagination!" said Dr. Goldcap. "Do I get a lollypop?" asked his nervous patient. (The Museum of Modern Art / Film Stills Archives.)

Genetics: Yes   Such people are born with a special combination of high creative ability, extraordinary drive, and a strong sense of vision and destiny that leads them to realize their dreams and make the world a better place. They also acquire great depth of knowledge in their chosen fields.

Learning: Yes

However, it also is absolutely true that every individual can raise his or her creative skill, creative productivity, and creative living to a higher level. An irrefutable argument for the trainability of creativity is simply that, with interest and effort, all of us can make better use of the creative abilities we were born with.

What does creativity guru Torrance (1987b) say about whether creativity can be taught?

Torrance: Yes

> I know that it is possible to teach children to think creatively and that it can be done in a variety of ways. I have done it. I have seen my wife do it; I have seen other excellent teachers do it. I have seen children who had seemed previously to be "non-thinkers" learn to think creatively, and I have seen them continuing for years thereafter to think creatively. . . . Their parents have told me that they saw it happening. Many of the children, now adults, say that it happened (p. 189).

Creativity Can
Be Taught:
Torrance

In 1972 Torrance itemized 142 studies describing efforts to "teach creativity" via brainstorming and divergent thinking exercises, training in the Osborn/Parnes Creative Problem Solving (CPS) model, training in creative art or writing, establishing a creative climate, or using various creativity training workbooks or programs (see Torrance, 1987b). Almost all of the research projects were successful in raising creativity, as measured, usually, by the *Torrance Tests of Creative Thinking.* In 1983 Torrance reviewed 166 studies at the elementary and secondary level plus 76 at the college and adult level. Success rates (Torrance Test scores, creative products, creative self-perceptions) were lower than those de-

Massive
Evidence

scribed in the earlier review, but still good. "Massive evidence" was the phrase Torrance (1987b) used to describe the convincing results of these efforts to teach creative thinking. CPS, FPS, and OM were especially recommended.

Individual Differences in Responsiveness to Creativity Training

Differences in
Receptiveness
to Training

No Sir, You
Can't Make Me
More Creative!

Just as there are immense individual differences in cognitive abilities and affective predispositions for creativity, there also are individual differences in *receptiveness* to creativity training. That is, receptiveness to adopting and internalizing the required affective orientation toward thinking creatively and doing creative things. Some children and adults respond quickly and positively to such training. They learn that, yes indeed, they can imagine, visualize, create, and solve problems better than they expected—the capability was there all along, they just never attempted to use it. Others seem impervious to creativity training, due to some combination of disinterest, rigidity, insecurity, conformity, or other traits and barriers that are incompatible with creative thinking and behavior.

College Course:
Improved
Affective
Components

Your author teaches undergraduate and graduate courses in creative thinking that have two purposes. First is the academic goal of transmitting a body of knowledge about issues, theories, characteristics, processes, tests, and techniques of creativity, along with strategies for teaching for creative growth. The second purpose is to help students become more creatively productive by raising their creativity consciousness, explaining how others use creativity techniques, and motivating them to use their creative abilities. One of our studies showed that, *on average,* students who completed the course improved in their affective creative traits—creative attitudes, predispositions, and self-ratings of creativity—significantly more than students who had registered for but had not yet taken the course (Davis & Bull, 1978).

Memorize the
Stuff, Take the
Tests

However, in these courses there always are substantial differences in the degree to which students' creative potential is affected by the exposure. Some students register for the course, meet the requirements, but remain untouched by the potentially life-changing principles and concepts. Other students experience changes in their self-perceptions of creativeness and their actual creative

Some Are
Profoundly
Influenced

output; they discover capabilities they did not know they had. As a few examples, one person wrote her first and potentially publishable children's book as a direct result of the class; another invented an educational game that was sold to Fisher Price Toys; and another began writing poetry, and lots of it, for the very first time. One memorable testimony was, "Now I do weird things!"

Be Ready for
Differences in
Responsiveness
to Training

There are wide differences then, not only in creative predispositions and innate creative abilities, but in responsiveness to creativity training. Teachers of creativity should be prepared for these differences, and perhaps ready to work a little harder with low-receptivity students.

Individual Differences in Motivation to Create

Motivation
Differences

There also are large differences in motivation for creativity. As we saw in Chapter 3, a high energy level, which may take the form of total involvement in and commitment to a project, is a common characteristic of creatively productive people. Related traits are high levels of curiosity, adventurousness, spontaneity, creative risk-taking, and wide interests.

RAS Theory

Some motivation theorists, most notably Berlyne (1961) and Farley (1986), assume that the high level of energy and arousal-seeking that is so common among creative people is governed by the reticular activating system (RAS) in the brain stem. According to this theory, creative and adventurous activities are sought out in order to raise an uncomfortably low level of RAS activity to a higher, more optimal state.

Raise Interest,
Involve
Students

There is not much we can do about students' reticular activating systems. However, the RAS hypothesis does not prevent a teacher from working to elevate students' interest in creative thinking, while concurrently exercising creative skills and abilities and engaging students in challenging and satisfying artistic, scientific, and other entrepreneurial work.

Creative Atmosphere

Psychological
Safety

We do not need a long discussion of the focal importance of a receptive and reinforcing creative atmosphere.
Carl Rogers (1962) called it *psychological safety;* in
brainstorming it is known as *deferred judgment.* We saw
in Chapter 2 that if creative ideas are not reinforced—or

Deferred
Judgment

worse, if they are criticized or squelched—normal children and adults simply will not produce creative ideas in
those unreceptive circumstances. One of our five main
goals of creativity training will be fostering creativity
consciousness and creative attitudes, which continues this
atmospheric theme.

Must Creativity Be Taught within a Content Area?

Logical, but
Misleading

A common (and mildly irksome) argument is that creativity must be taught within a subject matter (Keating,
1980; Schiever & Maker, 1991). The assumption is simply
that students must have something to think about and
create with. While this viewpoint sounds logical, it is in-
accurate and misleading. Effective creativity training may
be content free *or* it may be embedded within a specific
content or subject area.

SA and ST
Creativity

The issue will be more clear if examined in the context
of that marvelous creativity concept, Maslow's (1954)
distinction between *self-actualized* and *special talent*
creativity, which we reviewed in Chapter 1. While it includes much more, self-actualized creativity essentially
is the mentally healthy tendency to approach all aspects
of one's life—personal, professional, avocational—in a
creative fashion. Self-actualized creativity is thus a general creativeness; it is content free.

Can Teach
General,
Content-Free
Creativity

Many successful creativity courses, programs, workshops, and educational workbooks try to teach a general
creativeness by strengthening creative attitudes and
awarenesses, exercising creative abilities, including analytic and evaluation abilities, teaching creativity techniques, and perhaps teaching the CPS model (Davis,

1989a). These efforts help the learner to understand creativity and to approach personal, academic, and professional problems in a more creative fashion. The approach is sensible, common, and effective (e.g., Davis & Bull, 1978; Edwards, 1968; Parnes, 1978, 1981; Smith, 1985; Stanish, 1977, 1981, 1988; Torrance, 1979; Torrance & Myers, 1970; Von Oech, 1983). Such training is not tied to a particular subject or content.

FPS, OM

CPS

For elementary and secondary students, the Future Problem Solving and Odyssey of the Mind programs, described in Chapter 9, are two excellent examples of successful efforts to teach a general, self-actualized type of creativeness. A highly recommended program for adults is the one-week Creative Problem Solving Institute held in Buffalo, New York, each June. Most participants return home as different, more creative, and more self-actualized persons.[1]

Special Talent Creativity

On the other hand, special talent creativity, as the name implies, refers to an obviously outstanding creative talent or gift in art, literature, music, theatre, science, business, or other area. Obviously, special talent creativity presumes some mastery of that area; and the greater the sophistication the more likely are creative contributions. Snow (1986), for example, referring to artistic, musical, literary, and scientific creativity—that is, special-talent creativity—stated that "A rich store of knowledge in a field is required as a base for idea production . . . Creativity . . . is an accomplishment born of intensive study, long reflection, persistence, and interest" (p. 1033).

Goals: Strengthening Creative Thinking Skills, Mastering Content and Technical Skills

Independent Projects

As for teaching special talent creativity, the two goals are strengthening creative thinking and problem solving skills while concurrently guiding students in mastering content and technical skills, for example, in such areas as creative writing, photography, theatre, botany, architecture, astronomy, journalism, and so forth. With the typical independent projects approach, students are given (or find) a high-interest project or problem. They proceed to clarify it, consider various approaches, find a main solution or resolution, and then create or prepare the project or problem for presentation. Throughout, students

[1]For information write to: Creative Education Foundation, 1050 Union Road, Buffalo, NY 14224.

A Common
G/T
Strategy

identify and resolve numerous subproblems; they evaluate their methods and results; they acquire knowledge and develop technical skills; and they develop content-related creative problem solving skills and abilities. The independent projects strategy nicely fits Maslow's category of special talent creativity.

SA and ST
Creativity
Overlap

As the reader might guess, some amount of *special talent* creativity may be strengthened while teaching a general, *self-actualized* type of creativeness, and vice versa. For example, within a primarily content-free creativity session students might brainstorm a science-, history- or math-related problem or they might do creative writing, creative dramatics, or art activities. Conversely, creative projects in a subject area (special talent creativity) are very likely to help develop general creative abilities and attitudes (self-actualized creativity) that extend beyond the specific topic at hand.

THIS BOOK SO FAR

In our first 10 chapters we have seen many concepts and principles related to becoming a more imaginative, flexible, creative thinker. It will be worth a little paper and ink to review them.

Chapter 1

Creativity
Consciousness

Chapter 1 sought mainly to increase your creativity consciousness by stressing the importance of creativity both to yourself as a self-actualizing person and to society. The chapter was short but important in its message. Nothing can be more important to life satisfaction—your life satisfaction—than becoming self-actualized: becoming what you are capable of becoming, being an independent, forward-growing, fully-functioning, democratic-minded, and mentally healthy individual.

Self-
Actualization

Chapter 2

Blocks and
Barriers

A Few Whacks
and Squelchers

Chapter 2 looked at creativity training not from a how-to-do-it view, but from the what-stops-it perspective—blocks and barriers that prevent us from thinking and behaving more creatively. We reviewed the effects of habit and learning, rules and traditions, perceptual blocks, cultural blocks (especially conformity), emotional blocks, and even resource barriers. We noted that creativity expert Von Oech recommended a "whack in the side of the head" to jolt us out of our mental blocks—habits and attitudes relating to finding one right answer; being logical, practical, and correct; avoiding ambiguity, play, and foolishness; and assuming "I'm not creative!" The chapter ended with a list of ways to squelch other people's creative thinking—the idea squelchers.

Chapter 3

Definitions,
Theories
Increase Our
Understanding,
Awareness

Reinforce
Creativity

Most of the definitions and theories in Chapter 3 tell us very little about directly teaching for creative growth. However, the chapter increases our understanding of creativity and creative ideas, which indirectly contributes to creativity consciousness. The emphasis of many definitions on *combining* ideas implicitly justifies the use of deliberate creativity techniques, techniques that basically force new idea combinations. The ancient learning theory concept of strengthening behavior through reinforcement definitely applies to creativity: Children (and adults) will do what they are rewarded for doing, including thinking creatively instead of convergently.

Chapter 4

Reinforce Traits
of Creativity

Chapter 4 described personality and biographical characteristics of creative people. We normally do not speak of "teaching personality traits." However, it may be sensible to recommend rewarding and encouraging, and cultivating in oneself, these (positive) kinds of creative traits, habits, and behaviors: confidence, independence, willingness to take a creative risk, enthusiasm, adventurousness, curiosity and wide interests, humor and playfulness, attraction to the complex and mysterious, and setting aside some alone time—time to incubate and create. The number one trait to encourage is, of course, a creativity consciousness. Teachers also should encourage aesthetic interests and involvement in creative activities.

Encourage Involvement

As we noted in Chapter 4, the main difference between people who *have* creative abilities and those who *use* their creative potential lies in affective traits that predispose some people to think and behave in creative ways.

Chapter 5

Use Visual Puzzles

Chapter 5 looked at creativity as a "change in perception"—"seeing" new meanings, relationships, combinations, and transformations—and described stage analyses of creativity. A teacher can use optical illusions and visual puzzles to illustrate how, with a little effort, one can always "see different things" and find more ideas.

CPS Models: Yes

The BIG contribution of Chapter 5, of course, is the remarkable CPS model—whose five steps almost always produce good, creative problem solutions. A relevant book is *CPS For Kids* (Eberle & Stanish, 1985).

Chapter 6

Analogical Thinking: Pervasive Technique

The crowning creative thinking technique is analogical thinking. Most of the personal creative thinking techniques described in Chapter 7 involve "seeing a connection" between the problem at hand and the solution to another situation, or transferring ideas from one situation to another. Try the analogical thinking exercises in Chapter 6 (Inset 6.2). Show students how it works.

Also
Enlightening

Practice the clever synectics variations (direct analogy, personal analogy, fantasy analogy, compressed conflicts) and the analogical thinking exercises at the end of Chapter 6. Combined with the techniques of Chapter 7, you and your students will feel that you better understand how creative people think, and are better able to produce new idea combinations and problem solutions on demand.

Chapter 7

Techniques

When it comes to "teaching creativity," the techniques described in Chapter 7 represent teachable ways that real, honest-to-goodness creative people find creative idea combinations. Brainstorming, attribute listing, morphological synthesis, idea checklists, and others all were derived from creatively productive people. Most of these adult/professional techniques are finding their way into elementary and secondary classrooms via workbooks (Davis & DiPego, 1973; Stanish, 1981, 1988), one computer program (Davis, 1985), and teachers who have done their homework on "teaching creativity."

Chapter 8

Testing

The creativity testing material in Chapter 8 presents precious little related to improving creativeness. An examination of the underlying assumptions regarding what is being evaluated may help one's understanding of creativity. Guilford (1962, 1986) suggested that to strengthen creative abilities, one might practice doing exercises similar to the tests that measure the particular abilities. That is, if listing unusual uses for a brick measures ideational fluency, then ideational fluency itself might be strengthened by practicing listing unusual uses. (Read that word salad again.)

Chapter 9

Gifted
Education Aims
at Fostering
Creative
Development

Renzulli

Feldhusen &
Kolloff

Chapter 9 was the G/T chapter. Most of the program models and the enrichment and acceleration strategies have as one main goal the strengthening of creative thinking and problem solving skills and abilities. For example, the Future Problem Solving and Odyssey of the Mind programs were designed entirely to foster creative development. Renzulli's Type II Enrichment includes creativity training (exercises, techniques), and his Type III Enrichment highlights creative involvement in individual research projects. The Feldhusen and Kolloff three-stage model explains that creativity training should begin with basic divergent thinking exercises, progress to more advanced creativity techniques and problem solving strategies, and finally include independent problems and projects.

Chapter 10

Creative
Dramatics; for
Kids of All Ages

The creative dramatics exercises in Chapter 10 all aim at loosening up the creative juices. If the reader is a proper adult and a non-teacher, you may feel this stuff is not for you. Possibly true. However, some corporate creativity techniques described by Smith (1985) included the following—designed to shake up a few neurons and stimulate some regression: "Now let's have the 'chicken cheer' . . . A dozen managers shed their jackets and stand up . . . The leader starts. One by one, others join in. They flap their arms and scratch at the floor with their feet. Finally, the room fills with crowing sounds a rooster would envy."

Is creative dramatics only for teachers and kids?

This Chapter

The remainder of this chapter is built around five main affective and cognitive objectives related to becoming a more creative person and teaching others to become more creative thinkers and producers. The points will review and extend ideas from earlier chapters. The objectives are not complicated, and the list is short. We will look at:

Five Goals

1. Fostering creativity consciousness and creative attitudes
2. Improving students' metacognitive understanding of creativity
3. Exercising creative abilities
4. Teaching creative thinking techniques
5. Involving students in creative activities

CREATIVITY CONSCIOUSNESS AND CREATIVE ATTITUDES

Creativity Consciousness

Increasing creativity consciousness and creative attitudes is the single most important component of teaching for creative growth. Every creative person is aware of creativity and his or her own creativeness. The single best item on adult creativity inventories is the question "Are you creative?" Creative people make conscious decisions: "Today I'm going to think creatively and do some creative work!"

Very Important, Easy to Teach

Ironically, creativity consciousness is both the most important aspect of becoming more creatively productive, yet also the easiest to teach. Creativity consciousness will be a natural outgrowth of virtually any type of creativity exercises and activities.

Awareness

Creativity consciousness and creative attitudes includes:

An awareness of the importance of creativity for personal development (self-actualization), and for solving personal and professional problems.

An appreciation of the role of creative ideas and creative people in the history of civilization—which may be seen as a history of creative innovations in every field.

Barriers

An awareness of barriers to creativity—habits, traditions, rules, policies, and particularly social expectations and conformity pressures.

Receptiveness

A receptiveness to the novel, unconventional, even zany and farfetched ideas of others.

Involvement

A predisposition to think creatively, play with ideas, and become involved in creative activities.

Risk-Taking

A willingness to take creative risks, make mistakes, and even fail.

Courses
Stimulate
People to Use
Their Abilities

Every college course in creativity and every professional workshop stresses creativity consciousness, appropriate creative attitudes, and common barriers to creative thinking and behavior. Regardless of whether innate abilities can be changed, by changing attitudes and awareness in a more creative direction we stimulate people to use the creative abilities which they already have.

Creative
Atmosphere

Note that the concept of a creative atmosphere, mentioned earlier, fits in exactly here. A creative atmosphere rewards creative thinking and helps it become habitual. It includes Rogers' concept of psychological safety, the deferred judgment concept of brainstorming, and good old-fashioned reinforcement theory.

The reader may wish to look again at the *idea squelchers* of Chapter 2. This is what a creative atmosphere and a creative person are not.

Creativity
Consciousness
Important

Increasing creativity consciousness and fostering favorable attitudes toward creative thinking is truly item number 1 in becoming a more creative person and helping others to develop and use their creative potential.

METACOGNITIVE UNDERSTANDING OF CREATIVITY

Thinking about
Thinking

Metacognition is thinking about thinking—or in this case, thinking about *creative* thinking. The predisposition to think creatively will take a giant step forward if a person knows more about the topic. In fact, a major purpose of this book is to expand the reader's metacognitive understanding of creative thinking. An increased understanding of creativity will help raise creativity consciousness, demystify creativity, and convince students that given their present abilities they are perfectly capable—with interest and effort—of hatching creative ideas and producing creative things.

Lesson Content A few lessons on creativity might include such topics as:

Importance The importance of creativity to self and society.

Creative Ideas The nature of creative ideas as modifications of existing ideas, new combinations of ideas, and products of analogical thinking.

Characteristics of Creative People Biographies and characteristics of creative people; that is, attitudes, personality, and biographical traits that contribute to one's creative imagination and creative productivity, for example, creativity consciousness, confidence, risk-taking, adventurousness, humor, open-mindedness, curiosity, wide-interests, needs for alone time, plus a supportive environment and depth of knowledge.

Techniques How creative people use deliberate techniques, including analogical thinking, to extend their intuition and spontaneous imagination (Chapters 6 and 7).

Rationale of Tests What is measured by tests of creativity, such as the *Torrance Tests of Creative Thinking* (Torrance, 1966); tests may be taken and explained (e.g., the meaning of fluency, flexibility, originality, and elaboration).

Creative Process The nature of the creative process, as represented in the Wallas (1926) *preparation, incubation, illumination,* and *verification* stages or the more useful CPS model (Chapter 5). The creative process also can be viewed as a "change in perception" or a mental transformation. As we mentioned earlier, visual puzzles, optical illusions, and even *Far Side* cartoons can be used to illustrate this sudden "seeing" of new ideas, new meanings, new combinations, or new modifications. Creativity techniques illustrate conscious creative idea-finding processes.

Definitions, Theories Depending upon their age and ability, students also can learn about definitions and theories of creativity; abilities that underlie creative expression; and habits and social pressures that block or squelch creativity.

Computer Disk Principles The Apple II Computer disk *Creative Thinking and Problem Solving* (Davis, 1985), along with fostering creative attitudes and teaching idea-finding techniques, tries to increase elementary students' metacognitive understanding of creativity by emphasizing these points in the

Table 11.1
Creative Abilities

Fluency	Analogical Thinking
Flexibility	Analysis
Originality	Synthesis
Elaboration	Evaluation
Sensitivity to Problems	Transformation
Problem Defining	Predicting Outcomes
Visualization	Resisting Premature Closure
Imagination	Logical Thinking

important opening lesson: Creativity is important for everyone, it will help you live a more interesting, successful, and enjoyable life; creative ideas usually are modifications and combinations of other ideas; creative people are not rigid, they see things from different points of view and are aware of pressures to conform; creative people take risks, play with possibilities—and make mistakes; they consider lots of ideas, use idea-finding techniques, think analogically, and evaluate their ideas. They use their talents, not waste them.

EXERCISING CREATIVE ABILITIES

Strengthening Creative Abilities Through Exercise

This section will take a little longer.

In Chapter 4 we itemized abilities that logically underlie creativity, each with a brief definition. It is a common and reasonable strategy to try to strengthen creative abilities through practice and exercise, the same way we strengthen skills of reading, typing, solving chemistry problems, and shooting baskets. We will look at most of these abilities (see Table 11.1), noting strategies, exercises, or materials that aim at strengthening that ability.

Fluency, Flexibility, Originality, Elaboration

Fluency, Flexibility, Originality, and Elaboration. You should recognize these as the abilities measured by the *Torrance Tests of Creative Thinking* (Chapter 8). Many exercises and workbooks use open-ended, think-of-all-you-can divergent thinking problems to try to improve

Divergent
Thinking
Exercises

Use to Teach
Values

What Would
Happen If?

these abilities. Note that such exercises also intrinsically raise creativity consciousness and teach creative attitudes—valuing creativity, looking for unusual ideas, and being receptive to creative ideas of others. Further, some exercises can be used to teach constructive and socially proper values—honesty, manners, promptness, cleanliness, conservation, etc.—while strengthening these four creative abilities (Davis, 1990).

Most divergent thinking exercises fall into just three categories. First, exercises of the *"What would happen if . . . ?"* variety are an old standby. They appear in workbooks for children by Stanish (1977), Helman and Larson (1980), Myers and Torrance (1965, 1966a, 1966b), and many others, and in texts about teaching for creativity and futuristic thinking (Shallcross, 1981; Torrance & Myers, 1970; Torrance, Williams, Torrance, & Horng, 1978). You can create problems of your own which may be tied to virtually any subject matter or business problem. As some examples, "What would happen . . .":

If we did not have arithmetic?

If we had no books?

If people were suddenly unable to write a comprehendable sentence?

If all the pens and pencils in the world disappeared?

If the British had won the Revolutionary War?

If people with blond hair were not allowed in hotels or restaurants, and could not vote?

If the only musical instruments were drums?

If people could not solve problems and create?

If Edison had become a plumber and did not invent lightbulbs?

If the Wright brothers stuck to bicycles?

If the computer chip were not invented?

If there were no corn crop in the Midwest this year?

If Miami Beach became the North Pole?

If everyone looked exactly alike?

If no one ever smiled?

If union wages were doubled?

If our main raw material (wood, steel, corn, nylon) became unavailable?

If a totally new product made our biggest seller obsolete?

If company management were decentralized, and 25 vice presidents and supervisors were asked to relocate?

If the company were taken over by IBM?

If parts could not be made in Taiwan?

If there were no McDonalds? No peanut butter? No candy? No cars? No electricity? No nuclear bombs?

If there were no gravity in this room?

If you had an eye in the back of your head?

If no one told the truth?

If everyone were dishonest?

If everyone were a litterbug?

If everyone were rude to everybody else?

If everyone wasted school supplies?

If the school building were vandalized three nights per week and twice on Saturday?

Unusual Uses

A second traditional divergent thinking problem is asking learners to think of *unusual uses* for any common object, for example, discarded tires, ping pong balls, a tea cup, a tennis racquet, a chair, a piece of chalk, a clothes pin, a wink (Stanish, 1977), a new material, a new product, or a new process. Again, it's easy to make up your own problems.

Product Improvements

Third, *product improvement* problems ask students to list ways to change or improve a familiar object, such as a bath tub, *Cracker Jacks,* a drinking fountain, a bicycle, a TV set, or a pencil or pen. Such exercises can deal with business related problems, such as thinking of ways to improve efficiency, hiring practices, morale, product quality, etc.

Design Problems

Another category, *design* problems, can be similar to product improvement problems. For example, designing a bathtub is about the same as thinking of improvements for a bathtub. Other design problems would ask students, for example, to design a dog walking machine, a new trash collection procedure, a safer traffic intersection, a cat petter, an airplane for animals (Helman & Larson, 1980), a burglary-prevention system, a theft-proof computer, or children who are never late.

There are, of course, limitless open-ended questions and problems that would exercise the learner's fluency, flexibility, originality, and elaboration abilities. Some exercises try to focus on just one or another of these four abilities. For example, *fluency* is exercised by asking students to list things that are round, square, sweet, sour, blue, white, made of metal, made of wood, long and slender, short and stubby, smell good, taste bad, or have sharp edges. Some *flexibility* exercises try to have students look at things from different perspectives, for example:

Fluency Exercises

Flexibility Exercises

> How does this room look to a tidy housekeeper? A hungry mouse? An alien from outer space?
>
> How does an old wooden chair look to a tired person? A termite? An antique collector?
>
> How does a train station look to a train? To a duck flying overhead? To a passenger arriving too late for the train?
>
> How does a highway look to a tire? To a crow? To a lost pilot?
>
> How does our health food line look to a nine-year old? A teenager? A college student? A health nut? A jogger? A middle-aged person (who has the cash)? The elderly?

Elaboration Exercises

Elaboration exercises require the learner to build upon a basic idea, for example, developing the dog walking or cat petting machine or the new bathtub in specific detail— measurements, materials, costs. Or writing a story built upon a specified theme, for example, a fish who cannot swim, a child with no hair, or a town with no rules or laws. Or developing the marketing or morale-improvement plan to the last detail.

Some Problems
Ask for
Solutions

Fluency, flexibility, originality and elaboration abilities also can be exercised with relatively complex brainstorming-type problems. Some problems ask for *solutions*, for example:

> How can we make school more interesting?
>
> How can the lunch menu be improved?
>
> How can bicycle theft be eliminated?
>
> How can the school (or home or business) electric bill be reduced?
>
> How can we prevent the best teachers from quitting?
>
> What can we do for a parent on his or her birthday for under five dollars?
>
> Improved medical technology has created an enormous population of elderly people who consume food and energy and require care. Is this a problem? What are solutions?
>
> How can our company benefit from the increasing numbers of retired persons and help them at the same time?

Others Ask for
Explanations

Other problems ask for *explanations,* for example:

> The grass behind a Wyoming billboard is extra lush and green. Why?
>
> The principal unexpectedly cancels gym classes for two weeks. What are some explanations?
>
> Ten paintings were discovered missing from the art gallery on Monday morning, but there was no sign of a break-in. How could they have disappeared?
>
> Sales suddenly dropped 30 percent. What are some explanations?

Ambiguities,
Paradoxes
Stimulate
Creativity

Note that these latter exercises involve presenting students with incompleteness, ambiguities, and paradoxes, all of which raise tension and motivate students to look for new combinations and relationships and to "synthesize relatively unrelated elements into coherent wholes" (Torrance, 1987b).

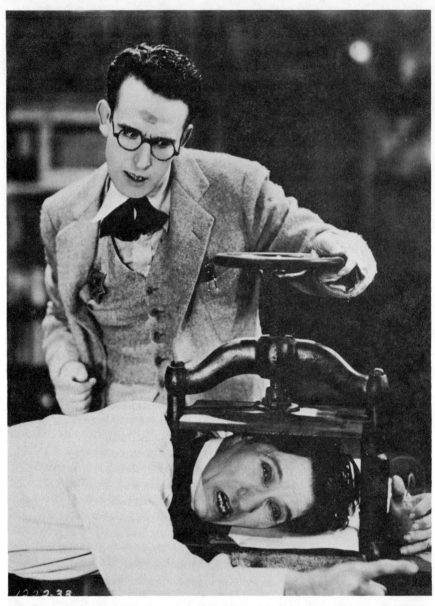

This enthusiastic teacher is trying to convince his principal of the pressing need for more creativity training in the curriculum. ''Okay, Okay! We'll add art! We'll brainstorm! We'll do 'What would happen if?' '' agrees principal Florence Flathead. (The Museum of Modern Art / Film Stills Archive.)

We mentioned earlier that it also is possible to teach constructive attitudes and values while strengthening fluency, flexibility, originality, and elaboration. In fact, some attitude-related exercises appeared in the "What would happen if . . . ?" section above. Students can work on such *brainstorming* problems as:

Teaching Values with Brainstorming

> Why is it good to be honest?
> Think of ways to show respect to the elderly.
> Think of ways to show friendliness in the classroom.
> How many different safety rules can you think of?

And Reverse Brainstorming

Or with *reverse brainstorming:*

> Think of ways to be unpleasant to new students.
> How can we create more work for the school custodian? For production workers? Managers? Secretaries?
> How might we waste lots and lots of electricity in our school building or company?
> How can we avoid thinking creatively?

See Davis' (1990) *The Good Person Book: Creative Teaching of Values and Moral Thinking* for hundreds of creativity-based exercises for teaching constructive attitudes and values.

Problem Sensitivity

Sensitivity to problems. Torrance considers problem sensitivity to be a very important creativity ability; it is, in fact, the first part of his definition of creativity (Chapter 3). Exercises aimed at strengthening problem sensitivity should have the learners find problems, detect difficulties, or detect missing information. One type of exercise aimed at increasing problem sensitivity is having students *ask questions* about an ambiguous situation or even a common object. What questions could you ask about clouds? Computers? The sun? The ocean? Weather? The competitor's products? Increasing creative thinking? A variation would begin with "What don't we know about . . . ?" Question asking also may be placed in a

Practice Asking Questions

fictitious TV interview context (Myers & Torrance, 1964): What three questions might you ask a Latin American dictator who has been driven from office? The mother of eight children just named "Mother of the Year"? A bus driver who refused to stop working after winning a five million dollar lottery?

Problem Defining

Problem defining. Problem defining is a complex ability. Relevant exercises would evolve around:

Identifying the Real Problem

1. Identifying the *real* problem and simplifying and clarifying the problem, for example, "What is the 'basic' problem here?" "What are we trying to do?" "What is it that really needs attention?"

Important Aspects

2. Isolating important aspects of a problem, for example, "What are the important parts of this problem?" "What should we focus on?"

Identify Subproblems

3. Identifying subproblems, for example, "What problems are related to this main problem?" "What problems will follow from each solution?"

Alternative Definitions

IWWMW

4. Proposing alternative problem definitions, for example, "How else can we define the problem?" Remember the "In What Ways Might We . . . ?" statements in Chapter 5?

Broaden Problem with "Why" Questions

5. Defining a problem more broadly to open new possibilities, perhaps by asking "Why?" after each problem definition.

Visualization, Imagination

Visualization and imagination. These are rather obviously important creative abilities. In fact, *imagination* sometimes is used interchangeably with *creativity.* Many exercises stimulate visualization and imagination. Two books, *Put Your Mother on the Ceiling* (DeMille, 1973) and *Scamper* (Eberle, 1971), are built upon the principle that imagination can be strengthened with exercise. Both ask the listeners to relax, shut their eyes, and visualize the substance of some colorful narrations, for example: "Now

Flying High!

put a light bulb in each hand, hold your hands straight out to the side, pretend that your light bulbs are jet engines and run down the street for a take off!" (Eberle, 1971).

Wild Stories from Headlines Elicit Visualization

Another exercise guaranteed to elicit visualization (and elaboration) is a creative writing task suggested by Helman and Larson (1980): "Cut out headlines from a newspaper dealing with unusual stories and have the kids make up the stories." Some recent grocery store rags included the following visualization-prodding winners: "Navy Raises UFO from Puget Sound: Crashed Starship Looks Like Solid Gold, Says Diver"; "5,000 Bodies Vanish From Old Cemetery"; "Baby Born Talking Gives Dad Winning Lottery Numbers . . . And He Becomes A Millionaire!"; "Bigfoot Saves Hunter Stuck in Quicksand"; "Titanic Survivor Has Been Afloat 76 Years!"; "We'll Keep Our Two-Headed Baby, Say Proud Parents"; "Lightening Bolt Zaps Coffin—And Corpse Comes Back to Life!"; "Farmer Dies in Suicide Pact With 46 Cows!"; "Female Vampires Terrorize Town!"; "Teacher Picks Up Hitchhiking Ghost"; and "Amazing Duck Man Lays Real Egg (No Yolk!)." (Some people do not believe these stories!)

Analogical Thinking. Exercises for practicing analogical thinking appear in Chapter 6. Stanish's (1977) *Sunflowering* and Gordon's (1974a) *Making it Strange* are loaded with exercises in analogical thinking.

Analysis, synthesis, evaluation. These, of course, are higher-level thinking skills in Bloom's taxonomy of educational objectives. Exercises include asking students to *analyze* components, relationships, hypotheses, patterns, and causes and effects; *synthesize* parts into plans, theories, generalizations, designs, and compositions; and *evaluate* the accuracy, value, efficiency, or utility of alternative ideas or courses of action.

Other evaluation exercises ask students, including adult students, to list what is *good* about an idea (or plan or experience), and what is *bad* about the idea (or plan or experience). Students can learn to use an evaluation matrix, as described in Chapter 5 (see Figure 5.2). Parnes (1981) recommends looking at a creative problem solution from other people's perspectives, or else imagining them reacting to the idea as you explain it.

Transformation. Transformation abilities are related to visualization, imagination, and creativity in general. Students can practice making mental transformations with complex visual puzzles of the type shown in chapter 5. What else can they see in the picture? The personal observation that people (of all ages) differ vastly in their ability to "see" other meanings and perceptions (specifically, the cow in Chapter 5) suggests that many do need

Margin notes:

Strangely Believe It!

Analogical Thinking

Analysis, Synthesis, Evaluation Exercises

What's Good?

What's Bad?

Transformation

Use Visual Puzzles

practice with this particular ability. Sounds, such as crumpling paper, also can elicit different meanings and transformations.

Predicting Outcomes: What Would Happen If?

Predicting outcomes. Predicting outcomes is related to evaluation abilities in the sense that evaluating problem solutions amounts to predicting their utility. Also, exercises of the "What would happen if . . . ?" variety give students practice at predicting outcomes. It's a form of futuristic thinking (Torrance & Torrance, 1978).

Grabbing First Idea: No

Emphasize Deferred Judgment

Resisting premature Closure. Most people, at all ages, are too fast in grabbing the first idea that presents itself. Yet considering lots of ideas and deferring judgment are two of the most basic principles of creative problem solving. Practice with brainstorming, with heavy emphasis on the rationale behind deferring judgment, should help with this pivotal ability.

Logical Thinking

Logical thinking. Logical thinking is vastly underrated as a central creative ability. Logical thinking is involved in clarifying the problem, figuring out solution requirements, and relating proposed ideas to those solution requirements. Interestingly, there seem to be few exercises specifically designed to strengthen logical thinking abilities, other than syllogistic reasoning and related problems, such as "If Tom is taller than Janice and Janice is shorter than Wilt Chamberlain, who is the best bowler?" An early workbook by Myers and Torrance (1966b) included exercises in logic that could serve as models for similar teacher-constructed activities. For example, explain why each of the following is *true* or *false*:

Logic Exercises

If something is beautiful, it has to be valuable.

Joe has one sister, but three brothers-in-law.

An object has color or else it has no color.

Joe, a strict vegetarian, prefers fish to beef.

The twins rode into town by themselves, with Chuck in the middle.

The headlights of the oncoming car blinded its driver, causing him to run off the road.

> Diamonds are more expensive than pearls, therefore pearls are more expensive than rubies.

A few exercise books try to strengthen logical thinking with syllogistic reasoning problems and other types of deductive and inductive reasoning problems (e.g., Black & Black, 1984; Harnadek, 1978, 1979; see also Clasen, 1985).

Many Abilities Contribute to Creativity

The present list of creative abilities appear central to creative thinking, and we have described some exercises that may help strengthen them. It is not, however, a complete and exhaustive list of creative abilities. As noted in Chapter 4, it would be extremely difficult to identify a cognitive ability that is *not* in some way involved in the complex requirements of creative thinking. Other lists of creative abilities overlap with our present list. In Chapter 10, for example, we reviewed Taylor's (1986, 1988)

Taylor's Talents

multiple-talent totem pole (creative) thinking talents of *productive thinking, communicating, forecasting, decision making,* and *planning;* and his getting-ideas-into-action talents of *implementing, human relations,* and *discerning opportunities.* These can be taught (see Slichter, 1986). Tardif and Sternberg (1988) described as important creative abilities *decision making, independence of*

More Abilities

judgment, coping with novelty, ability to escape perceptual sets, ability to find order in chaos, aesthetic ability (taste and judgment), and *versatility.* Many of these are disguised versions of the present creative abilities or the personality characteristics described in Chapter 4.

CREATIVE THINKING TECHNIQUES

We have devoted enough space to *techniques* of creative thinking in Chapters 6 and 7. Teaching students to use such techniques not only provides them with strategies for generating ideas, but helps them to understand the nature of creative ideas and the creative processes used by others. Children's versions of the techniques are found in Davis and DiPego (1973), Davis (1985), Stanish

Direct involvement in aesthetic and scientific activities promotes creative interests and skills. These two students are absorbed in violin lessons and hygiene research. (The Museum of Modern Art / Film Stills Archive.)

(1977, 1981, 1988), Gordon (1974a), and Gordon and Poze (1972a, 1972b).

As a caution, it is not easy for adults or children to quickly adopt an unfamiliar thinking or problem-solving method. Nonetheless, creative people do use such techniques, consciously or unconsciously, and the techniques work. Personally, your author found ideas for the more-or-less comical dialogues of this book and another (Davis, 1983) by creating checklists of well-known children's stories (Alice in Wonderland, Cinderella), movies (Rambo), famous people and comedians (e.g., Sigmund Freud, Woody Allen, Barbara Walters, Don Rickles, Rodney Dangerfield, Norm Crosby), and myths and legends (Frankenstein, the devil, an oracle), and using these as analogical sources. The morphological synthesis (matrix) technique helped generate approximately 900 exercises that use creativity procedures (brainstorming, analogical thinking, "What would happen if . . . ?", visualization) to teach values and moral thinking (Davis, 1990).

INVOLVEMENT IN CREATIVE ACTIVITIES

Leonardo DaVinci did not become a great painter by practicing shuffleboard, nor did Hemingway spend much time on juggling skills. The strongest and most logically sound, recommendation for strengthening creativity is simply to involve yourself or your students in activities that intrinsically require creative thinking and problem solving. It is virtually assured that creative attitudes, abilities, and skills will be strengthened in the course of actual creative involvement.

For example, Renzulli's Type III Enrichment and his Schoolwide Enrichment Model focus on individual or small group projects and investigations of real problems. The variety of potential projects is unlimited. Reis and Burns (1987) itemized several hundred possibilities (partly reproduced in Davis and Rimm, 1989) in the categories of visual arts and performing arts; math, science, and computers; literature, writing, and communication; social sciences, culture, and language; business and economics; and miscellaneous (e.g., bridge, chess, horses, karate, magic, and sailing). The *Future Problem Solving* and *Odyssey of the Mind* programs also involve students in real creative activity.

Comment

In addition to reviewing a few issues pertaining to "teaching creativity," plus contributions from earlier chapters, the main focus of this chapter was on five core objectives of creativity training and their related strategies. As for which approach or combination of approaches produces the greatest gains the most quickly and efficiently, the variety of ages, abilities, interests, and needs of the particular students—along with a virtual absence of relevant research—make it impossible to specify an all-around ideal recipe. Your author recommends using *all* of the goals/activities in approximately the order they were presented. Students need to be aware of creativity and acquire attitudes that predispose them to thinking creatively; they need to metacognitively understand creative people and creative thinking; their creative abilities and skills should be exercised; they should learn brainstorming and other idea-finding techniques; and they certainly should be involved in activities that require creative thinking and problem solving.

Very little in your own personal development or in the education of your children or students is as critical as strengthening creative potential. Creative self-actualization is much too important to be left to chance.

SUMMARY

While heredity plays a large role, creativity can be taught and learned. There is "massive evidence" for the teachability of creativity, said Torrance.

There also are individual differences in responsiveness to creativity training.

Differences in motivation to create—arousal-seeking tendencies—are thought to be governed by the brain's reticular activating system.

The psychological safety (Rogers) of a receptive and reinforcing creative atmosphere is essential.

Teaching a general, self-actualized creativity can include strengthening creative attitudes, abilities, techniques, teaching the CPS model, and involving students in FPS and OM. Such training is mostly content-free. Teaching special talent creativity, however, which requires a depth of knowledge and content-specific skills, must take place within a content area. Independent projects is a good strategy.

Earlier chapters made the following contributions to the teaching of creativity.

Chapter 1 stressed the importance of creativity to the (self-actualized) individual and society.

Chapter 2 reviewed blocks and barriers to creativity, including Von Oech's 10 mental blocks, and a whole bunch of idea squelchers.

Chapter 3 looked at definitions and theories, which can increase one's understanding of creativity.

Chapter 4 reviewed characteristics of creative people, many of which can be reinforced or otherwise cultivated.

Chapter 5 illustrated perceptual change as a process and discussed the effective CPS model.

Chapter 6 covered the most common and useful creative thinking process/technique of all, analogical thinking.

Chapter 7, a central one in creativity training, described other creative thinking techniques.

Chapter 8 reviewed published creativity tests, which can contribute to one's understanding of creativity.

Chapter 9 summarized G/T program models and enrichment and acceleration strategies that feature creative development as a main goal (FPS, OM, Type II and Type III Enrichment, Feldhusen/Kolloff three-stage model).

Chapter 10, creative dramatics, contributes to more flexible thinking.

This chapter emphasized five main points (goals, strategies) related to increasing creative potential:

First, we should increase students' creativity consciousness and creative attitudes, especially, an appreciation for creative ideas and a predisposition to think creatively.

Second, we should help students metacognitively understand the topic of creativity (nature of creative ideas, creative characteristics, techniques, rationale of creativity tests, creative process, CPS model, definitions and theories).

Third, we should help strengthen creative abilities. Many divergent thinking types of exercises and brainstorming problems were suggested for strengthening fluency, flexibility, originality, and elaboration.

Problem sensitivity may be exercised by having students ask questions about a phenomena.

Problem defining exercises can focus on identifying the "real" problem, isolating important aspects of a problem, identifying subproblems, or thinking of alternative problem definitions.

Guided visualization can be used to exercise visualization and imagination abilities. Also, writing stories for bizarre newspaper headlines exercises visualization and elaboration abilities.

Many analogical thinking exercises appear in Chapter 6.

Regarding Bloom's higher-level abilities, students can analyze components, patterns, causes and effects; synthesize parts into plans and designs; and evaluate accuracy, value, or utility. Students also can practice evaluation skills by thinking of what is "good" and "bad" about an object or experience, using an evaluation matrix, or looking at an idea from other people's perspective.

Student can practice mental transformations with complex visual puzzles of the type shown in Chapter 5.

Emphasizing the deferred judgment principle should strengthen the ability to resist premature closure.

Logical thinking is important to creative potential. Some thinking skills workbooks exercise inductive and deductive logic.

Other creative thinking abilities that may be strengthened are Taylor's totem pole thinking talents and idea-implementing talents.

The fourth main goal of creativity training is teaching creative thinking techniques.

Fifth, we should involve students in creative thinking and problem solving activities.

It is recommended that creativity training proceed in the sequence in which the five points were presented.

Because creative development is tied to self-actualization, it is extremely important.

References

Alexander, T. (1978). Inventing by the madness method. In G. A. Davis & J. A. Scott (Eds.), *Training creative thinking.* Melbourne, FL: Krieger.

Allen, M. S. (1962). *Morphological creativity.* Englewood Cliffs, NJ: Prentice-Hall.

Allen, M. S. (1966). *Psycho-Dynamic Synthesis.* West Nyack, NY: Parker.

Al-Sabaty, I., & Davis, G. A. (1989). Relationship between creativity and right, left, and integrated thinking styles. *Creativity Research Journal, 2,* 111–117.

Amabile, T. M. (1987). The motivation to create. In S. G. Isaksen (Ed.), *Frontiers of creativity research: Beyond the basics.* Buffalo, NY: Bearly Limited.

Arietti, S. (1976). *Creativity: The magic synthesis.* New York: Basic Books.

Barron, F. (1955). The disposition toward originality. *Journal of Abnormal and Social Psychology, 51,* 478–485.

Barron, F. (1961). Creative vision and expression in writing and painting. In D. W. MacKinnon (Ed.), *The creative person* (pp. 237–251). Berkeley, CA: Institute of Personality Assessment Research, University of California.

Barron, F. (1965). The psychology of creativity. In F. Barron, W. C. Dement, W. Edwards, H. Lindman, L. D. Phillips, J. Olds, & M. Olds, *New directions in psychology II.* New York: Holt.

Barron, F. (1968). *Creativity and personal freedom.* Princeton, NJ: Van Nostrand.

Barron, F. (1969). *Creative person and creative process.* New York: Holt, Rinehart & Winston.

Barron, F. (1978). An eye more fantastical. In G. A. Davis & J. A. Scott (Eds.), *Training creative thinking.* Melbourne, FL: Krieger.

Barron, F. (1988). Putting creativity to work. In R. J. Sternberg (Ed.), *The nature of creativity* (pp. 76–98). New York: Cambridge University Press.

Barlett, M. M., & Davis, G. A. (1974). Do the Wallach and Kogan tests predict real creative behavior? *Perceptual and Motor Skills, 39,* 730.

Bass, A. R., Hatton, G. I., McHale, T. J., & Stolurow, L. W. (1962). Originality, intelligence, and performance on problem solving tasks: A pilot study of their relationship. (Tech. Rep. No. 2). Urbana, IL: University of Illinois.

Bem, S. L. (1974). The measurement of psychological androgyny. *Journal of Consulting and Clinical Psychology, 42,* 155–162.

Benbow, C. (1991). Mathematically talented children: Can acceleration meet their educational needs? In N. Colangelo & G. A. Davis (Eds.), *Handbook of gifted education.* Needham Heights, MA: Allyn & Bacon.

Berlyne, D. E. (1961). *Conflict, arousal, and curiosity.* New York: McGraw-Hill.

Betts, G. (1985). *Autonomous learner model.* Greeley, CO: Autonomous Learning Publications and Specialists.

Betts, G. (1991). *Autonomous learner model.* In N. Colangelo & G. A. Davis (Eds.), *Handbook of gifted education.* Needham Heights, MA: Allyn & Bacon.

Biondi, A. M. (1980). About the small cage habit. *Journal of Creative Behavior, 2,* 75–76.

Black, H., & Black, S. (1984). *Building thinking skills.* Pacific Grove, CA: Midwest Publications.

Briskman, L. (1980). Creative product and creative process in science and art. *Inquiry, 23,* 83–106.

Brittain, W. L., & Beitel, K. R. (1961). A study of some tests of creativity in relationship to performance in the visual arts. *Studies in Art Education, 2,* 54–65.

Bronowski, J. (1961). *Science and human values.* London: Hutchinson.

Buckmaster, L. R., & Davis, G. A. (1985). ROSE: A measure of self-actualization and its relationship to creativity. *Journal of Creative Behavior, 19,* 30–37.

Callahan, C. M. (1991). The assessment of creativity. In N. Colangelo & G. A. Davis (Eds.), *Handbook of gifted education.* Needham Heights, MA: Allyn & Bacon.

Cattell, R. B. (1955). *Handbook for the objective-analysis test battery.* Champaign, IL: Institute for Personality and Ability Testing.

Cattel, R. B. (1956). *Objective-analytic test battery.* Champaign, IL: Institute for Personality and Ability Testing.

Clark, C. H. (1958). *Brainstorming.* Garden City, NY: Doubleday.

Clasen, D. R. (Ed.) (1985). *Teaching for thinking: Creativity in the class-room.* Madison, WI: University of Wisconsin–Extension.

Cohn, S. J. (1981). What is giftedness: A multidimensional approach. In A. H. Kramer (Ed.), *Gifted children: Challenging their potential.* New York: Trillium Press.

Cohn, S. J. (1991). Talent searches. In N. Colangelo & G. A. Davis (Eds.), *Handbook of gifted education.* Needham Heights, MA: Allyn & Bacon.

Compton, A. H. (1952). Case histories: Creativity in science. In F. Olsen (Ed.), *The nature of creative thinking* (pp. 23–31). New York: Industrial Research Institute.

Cooper, L. (Trans.); Hamilton, E., & Cairns, H. (Eds.). (1961). *The collected dialogues of Plato.* Princeton, NJ: Princeton University Press.

Covington, M. V., Crutchfield, R. S., Olton, R. M., & Davies, L. (1972). *Productive thinking program.* Columbus, OH: Charles E. Merrill.

Cox, C. M. (1926). *The early mental traits of three hundred geniuses.* Stanford, CA: Stanford University Press.

Cox, J., Daniel, N., & Boston, B. A. (1985). *Educating able learners: Programs and promising practices.* Austin, TX: University of Texas Press.

Crabbe, A. (1985). Future problem solving. In A. L. Costa (Ed.), *Developing minds: A resource book for teaching thinking.* Alexandria, VA: Association for Supervision and Curriculum Development.

Craig, R. (1966). Trait lists and creativity. *Psychologia, 9,* 107–110.

Crawford, R. P. (1978). The techniques of creative thinking. In G. A. Davis & J. A. Scott (Eds.), *Training creative thinking.* Melbourne, FL: Krieger.

Cropley, A. J. (1971). Some Canadian creativity research. *Journal of Research and Development in Education, 4*(3), 113–115.

Cropley, A. J. (1972). A five-year longitudinal study of the validity of creativity tests. *Developmental Psychology, 6,* 119–124.

Cropley, C. (1986). *Divergent thinking in young handicapped children.* Unpublished doctoral dissertation, University of Washington, Seattle, WA.

Csikszentmihalyi, M. (1988). Society, culture, and person: A systems view of creativity. In R. J. Sternberg (Ed.), *The nature of creativity* (pp. 325–339). New York: Cambridge University Press.

Dacey, J. S. (1989). *Fundamentals of creative thinking.* Lexington, MA: Lexington Books.

Damm, V. J. (1970). Creativity and intelligence: Research implications for equal emphasis in high school. *Exceptional Children, 36,* 565–570.

Davis, G. A. (1971). Instruments useful in studying creative behavior and creative talent, Part II: Noncommercially available instruments. *Journal of Creative Behavior, 5,* 162–165.

Davis, G. A. (1973). *Psychology of problem solving.* New York: Basic Books.

Davis, G. A. (1975). In frumious pursuit of the creative person. *Journal of Creative Behavior, 9,* 75–87.

Davis, G. A. (1983). *Student study guide to accompany Educational Psychology: Theory and Practice.* New York: Random House.

Davis, G. A. (1985). *Creative thinking and problem solving* (computer disk and manual). Buffalo, NY: Bearly Limited.

Davis, G. A. (1989a). Objectives and activities for teaching creative thinking. *Gifted Child Quarterly, 33,* 81–84.

Davis, G. A. (1989b). Testing for creative potential. *Contemporary Educational Psychology, 14,* 257–274.

Davis, G. A. (1990). *The good person book: Creative teaching of values and moral thinking.* Buffalo, NY: DOK.

Davis, G. A. (1991a). *How do you think: Administration and technical manual.* Cross Plains, WI: Badger Press.

Davis, G. A. (1991b). Teaching creative thinking. In N. Colangelo & G. A. Davis (Eds.), *Handbook of gifted education.* Needham Heights, MA: Allyn & Bacon.

Davis, G. A. & Belcher, T. L. (1971). How shall creativity be measured? Torrance Tests, RAT, Alpha Biographical, and IQ. *Journal of Creative Behavior, 3,* 153–161.

Davis, G. A. & Bull, K. S. (1978). Strengthening affective components of creativity in a college course. *Journal of Educational Psychology, 70,* 833–836.

Davis, G. A., & DiPego, G. (1973). *Imagination Express: Saturday subway ride.* Buffalo, NY: DOK.

Davis, G. A., Helfert, C. J. & Shapiro, G. R. (1973). Let's be an ice cream machine!: Creative dramatics. *Journal of Creative Behavior, 7,* 37–48.

Davis, G. A., Peterson, J. M. & Farley, F. H. (1973). Attitudes, motivation, sensation seeking, and belief in ESP as predictors of real creative behavior. *Journal of Creative Behavior, 7,* 31–39.

Davis, G. A., & Rimm, S. (1980). *Group inventory for finding interests. II.* Watertown, WI: Educational Assessment Service.

Davis, G. A., & Rimm, S. (1982). Group inventory for finding interests (GIFFI) I and II: Instruments for identifying creative potential in the junior and senior high school. *Journal of Creative Behavior, 16,* 50–57.

Davis, G. A., & Rimm, S. (1989). *Education of the gifted and talented.* Second ed. Englewood Cliffs, NJ: Prentice-Hall.

Davis, G. A., & Rudmanis, I. (1986). Teaching creativity with a computer. Unpublished manuscript, Department of Educational Psychology, University of Wisconsin, Madison.

Davis, G. A., & Subkoviak, M. J. (1978). Multidimensional analysis of a personality-based test of creative potential. *Journal of Educational Measurement, 12,* 37–43.

DeMille, R. (1973). *Put your mother on the ceiling.* New York: Viking/ Compass.

Dewey, J. (1933). *How we think.* Lexington, MA: D.C. Heath.

Domino, G. (1970). Identification of potentially creative persons from the Adjective Check List. *Journal of Consulting and Clinical Psychology, 35,* 48–51.

Eberle, B. (1971). *Scamper.* Buffalo, NY: DOK.

Eberle, B., & Stanish, B. (1985). *CPS for kids.* Carthage, IL: Good Apple.

Edwards, M. O. (1968). A survey of problem solving courses. *Journal of Creative Behavior 2,* 33–51.

Eisenman, R. (1964). Birth order and artistic creativity. *Journal of Individual Psychology, 20,* 183–185.

Evans, E. D. (1986). Review of *Thinking Creatively in Action and Movement.* In D. Keyser & R. Sweetland (Eds.), *Test critiques* (Vol. V, pp. 505–512). Kansas City, MO: Testing Corporation of America.

Fabun, D. (1968). *You and creativity.* New York: Macmillan.

Farley, F. H. (1986, May). The big T in personality. *Psychology Today,* 47–52.

Fekken, G. C. (1985). Review of *Creativity Assessment Packet.* In D. Keyser & R. Sweetland (Eds.), *Test critiques* (Vol. V, pp. 211–215). Kansas City, MO: Testing Corporation of America.

Feldhusen, J. F., & Kolloff, P. B. (1981). In R. E. Clasen, B. Robinson, D. R. Clasen, & G. Libster (Eds.), *Programming for the gifted, talented and creative: Models and methods.* Madison, WI: University of Wisconsin–Extension.

Feldhusen, J. F., & Kolloff, P. B. (1986). The Purdue three-stage enrichment model for gifted education at the elementary level. In J. S. Renzulli (Ed.), *Systems and models for developing programs for the gifted and talented* (pp. 126–152). Mansfield Center, CT: Creative Learning Press.

Fleming, E. S., & Weintraub, S. (1962). Attitudinal rigidity as a measure of creativity in gifted children. *Journal of Educational Psychology, 53,* 81–85.

Folmer, P. (1975). Creativity: The search for a definition. *Educational Media International, 2,* 2–7.

Freeman, J., Butcher, H. J., & Christie, T. (1968). *Creativity: A selective review of research.* London: Society for Research into Higher Education Ltd.

Gagné, F. (1985). Giftedness and talent: Reexamining a reexamination of the definitions. *Gifted Child Quarterly, 29,* 103–112.

Gagné, F. (1991). Toward a differentiated model of giftedness and talent. In N. Colangelo & G. A. Davis (Eds.), *Handbook of gifted education.* Needham Heights, MA: Allyn & Bacon.

Getzels, J. W., & Jackson, P. W. (1962). *Creativity and intelligence.* New York: Wiley.

Ghiselin, B. (1952). Wolfgang Amadeus Mozart: A letter. In B. Ghiselin (Ed.), *The creative process.* New York: Mentor.

Gordon, W. J. J. (1961). *Synectics.* New York: Harper & Row.

Gordon, W. J. J. (1974a). *Making it strange.* Books 1–4. New York: Harper & Row.

Gordon, W. J. J. (1974b). Some source material in discovery by analogy. *Journal of Creative Behavior, 8,* 239–257.

Gordon, W. J. J., & Poze, T. (1971). *Metaphorical way of learning and knowing.* Cambridge, MA: SES Associates.

Gordon, W. J. J., & Poze, T. (1972a). *Teaching is listening.* Cambridge, MA: SES Associates.

Gordon, W. J. J., & Poze, T. (1972b). *Strange and familiar.* Cambridge, MA: SES Associates.

Gordon, W. J. J., & Poze, T. (1980a). SES synectics and gifted education today. *Gifted Child Quarterly, 24,* 147–151.

Gordon, W. J. J., & Poze, T. (1980b). *The new art of the possible.* Cambridge, MA: Porpoise Books.

Gough, H. G. (1952). *Adjective check list.* Palo Alto, CA: Consulting Psychologists' Press.

Griggs, S., & Dunn, R. (1984). Selected case studies of the learning style preferences of gifted students. *Gifted Child Quarterly, 28,* 115–119.

Gruber, H. E., & Davis, S. N. (1988). Inching our way up Mount Olympus: The evolving-systems approach to creative thinking. In R. J. Sternberg (Ed.), *The nature of creativity* (pp. 243–270). New York: Cambridge University Press.

Guilford, J. P. (1967). *The nature of human intelligence.* New York: McGraw-Hill.

Guilford, J. P. (1977). *Way beyond the IQ.* Buffalo, NY: Creative Education Foundation.

Guilford, J. P. (1979). Some incubated thoughts on incubation. *Journal of Creative Behavior, 13,* 1–8.

Guilford, J. P. (1986). *Creative talents: Their nature, uses and development.* Buffalo, NY: Bearly Limited.

Guilford, J. P. (1988). Some changes in the structure-of-intellect model. *Educational and Psychological Measurement, 48,* 1–4.

Hadamard, J. (1945). *An essay on the psychology of invention in the mathematical field.* New York: Dover.

Haefele, J. W. (1962). *Creativity and innovation.* New York: Reinhold.

Harmon, L. R. (1956). Social and technological determiners of creativity. In C. W. Taylor (Ed.), *The 1955 University of Utah research conference on the identification of creative scientific talent* (pp. 42–52). Salt Lake City, UT: University of Utah Press.

Harnadek, A. (1978). *Mind benders B1: Deductive thinking skills.* Pacific Grove, CA: Midwest Publications.

Harnadek, A. (1979). *Inference B: Inductive thinking skills.* Pacific Grove, CA: Midwest Publications.

Helman, I. B., & Larson, S. G. (1980). *Now what do I do?* Buffalo, NY: DOK.

Hetherington, E. M., & Parke, R. D. (1979). *Child psychology: A contemporary viewpoint.* New York: McGraw-Hill.

Hilgard, E. R., Atkinson, R. L., & Atkinson, R. C. (1979). *Introduction to psychology.* Seventh ed. New York: Harcourt, Brace, Jovanovich.

Hoepfner, R., & Hemenway, J. (1973). *Test of creative potential.* Hollywood, CA: Monitor.

Honorton, C. (1967). Creativity and precognition scoring level. *Journal of Parapsychology, 31,* 29–42.

Isaksen, S. G. (1987). *Introduction: An orientation to the frontiers of creativity research.* In S. G. Isaksen (Ed.), *Frontiers of creativity research: Beyond the basics* (pp. 1–26). Buffalo, NY: Bearly Limited.

Isaksen, S. G., & Treffinger, D. J. (1985). *Creative problem solving: The basic course.* Buffalo, NY: Bearly Limited.

Jamison, K. R. (1989). Manic-depressive illness and accomplishment: Creativity, leadership and social class. In F. K. Goodwin and K. R. Jamison (Eds.), *Manic-depressive illness.* New York: Oxford University Press.

Jones, C. A. (1960). Some relationships between creative writing and creative drawing of sixth grade children. Unpublished doctoral dissertation, Pennsylvania State University, University Park, PA.

Jung, C. G. (1933). *Psychological types.* New York: Harcourt, Brace and World.

Jung, C. G. (1959). The archetypes and the collective unconscious. *Collected works.* New York: Pantheon.

Jung, C. G. (1976). On the relation of analytic psychology to poetic art. In A. Rothenberg & C. R. Hausman (Eds.), *The creativity question* (pp. 135–143). Durham, NC: Duke University Press.

Kaltsoonis, B. (1971). Instruments useful in studying creative behavior and creative talent, Part I: Commercially available instruments. *Journal of Creative Behavior, 5,* 117–126.

Kaltsoonis, B. (1972). Additional instruments useful in studying creative behavior and creative talent, Part III: Noncommercially available instruments. *Journal of Creative Behavior, 6,* 268–274.

Kaltsoonis, B., & Honeywell, L. (1980). Additional instruments useful in studying creative behavior and creative talent, Part IV: Noncommercially available instruments. *Journal of Creative Behavior, 14*, 56–67.

Kang, C. (1989). Gender differences in Korean Children's responses to the Torrance Tests of Creative Thinking from first to sixth grade. Unpublished masters thesis, University of Wisconsin, Madison, WI.

Katz, A. N. (1980). Do left-handers tend to be more creative? *Journal of Creative Behavior, 14*, 271.

Keating, D. P. (1980). Four faces of creativity: The continuing plight of the intellectually underserved. *Gifted Child Quarterly, 24*, 56–61.

Kingsley, H. L., & Garry, R. (1957). *The nature and conditions of learning.* Second edition. Englewood Cliffs, NJ: Prentice-Hall.

Koestler, A. (1964). *The act of creation.* New York: Macmillan.

Kolloff, P. B., & Feldhusen, J. F. (1984). The effects of enrichment on self-concept and creative thinking. *Gifted Child Quarterly, 28*, 53–57.

Kris, E. (1952). On preconscious mental processes. In *Psychoanalytic explorations in art.* New York: International Universities Press. Reprinted in A. Rothenberg & C. R. Hausman (Eds.), *The creativity question.* Durham, NC: Duke University Press, 1976.

Kubie, L. S. (1958). *Neurotic distortion of the creative process.* Lawrence, KA: University of Kansas Press.

Leff, H. L. (1984). *Playful perception.* Burlington, VT: Waterfront Books.

Lichtenwalner, J. S., & Maxwell, J. W. (1969). The relationship of birth order and socioeconomic status of the creativity of preschool children. *Child Development, 40*, 1241–1247.

Lingemann, L. S. (1982) Assessing creativity from a diagnostic perspective: The creative attribute profile. Unpublished doctoral dissertation, University of Wisconsin, Madison.

Lombroso, C. (1895). *The man of genius.* London: Charles Schribner's Sons.

Lowes, J. L. (1927). *The road to Xanadu.* Boston: Houghton Mifflin.

MacKinnon, D. W. (1961). Creativity in architects. In D. W. MacKinnon (Ed.), *The creative person* (pp. 291–320). Berkeley, CA: Institute of Personality Assessment Research, University of California.

MacKinnon, D. W. (1976). Architects, personality types, and creativity. In A. Rothenberg & C. R. Hausman (Eds.), *The creativity question.* Durham, NC: Duke University Press.

MacKinnon, D. W. (1978a). Educating for creativity: A modern myth? In G. A. Davis & J. A. Scott (Eds.), *Training creative thinking.* Melbourne, FL: Krieger.

MacKinnon, D. W. (1978b). *In search of human effectiveness: Identifying and developing creativity.* Buffalo, NY: Creative Education Foundation.

Maltzman, I. (1960). On the training of originality. *Psychological Review, 67,* 229–242.

Manske, M. E., & Davis, G. A. (1968). Effects of simple instructional biases upon performance in the unusual uses test. *Journal of General Psychology, 79,* 25–33.

Marland, S. (1972). *Education of the gifted and talented, Volume I. Report to the Congress of the United States by the U.S. Commission of Education.* Washington, DC: U.S. Government Printing Office.

Martindale, C. (1975, July). What makes a person different? *Psychology Today,* 44–50.

Maslow, A. H. (1954). *Motivation and personality.* New York: Harper & Row.

Maslow, A. H. (1968). *Toward a psychology of being.* Second ed. Princeton, NJ: Van Nostrand.

Maslow, A. H. (1971). *The farther reaches of human nature.* New York: Viking Press.

Mason, J. G. (1960). *How to be a more creative executive.* New York: McGraw-Hill.

May, R. (1959). The nature of creativity. In H. H. Anderson (Ed.), *Creativity and its cultivation.* New York: Harper & Row.

McKee, M. G. (1985). Review of *Creativity Attitude Survey.* In D. Keyser & R. Sweetland (Eds.), *Test critiques* (Vol. V, pp. 206–208). Kansas City, MO: Testing Corporation of America.

Mednick, S. A. (1962). The associative basis of the creative process. *Psychological Review, 69,* 220–232.

Mednick, S. A. (1967). *Remote associates test.* Boston: Houghton Mifflin.

Mednick, M. T., & Andrews, F. M. (1967). Creative thinking and level of intelligence. *Journal of Creative Behavior, 1,* 428–431.

Meeker, M. (1969). *The structure of intellect: Its use and interpretation.* Columbus, OH: Merrill.

Meeker, M. (1976). *Basic teaching comprehension skills workbook.* Books 1–5. El Segundo, CA: SOI Institute.

Meeker, M. (1981). Teaching children to think—not parrot. In R. E. Clasen, B. Robinson, D. R. Clasen, & G. Libster (Eds.), *Programming for the gifted, talented and creative: Models and methods.* Madison, WI: University of Wisconsin-Extension.

Meeker, M. N., & Meeker, R. (1986). The SOI system for gifted education. In J. S. Renzulli (Ed.), *Systems and models for developing programs for the gifted and talented* (194–215). Mansfield Center, CT: Creative Learning Press.

Meeker, M. N., Meeker, R., & Roid, G. (1985). Structure-of-intellect learning abilities test (SOI-LA). Los Angeles: Western Psychological Services.

Mooney, R. L. (1963). A conceptual model for integrating four approaches to the identification of creative talent. In C. W. Taylor & F. Barron (Eds.), *Scientific creativity: Its recognition and development* (pp. 331–340). New York: Wiley.

Moss, M. A. (1991). The meaning and measurement of Jung's construct of intuition: Intuition and creativity. Unpublished doctoral dissertation, University of Wisconsin, Madison.

Moustakis, C. E. (1967). *Creativity and conformity.* Princeton, NJ: Van Nostrand.

Myers, R. E., & Torrance, E. P. (1964). *Invitation to thinking and doing.* Boston: Ginn.

Myers, R. E., & Torrance, E. P. (1965). *Can you imagine?* Boston: Ginn.

Myers, R. E., & Torrance, E. P. (1966a). *For those who wonder.* Boston: Ginn.

Myers, R. E., & Torrance, E. P. (1966b). *Plots, puzzles and ploys.* Boston: Ginn.

Newell, A., Shaw, J. C., & Simon, H. A. (1962). In H. E. Gruber, G. Terrell, & M. Wertheimer (Eds.), *Contemporary approaches to creative thinking.* New York: Atherton.

Nicholls, J. G. (1972). Creativity in a person who will never produce anything original and useful: The concept of creativity as a normally distributed trait. *American Psychologist, 27,* 717–727.

Norman, D. A. (1976). *Memory and attention: An introduction to human information processing.* Second edition. New York: Wiley.

Osborn, A. F. (1963). *Applied imagination.* Third ed. New York: Scribners.

Paffard, M. K. (1970). Creative activities and peak experiences. *British Journal of Educational Psychology,* 283–290.

Parnes, S. J. (1961). Effects of extended effort in creative problem solving. *Journal of Educational Psychology, 53,* 117–122.

Parnes, S. J. (1978). Can creativity be increased? In G. A. Davis & J. A. Scott (Eds.), *Training creative thinking.* Melbourne, FL: Krieger.

Parnes, S. J. (1981). *Magic of your mind.* Buffalo, NY: Bearly Limited.

Parnes, S. J., Noller, R. B., & Biondi, A. M. (1976). *Creative actionbook.* New York: Scribners.

Perkins, D. A. (1988). The possibility of invention. In R. J. Sternberg (Ed.), *The nature of creativity* (pp. 362–385). New York: Cambridge University Press.

Peterson, J. M., & Lansky, L. M. (1980). Success in architecture: Handedness and/or visual thinking. *Perceptual and Motor Skills, 50,* 1139–1143.

Piers, E. V., Daniels, J. M., & Quackenbush, J. F. (1960). The identification of creativity in adolescents. *Journal of Educational Psychology, 51,* 346–351.

Porshe, J. D. (October, 1955). Creative ability: Its role in the search for new products. Paper presented at the Special Conference on Managing Product Research and Development, American Management Association, New York.

Prince, G. (1968). The operational mechanism of synectics. *Journal of Creative Behavior, 2*, 1–13.

Prince, G. (1982). Synectics. In S. A. Olsen (Ed.), *Group planning and problem solving methods in engineering.* New York: Wiley.

Pryor, K. W., Haag, R., & O'Reilly, J. (1969). The creative porpoise: Training for novel behavior. *Journal of the Experimental Analysis of Behavior, 12,* 653–661.

Rank, O. (1945). *Will therapy, truth and reality.* New York: Knopf.

Read, G. M. (1955). Profile of human materials. Paper presented at the Centennial Symposium on Modern Engineering. University of Pennsylvania, Philadelphia, PA.

Reis, S. M., & Burns, D. E. (1987). A schoolwide enrichment team invites you to read about methods for promoting community and faculty involvement in a gifted educational program. *Gifted Child Today, 49*(2), 27–32.

Renzulli, J. S. (1977). *Enrichment triad model.* Mansfield, CT: Creative Learning Press.

Renzulli, J. S. (1983, Sept./Oct.). Rating the behavioral characteristics of superior students. *G/C/T,* 30–35.

Renzulli, J. S., & Reis, S. M. (1985). *The schoolwide enrichment model: A comprehensive plan for educational excellence.* Mansfield Center, CT: Creative Learning Press.

Renzulli, J. S., & Reis, S. M. (1991). The schoolwide enrichment model: A comprehensive plan for the development of creative productivity. In N. Colangelo & G. A. Davis (Eds.), *Handbook of gifted education.* Needham Heights, MA: Allyn & Bacon.

Renzulli, J. S., Reis, S. M., & Smith, L. H. (1981). *Revolving door identification model.* Mansfield Center, CT: Creative Learning Press.

Rhodes, M. (1961). Analysis of creativity. *Phi Delta Kappan, 42,* 305–310.

Rhodes, M. (1987). An analysis of creativity. In S. G. Isaksen (Ed.), *Frontiers of creativity research: Beyond the basics* (pp. 216–222). Buffalo, NY: Bearly Limited.

Rimm, S. B. (1976). *GIFT: Group inventory for finding creative talent.* Watertown, WI: Educational Assessment Service.

Rimm, S. B. (1983). *Preschool and kindergarten interest descriptor.* Watertown, WI: Educational Assessment Service.

Rimm, S. B., & Davis, G. A. (1976). GIFT: An instrument for the identification of creativity. *Journal of Creative Behavior, 10,* 178–182.

Rimm, S. B., & Davis, G. A. (1979). *Group inventory for finding interests. I.* Watertown, WI: Educational Assessment Service.

Rimm, S. B., & Davis, G. A. (1980). Five years of international research with GIFT: An instrument for the identification of creativity. *Journal of Creative Behavior, 14,* 35–46.

Rimm, S. B., & Davis, G. A. (1983, Sept./Oct.). Identifying creativity, Part II. *G/C/T,* 19–23.

Rogers, C. R. (1962). Toward a theory of creativity. In S. J. Parnes & H. F. Harding (Eds.), *A source book for creative thinking.* New York: Scribner's.

Rothenberg, A., & Hausman, C. R. (Eds.). (1975). *The creativity question.* Durham, NC: Duke University Press.

Rothenberg, A. (1975). The process of Janusian thinking in creativity. In A. Rothenberg & C. R. Hausman (Eds.), *The creativity question* (pp. 311–327). Durham, NC: Duke University Press.

Roweton, W. E. (1972). Creativity: A review of theory and research. Occasional Paper No. 7, Creative Education Foundation, Buffalo, NY.

Rugg, H. (1963). *Imagination: An inquiry into the sources and conditions that stimulate creativity.* New York: Harper & Row.

Runco, M. A. (1984). Teachers' judgments of creativity and social validation of divergent thinking tests. *Perceptual and Motor Skills, 59,* 711–717.

Runco, M. A., & Bahleda, M. D. (1986). Birth-order and divergent thinking. *Journal of Genetic Psychology, 148,* 119–125.

Runco, M. A., & Okuda, S. M., & Akau, B. T. (1988). Psychometric properties of four systems for scoring divergent thinking tests. *Journal of Psychoeducational Assessment.*

Runco, M. A., Okuda, S. M., & Hwang, S. R. (1987). Creativity, extracurricular activity, and divergent thinking as predictors of mathematics and science performance by talented students. Eric Document ED279523.

Schaefer, C. E. (1969). Imaginary companions and creative adolescents. *Developmental Psychology, 1,* 747–749.

Schaefer, C. E. (1970). *Biographical Inventory-Creativity.* San Diego, CA: Educational and Industrial Testing Services.

Schaefer, C. E. (1971). *Creativity attitude survey.* Jacksonville, IL: Psychologists and Educators, Inc.

Schiever, S., & Maker, C. J. (1991). Acceleration and enrichment practices: An overview. In N. Colangelo & G. A. Davis (Eds.), *Handbook of gifted education.* Needham Heights, MA: Allyn & Bacon.

Schuldberg, D., French, C., Stone, B. L., & Heberle, J. (1988). Creativity and Schizotypal traits: Creativity tests scores and perceptual aberration, magical ideation, and impulsive nonconformity. *Journal of Nervous and Mental Disease, 176,* 648–657.

Seidel, G. J. (1962). *The crisis in creativity.* Notre Dame, IN: University of Notre Dame Press.

Shallcross, D. J. (1981). *Teaching creative behavior.* Englewood Cliffs, NJ: Prentice-Hall.

Sheerer, M. (1963). *Problem solving.* Scientific American, *208*(4), 118–128.

Shields, S. (1989). Creativity of radio announcers. Unpublished Doctoral Dissertation, University of Wisconsin, Madison.

Shostrum, E. L. (1963). *Personal orientation inventory.* San Diego, CA: Educational and Industrial Testing Service.

Simberg, A. S. (1978). Blocks to creative thinking. In G. A. Davis & J. A. Scott (Eds.), *Training creative thinking* (pp. 119–135). Melbourne, FL: Krieger.

Simonton, D. K. (1988). Creativity, leadership, and chance. In R. J. Sternberg (Ed.), *The nature of creativity* (pp. 386–426). New York: Cambridge University Press.

Skinner, B. F. (1971). *Beyond freedom and dignity.* New York: Knopf.

Skinner, B. F. (1972). *Cumulative record: A selection of papers.* Third ed. Englewood Cliffs, NJ: Prentice-Hall.

Slichter, C. (1986). Talents unlimited: Applying the multiple talent approach. In J. S. Renzulli (Ed.), *Systems and models for developing programs for the gifted and talented* (pp. 352–390). Mansfield Center, CT: Creative Learning Press.

Smith, E. (1985, Sept. 30). Are you creative? *Business Week,* 80–84.

Smith, J. M. (1966). *Setting conditions for creative teaching in the elementary school.* Boston: Allyn & Bacon.

Snow, R. E. (1986). Individual differences and the design of educational programs. *American Psychologist, 41,* 1029–1039.

Somers, J. V., & Yawkey, T. D. (1984). Imaginary play companions: Contributions of creativity and intellectual abilities of young children. *Journal of Creative Behavior, 18,* 77–89.

Springer, S. P. & Deutsch, G. (1985). *Left brain, right brain.* Second ed. New York: Freeman.

Staats, A. W. (1968). *Learning, language, and cognition.* New York: Holt.

Staffieri, R. J. (1970). Birth-order and creativity. *Journal of Clinical Psychology, 26,* 65–66.

Stanish, B. (1977). *Sunflowing.* Carthage, IL: Good Apple.

Stanish, B. (1979). *I believe in unicorns.* Carthage, IL: Good Apple.

Stanish, B. (1981). *Hippogriff feathers.* Carthage, IL: Good Apple.

Stanish, B. (1988). *Hearthstone traveler.* Carthage, IL: Good Apple.

Stankowski, W. M. (1978). Definition. In R. E. Clasen & B. Robinson (Eds.), *Simple gifts.* Madison, WI: University of Wisconsin–Extension.

Stanley, J. C., & Benbow, C. P. (1986). Youths who reason exceptionally well mathematically. In R. J. Sternberg, & J. Davidson (Eds.), *Conceptions of giftedness* (361–387). New York: Cambridge University Press.

Sternberg, R. S. (1986). Intelligence, wisdom, and creativity: Three is better than one. *Educational Psychologist, 21,* 175–190.

Sternberg, R. S. (1988a). A three-facet model of creativity. In R. J. Sternberg (Ed.), *The nature of creativity* (pp. 125–147). New York: Cambridge University Press.

Sternberg, R. J. (Ed.) (1988b). *The nature of creativity.* New York: Cambridge University Press.

Sternberg, R. S. (1991). Giftedness according to the triarchic theory of human intelligence. In N. Colangelo & G. A. Davis (Eds.), *Handbook of gifted education.* Needham Heights, MA: Allyn & Bacon.

Striker, F. (1964). Creative writing workbook and the morphological approach to plotting. Unpublished manuscript, University of Buffalo, Buffalo, NY.

Tardif, T. Z., & Sternberg, R. J. (1988). What do we know about creativity? In R. J. Sternberg (Ed.), *The nature of creativity* (pp. 429–440). New York: Cambridge University Press.

Taylor, C. W. (1986). Cultivating simultaneous student growth in both multiple creative talents and knowledge. In J. S. Renzulli (Ed.), *Systems and models for developing programs for the gifted and talented.* Mansfield Center, CT: Creative Learning Press.

Taylor, C. W. (1988). Various approaches to and definitions of creativity. In R. J. Sternberg (Ed.), *The nature of creativity* (pp. 99–121). New York: Cambridge University Press.

Tegano, D. W., Moran, J. D., & Godwin, L. J. (1986). Cross-validation of two creativity tests designed for preschool children. *Early Childhood Research Quarterly, 1,* 387–396.

Terman, L. M. (1925). *Genetic studies of genius: Mental and physical traits of a thousand gifted children.* Stanford, CA: Stanford University Press.

Terman, L. M., & Oden, M. H. (1947). *Genetic studies of genius: The gifted child grows up.* Stanford, CA: Stanford University Press.

Thompson, J. (1942). *John Thompson's modern course for the piano.* Fifth grade book. Cincinnati, OH: Willis Music Co.

Torrance, E. P. (1962). *Guiding creative talent.* Englewood Cliffs, NJ: Prentice-Hall.

Torrance, E. P. (1965). *Rewarding creative behavior.* Englewood Cliffs, NJ: Prentice-Hall.

Torrance, E. P. (1966). *Torrance tests of creative thinking.* Bensenville, IL: Scholastic Testing Service.

Torrance, E. P. (1974). *Norms and technical manual: Torrance tests of creative thinking.* Revised ed. Bensenville, IL: Scholastic Testing Service.

Torrance, E. P. (1977). *Creativity in the classroom.* Washington, DC: National Education Association.

Torrance, E. P. (1979). *The search for satori and creativity.* Buffalo, NY: Creative Education Foundation.

Torrance, E. P. (1981a). Non-test ways of identifying the creatively gifted. In J. C. Gowan, J. Khatena, & E. P. Torrance (Eds.), *Creativity: Its educational implications.* Dubuque, IA: Kendall/Hunt.

Torrance, E. P. (1981b). *Thinking creatively in action and movement.* Bensenville, IL: Scholastic Testing Service.

Torrance, E. P. (1984a). Some products of 25 years of creativity research. *Educational Perspectives, 22*(3), 3-8.

Torrance, E. P. (1984b). Teaching creative and gifted learners. In M. E. Wittrock (Ed.), *Handbook of research on teaching.* Third ed. (pp. 630-647). Chicago: Rand McNally.

Torrance, E. P. (1987a). *The blazing drive: The creative personality.* Buffalo NY: Bearly Limited.

Torrance, E. P. (1987b). Teaching for creativity. In S. G. Isaksen (Ed.), *Frontiers of creativity research: Beyond the basics* (pp. 189-215). Buffalo, NY: Bearly Limited.

Torrance, E. P. (1988). The nature of creativity as manifest in its testing. In R. W. Sternberg (Ed.), *The nature of creativity* (pp. 43-75). New York: Cambridge University Press.

Torrance, E. P., & Ball, O. E. (1984). *Torrance tests of creative thinking: Streamlined (revised) manual, figural A and B.* Bensenville, IL: Scholastic Testing Service.

Torrance, E. P. & Dauw, D. C. (1965). Aspirations and dreams of three groups of creatively gifted high school seniors and a comparable unselected group. *Gifted Child Quarterly, 9,* 177-182.

Torrance, E. P., Khatena, J., & Cunnington, B. F. (1973). *Thinking creatively with sounds and words.* Bensenville, IL: Scholastic Testing Service.

Torrance, E. P., & Myers, R. E. (1970). *Creative learning and teaching.* New York: Dodd, Mead.

Torrance, E. P., & Torrance, J. P. (1978). The 1977-78 future problem-solving program: Interscholastic competition and curriculum project. *Journal of Creative Behavior, 12,* 87-89.

Torrance, E. P., Williams, S. E., Torrance, J. P., & Horng, R. (1978). *Handbook for training future problem-solving teams.* Athens, GA: Georgia Studies of Creative Behavior, University of Georgia.

Treffinger, D. T. (1987). Research on creativity assessment. In S. G. Isaksen (Ed.), *Frontiers of creativity research* (pp. 103–119). Buffalo, NY: Bearly Limited.

Treffinger, D. J., Isaksen, S. G., & Firestien, R. L. (1982). *Handbook of creative learning.* Volume 1. Williamsville, NY: Center for Creative Learning.

Treffinger, D. T., Renzulli, J. S., & Feldhusen, J. F. (1971). Problems in the assessment of creative thinking. *Journal of Creative Behavior, 5,* 104–112.

Van Gundy, A. B. (1987). Organizational creativity and innovation. In S. G. Isaksen (Ed.), *Frontiers of creativity research* (pp. 358–379). Buffalo, NY: Bearly Limited.

Vernon, P. E. (1970). *Creativity.* Harmondsworth, UK: Methuen.

Von Oech, R. (1983). *A whack in the side of the head.* New York: Warner Communications.

Walberg, H. A. (1988). Creativity and talent as learning. In R. W. Sternberg (Ed.), *The nature of creativity* (pp. 340–361). New York: Cambridge University Press.

Walberg, H. A., & Herbig, M. P. (1991). Developing talent, creativity, and eminence. In N. Colangelo & G. A. Davis (Eds.), *Handbook of gifted education.* Needham Heights, MA: Allyn & Bacon.

Wallach, M. A., & Kogan, N. (1965). *Modes of thinking in young children.* New York: Holt.

Wallas, G. (1926). *The art of thought.* New York: Harcourt, Brace & World.

Warren, T. F. (1974). How to squelch ideas. In G. A. Davis & T. F. Warren (Eds.), *Psychology of education: New looks.* Lexington, MA: Heath.

Way, B. (1967). *Development through drama.* London: Longman.

Weisberg, P. S., & Springer, K. J. (1961). Environmental factors in creative function. *Archives of General Psychiatry, 5,* 554–564.

Welch, L. (1946). Recombination of ideas in creative thinking. *Journal of Applied Psychology, 30,* 49–53.

Welsh, G. S., & Barron, F. (1963). *Barron-Welsh art scale.* Palo Alto, CA: Consulting Psychologists Press.

Williams, F. (1980). *Creativity assessment packet.* Buffalo, NY: DOK.

Witkin, H. A., Moore, C. A., Goodenough, D. R., & Cox, P. W. (1977). Field-dependent and field-independent cognitive styles and their educational implications. *Review of Educational Research, 47,* 1–64.

Yamamoto, K. (1963). Creative writing and school achievement. *School and Society, 91,* 307–308.

Yonge, G. D. (1975). Time experiences, self-actualizing values and creativity. *Journal of Personality Assessment, 39,* 601–606.

Zuckerman, M. (1975). *A manual and research report of the sensation seeking scale.* ETS Test Collection. Princeton, NJ: Educational Testing Service.

Name Index

Subject Index